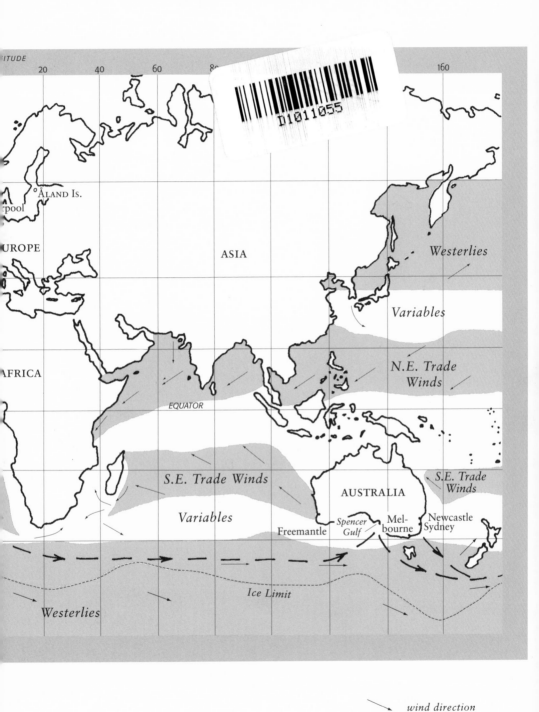

ITUDE

20   40   60   8...   160

ÅLAND IS.
pool

UROPE   ASIA   *Westerlies*

Variables

AFRICA   N.E. Trade
                                                         Winds
              EQUATOR

                                                         S.E. Trade
              S.E. Trade Winds   Winds

                                        AUSTRALIA
              Variables
                              Freemantle *Spencer* Mel-   Newcastle
                                          Gulf   bourne Sydney

                                          Ice Limit

Westerlies

                                        wind direction

                                        ship route

The Last of the Cape Horners

The Last of the Cape Horners

Firsthand Accounts from the Final Days of the Commercial Tall Ships

Edited by Spencer Apollonio

BRASSEY'S
Washington, D.C.

Library of Congress Cataloging-in-Publication Data
The last of the Cape Horners : firsthand accounts from the final days
of the commercial tall ships / edited by Spencer Apollonio—1st ed.
    p. cm.
  Includes bibliographical references and index.
  ISBN 1-57488-283-x (alk. paper)
    1. Seafaring life. 2. Merchant mariners—Biography.
  3. Sailing ships. 4. Merchant ships. I. Apollonio, Spencer.
  VK149 .L38 2000
  910.4'5—dc21   00-056445

ISBN 1-57488-283-x (alk. paper)

Printed in the United States of America on acid-free paper that
meets the American National Standards Institute Z39-48 Standard.

Brassey's
22841 Quicksilver Drive
Dulles, Virginia 20166

First Edition

10 9 8 7 6 5 4 3 2 1

Unchanged, unchanging, in a world of change,
She shall endure, though all things else grow strange,
And though her bones to rust and dust be gone,
Find in men's dreams her resurrection.

Resurrection, C. Fox Smith

Contents

PREFACE

This book is about life in the last big, commercial, square-rigged sailing ships—the Cape Horners—almost all within the first half of the twentieth century. It is about the reality of seafaring that was fast disappearing, never to be repeated within human experience, but that still existed within the lifetime of many of us. Even in my early years, two dozen great sailing ships—ghosts of the past—voyaged every year around the world, out from Europe and then home again around Cape Horn or the Cape of Good Hope, deep loaded with the grain of Australia. They sailed without engines or mechanical power, without electronics, without any contact with the world for the hundred days or more that were usual for their voyages.

Alan Villiers, an undoubted authority and the most prolific chronicler of the last days of cargo-carrying, square-rigged ships, once wrote that anyone may write a sea book. "All that is necessary is to buy copies of the other sea books already written, and then to compile from those a book that is more or less your own. You need never have gone to sea," he wrote, "you need not even have wanted to go. You need have no information of your own, nor seek any.

"But," he continued, "that is a poor way to write books. There are works enough of that scissors-and-paste kind, surely books enough that are made from other books. There is no need to compile sea material of that kind: there is new stuff for the making of a hundred good stories if only someone will see it and go after it." [1]

This book is, alas, of that scissors-and-paste kind. I have done exactly what Captain Villiers deplored. It has to be; I have no choice. The last commercial (but subsidized) voyage of those ships ended in

1. A. J. Villiers, *Modern Mariners* (Garden City, NY: Garden City Publishing Co., Inc., 1937), ix.

1957, before many from the current generation were born, when the *Pamir* sank in an Atlantic hurricane, drowning most of her crew. The days of commercial sail are gone and will not return. There will never again be "new stuff" from those old ships for one to go and seek. All we can do now, those of us who may be interested, is to retell and reinterpret what we can never experience for ourselves, relying on the writings of mariners who knew very well that they were recording the last of sail—truly the end of an era of human history. There is little enough even of oral tradition still to be retrieved; there are very few survivors now of those voyages to pass on their memories.

Since the loss of the *Pamir*, there has been a remarkable resurgence of large sailing ships, many of them square-rigged though newly built, some of them peculiar in rig or hull, and all of them with engines. It is now a mark of status for a country to have its own "tall ship" however slight may be its maritime tradition. Thousands of people flock to gatherings of tall ships held round the world at quite frequent intervals.

"It is doubtful if this late twentieth century interest in sail would exist had it not been for the survival of the merchant sailing vessel into the middle, indeed into the second half, of this century," wrote Basil Greenhill and John Hackman in their *The Grain Races: The Baltic Background*. "If such vessels had not lasted just into the beginning of the era of mass communication through the media it is doubtful if there would be much interest in sailing vessels now. The fascination is stronger because it has its roots in reality still within living memory."

There are at least thirty large (over 150 feet long) square-rigged tall ships sailing today, more than there were of cargo-carrying Cape Horners in their last three decades (the 1930s through the 1950s). There are many more than that of smaller vessels of both fore-and-aft and square rigs. And more are launched every year. Thousands of people each year have some experience aboard these vessels, from a few days to perhaps several months. Most of them sail in summer months or in warm climes. This is all to the good and to be encouraged and cheered. There is no grander sight than a ship under way in a whole-sail breeze, and no better way than to sail such a ship to develop one's personal confidence and competence to respond to the challenges of the sea and of life. I was the mate, once, briefly, of a handsome and very smart schooner of eighty-odd feet. Even in the benign bays in which we sailed, she was grand, indeed, under full sail in a strong breeze. More than once I found enough to do to respond properly and quickly to the captain's quiet but emphatic orders. And so this resurgence of sail has awakened interests and capabilities in so many people who would not otherwise be so uniquely challenged and tested.

But this tall-ships experience does not re-create life as it was under commercial sail. It is a very different experience, for the ships now cater to the fantasies and aspirations of their passengers. The crews now are the reasons for the ships; the ships serve the crews. The crews of the old ships served the ships, and never did the officers allow the crews to forget it.

This book is not about life as it is in today's tall ships, but rather about life at sea when the crews served the ships. It is a compilation of personal experiences; the mariners here speak for themselves. I have looked through all the books about those ships that I could find that have been published in English in the last hundred years, and I have taken those parts that seem to best describe that life under sail at the end of the sailing-ship era. I have taken selections only from first-person accounts of the authors' own experiences. The books were written by professional sailors, a shipmaster in sail, passengers, apprentices who later became masters in sail and steam (and some who didn't), journalists, an artist, and a few who made a single voyage, or even two, just to experience deep-sea sail. One book is by a young woman and two by a professional Finnish sailing-ship officer.

The authors, obviously, brought very different perspectives to their accounts and had very different reactions to their experiences, from lifelong enthusiasm that survived the good and the bad of a number of voyages to bitter disappointment and disillusionment from just one voyage. This was, in part, a matter of personalities of both people and ships. Some authors joined a ship having no idea what to expect and were clearly not suited for life under sail. Some, in spite of recording hardships faithfully, were enthusiastic about the experience. And there is no doubt that the ships had idiosyncracies: *Lawhill* was known to be a singularly lucky vessel; *Winterhude* had a bad reputation. *Pommern* was fast and trouble free; *Olivebank* was frequently in trouble and ended tragically early in the Second World War. Authors' experiences were also, in part, the luck of the draw. The usually reliable and steady trade winds could be fickle, or some ships slipped through the often tedious doldrums with hardly a pause. Adverse winds might be persistent on the run eastward from Australia, greatly prolonging the duration and misery of the passage around Cape Horn. There are both good and bad in these accounts, just as there were in the ships themselves and in the conditions in which they sailed. I have included both, but I have not tried to tip the balance one way or the other. "Good" and "bad," we should remember, are often a matter of perspective, not only among individuals but also with the passage of time. What we today might consider "bad" was perhaps considered only normal and hardly worth mention one hundred years ago, as one author makes clear. I have tried only to select interesting and revealing parts of all the accounts and to let the total speak for itself.

I should note that Alan Villiers had a low opinion of many of the books written about the last days of sail. In his *The War with Cape Horn*, he wrote: "These books follow a fairly general pattern—the older are written by former apprentices who at least served four or five years in deep-sea limejuice *[British]* sail and, being grounded in it, know their business: the newer are from the typewriters of passengers and one-voyage cadets in the big Finnish Cape Horners. These are ninety per cent useless, as far as gaining any real knowledge of or insight into the sailing-ship era may be concerned, for the writers had neither." His condemnation would not include all the books I have used; indeed, he wrote introductions for several of them, and he wrote several himself. But however deficient may be some of the books for a real "insight into the sailing-ship era," undoubtedly they give an honest insight into what the authors *thought* about the sailing-ship era— and that is a good part of my purpose. And I can add that I have not found serious discrepancies between the older books written by former apprentices and the newer books that Captain Villiers found mostly useless.

Others might have taken different selections than I did. Many of those books contain similar descriptions of catching sharks and albatrosses, and of hauling Portuguese men-o'-war on board. Many contain accounts of traditional ceremonies when crossing the equator. Because these descriptions may be found almost anywhere, I have passed over them. Similarly, storms and the labors of handling sail in storms are common themes and occupy much space in nearly all of the books (but one passenger-author hardly mentions heavy weather, perhaps because he did not have to turn out in the middle watch to manhandle a topsail). I have not included a proportionate amount of such storm description here. Everyone expects those descriptions, even though many voyages were not tormented by storms. In fact, many voyages were almost uneventful with respect to the weather. Captain James William Holmes wrote that in the *Cimba* in 1904 "from outside the Channel to Tasmania I had had the royals in for one hour."[2] He meant simply that the weather was so favorable that for all but an hour on a voyage halfway around the world his ship spread its full suit of sails. And rounding the notorious Cape Horn was not always a terrible

2. Royals were light, generally fair weather sails set high on the masts of square-riggers. Refer to the diagram on page xviii for the identification of sails, masts, and parts of the rigging; James William Holmes, *Voyaging: Fifty Years on the Seven Seas in Sail* (Lymington, Hampshire, U.K.: Nautical Publishing Company, 1970), 138.

experience. Captain Carl Granith reported that the *Pommern* rounded "the Corner" in 1933 "with the finest weather imaginable, a high and steady barometer and an exceptionally smooth sea." He summarized that particular circumnavigation as "the most pleasant round trip to Australia and back I have ever made—without a storm and any damages to the ship or loss of canvas."[3] Bad weather on the old vessels could be overdrawn. Most of their voyagings were not afflicted by storms.

I prefer to recall perhaps less familiar faces of life on the ships. My purpose is not to relate tales of high adventure at sea, but rather to distill the essence of the ships at sea, to include unusual and interesting experiences, and to record some technical detail as well as the spirit of life under sail. I want to combine a sense of what life was like with some sense of how the ships were sailed. I have included accounts of ship- and sail-handling when they are helpful in understanding how things were done. And there are some records of interesting natural phenomena of the sea that would not be seen from powered vessels.

The extracts, even though they occurred on a variety of voyages on differing tracks across the sea, are arranged as if they narrated a single voyage around the world. Of course, not all the events here would occur on any single real voyage. Our voyage begins at a port (which port is not important) in the northern hemisphere, as did almost all deep-sea voyages, and then proceeds south through the various climate zones, passing first through the westerly winds[4] of the northern hemisphere, then through the northeast trade winds and the doldrums about the equator until the southeast trades are encountered and traversed. Then the vessel enters the westerly winds of the southern hemisphere and races eastward toward Australia. The vessel stops at ports in southern Australia or continues on to ports on the west coast

3. Carl Granith, "A Round Voyage in the S. V. *Pommern*," *Sea Breezes* 18: 174 (May 1934): 101–105.
4. Winds at sea are named for the direction from which they come.

of South America. It then sails far south into subantarctic waters to round Cape Horn. Once around the Horn, the ship climbs up the South and North Atlantic Oceans, reversing the sequence of wind zones as it returns to a port in northern Europe or North America. This was a typical voyage in the last days of Cape Horners. The various extracts are set in sequence in those stages of the voyage for which they are appropriate.

The language of seamen, and particularly of sailors of sail, evolved out of necessity over centuries as shared experiences unique to the sea accumulated and as ships evolved in complexity. Sea language became highly specialized and precise. The order "lee fore clew-garnet," for example, while meaningless, perhaps, to landsmen, tells a sailor precisely where to go and what to do (and always with an implication to be quick about it). Such clarity and precision were essential for the safety of a ship if shouted orders were to carry over and through the uproar of wind and sea and clashing gear when quick and appropriate action was imperative. This book is full of such language. The authors, because of their training in sail, used it instinctively as the natural and clearest mode of expression in their narratives. Rather than interrupt the flow of narrative with frequent explanations, a glossary of technical terms is included, and the reader new to the language of the sea should use it. The diagram of a ship under sail and the glossary will help the reader become familiar with sailors' language. The reader may discover a logic and regularity in the technical terms that are part of the inherent precision of sea language. And perhaps some familiarity with sea language adds to that peculiar appeal of the old Cape Horners that touches us all.

ACKNOWLEDGMENTS

Robert Lane in Friendship and Cranberry Island, Douglas Bart on Ocean Point in Boothbay, and Peter Boehmer on Monhegan Island, all on the coast of Maine, kindly read the manuscript out of friendship and gave me their suggestions for improvements, for which I am grateful. Pat Roach in Virginia reviewed it with a sailor's eye. Don McKeon, the publisher at Brassey's, was immediately receptive on first receiving the draft outline, and was patient and helpful throughout the protracted process of publication. I thank them all.

Diagram of Sails and Rigging

From *Farewell Windjammer,* by Holger Thesleff

1. Foresail or forecourse
2. Fore lower topsail
3. Fore upper topsail
4. Fore lower topgallant
5. Fore upper topgallant
6. Fore royal
7. Mainsail or maincourse
8. Main lower topsail
9. Main upper topsail
10. Main lower topgallant
11. Main upper topgallant
12. Main royal
13. Crossjack or crojack
14. Mizzen lower topsail
15. Mizzen upper topsail
16. Mizzen lower topgallant
17. Mizzen upper topgallant
18. Mizzen royal
19. Fore topmast staysail
20. Inner jib
21. Outer jib
22. Flying jib
23. Main topmast staysail
24. Foremast
25. Mainmast
26. Mizzen topmast staysail
27. Mizzen-mast
28. Jigger-mast
29. Jigger staysail
30. Shrouds
31. Charthouse
32. Jigger, driver, or spanker
33. Gaff topsail, or spanker topsail
34. Flying-bridge
35. Midships section
36. Poop
37. Fo'c'sle head
38. Yard
39. Yard arm

The glossary appears on pages 275–86.

Just over fifty years ago, in 1948–49, two big square-rigged ships, the *Pamir* and the *Passat,* circumnavigated the earth and, together carrying nine thousand tons of wheat from Australia to England, made the last passages of commercial sail around Cape Horn. The *Pamir* arrived in England after 127 days at sea and the *Passat* after 110 days, both about average passages for the last of the windships. Later attempts to keep those vessels at sea, but with auxiliary power and heavily subsidized, were not successful. Their 1949 voyages thus ended the centuries-old era of ocean-going, cargo-carrying sailing ships. Never again would great ships circumnavigate the earth and travel immense distances—twenty-five thousand to thirty thousand miles—only once touching the land, sped on their ways solely by wind and sails. Never again could sailors experience the great power of those ships in the roaring forties or the sublime sailing experience on such ships in the trade winds. The era thus ended is perhaps unique in human experience. It cannot be revived nor truly re-created and so is gone forever, and perhaps we are the poorer for it.

There are still, surprisingly perhaps, about twenty Cape Horners in some better or lesser state of preservation in the world today, at the beginning of the twenty-first century. They are the sole survivors of several thousand that carried some of the world's commerce about the oceans about three generations ago. Alan Villiers estimated that in 1905 (which does not seem all that long ago to those of us born before 1950), there were 3,500 deepwater square-riggers. By nationality they were: British, 800; Norwegian, 550; French, 215; German, 250; Italian, 350; American, 150; Russian, 52; and many Spanish, Portuguese, South American, Austro-Hungarian, Danish, Swedish, and Belgian vessels.

The First World War brought about the violent destruction of many of these square-riggers, and the shipping slump and depression of the early 1920s caused many more to be broken up for scrap. Even so, as late as 1928, Villiers estimated, there were still a hundred large square-rigged ships in use or more or less fit to be commissioned. The great global economic depression and accidents at sea in the 1930s reduced them to two or three dozen working windjammers. Even the Second World War took its toll: *Olivebank* mined in the North Sea, *Penang* torpedoed, *Killoran* and *Reine Marie Stewart* sunk by gunfire of a surface raider and of a submarine. *Lawhill* and *Pamir*, miraculously, sailed throughout the war without damage, contributing to the available ocean-going tonnage in desperate shortage, the only square-riggers to do so. The *Pamir*, incidentally, probably encountered in poor visibility a surfaced Japanese submarine which, perhaps unwilling to strike down the majestic and defenseless old vessel, took no action and vanished into the murk.

Several were broken up for scrap metal after the war. Those twenty or so commercial square-riggers that remain now probably are safe, to be with us as long as the iron or steel of their hulls, masts, and rigging can be preserved against the disintegrations of time and weather. They will not be lost by collision with ice or another ship, or wrecked onshore, or dismasted, or taken to the shipbreakers, or burned at sea, or mined, or torpedoed, or sunk by gunfire, or just disappear at sea—all of which happened to those poor ships since 1928. In fact, *James Craig*, formerly *Clan Mcleod*, on which Alan Villiers served, has been rescued from disintegration on a mudflat and is being restored in Melbourne, Australia. *Polly Woodside* has been beautifully restored in Melbourne. *Pommern* lies at a quiet anchorage at Mariehamn, the homeport of the last Cape Horners in commission, in the Finnish Åland Islands. *Wavertree* and *Peking* are at South Street in New York. *Moshulu* is in Philadelphia. *Balclutha* and *Star of India*, formerly *Euterpe*, are in San Francisco and San Diego, respectively. *Falls of*

Clyde is partially restored in Honolulu. *Passat* is preserved in Hamburg. *Padua* is still sailing as the Russian *Kruzenstern*, and *Kommodore Johnsen*, formerly *Magdalene Vinnen*, sails as the Russian *Sedov*—both training ships. *Viking* is on public exhibition in Gothenborg, and *Rickmer Rickmers*, formerly *Sagres*, formerly *Rickmer Rickmers*, is a museum ship in Hamburg. *Elissa* sails out of Houston, and *City of Adelaide* and *Glenlee* are being restored at Irvine and Glasgow, Scotland. Though not a Cape Horner, one notes with pleasure that the beautiful little brig *Maria Asumpta*, built in 1856, sails in England. And, of course, the tea-clipper *Cutty Sark* is at Greenwich. The wooden bark *Sigyn* has been rebuilt in Turku, Sweden; *Suomen Joutsen*, formerly *Laennec*, is preserved at Helsinki; and *af Chapman*, formerly *G.D. Kennedy*, formerly *Dunboyne*, is in Stockholm.

These combine to include one four-masted, full-rigged ship, eight four-masted barks, six full-rigged ships, and six big barks, a grand representation of the big ships that were the culmination of commercial sail. There is also about an equal number of sailing-ship hulks, in various stages of disintegration, in Chile, New Zealand, the Falkland Islands, and elsewhere. They are mostly beyond the possibility of restoration.

The last of the Cape Horners were not at all like the fast and famous clipper ships of the mid–nineteeth century—the California gold-rush clippers or the English colonial or tea-clippers like the *Cutty Sark*—with towering sail plans, sharp hulls, and large crews to deliver valuable cargoes to their destinations as fast as possible—and never mind the cost. The clipper ships were *never* called "windjammers," a somewhat derogatory term coined for their less prestigious successors. The last ships, the windjammers, were built—some, but not all, like warehouses—to carry the largest possible cargo at the least possible cost; they had to if they were to survive against the ever-increasing competition of steam. Speed was not a consideration. Ever-smaller crews sailed ever-larger ships as the inevitability of competition with steam forced economies of size and crew costs to the limits. W. L. A. Derby compiled the following information on the evolution of the manning of sailing ships:[5]

Year	Ship	Tons	Length (ft)	Crew
1815	*Earl of Balcarres*	1,417	about 180	138
1852	*Sovereign of the Seas*	2,412	258	106
1866	*Sobraon*	2,131	272	69
1873	*British Ambassador*	1,794	262	47
1895	*Potosi*	4,026	366	40
1932	*Parma*	3,091	328	29

The *Herzogin Cecilie* (3,111 tons, 314 feet) in 1926 sailed around Cape Horn with only nineteen men on board, although not from choice. Nothing could better summarize the competitive struggle of the last square-riggers than these figures.

— · — · —

By the end of the nineteenth century, steamers were rapidly taking over the ocean commerce of the world. A few square-rigged, cargo-carrying ships were still being built (the last, *Padua*, in 1926), but because of the severe competition from powered vessels, most ship-owners scrapped or sold their sailing vessels as rapidly as possible in the 1910s, 1920s, and 1930s. Even in the 1930s, however, the Cape Horners could still compete with steamers in a very few trades and there was money to be made in sail *if* the vessels were operated with strictest economy. Scandinavian shipowners, particularly in Finland, bought sailing vessels that were in good condition, usually at prices equal to their scrap value. The *Moshulu*, a magnificent vessel, was bought in 1935 for twelve thousand dollars. The new owners rarely

5. W. L. A. Derby, *The Tall Ships Pass* (New York: Charles Scribner's Sons, 1937), 139–41.

insured their hulls; the premiums were not affordable and at the purchase prices, there was little or no depreciation. The owners then ran them with closest attention to costs. Crews were kept as small as possible, usually far less than when the vessels were new. Officers and essential skilled crew, such as sailmakers, had to be paid something. The captain of the *Moshulu* in 1938 received about a hundred dollars a month and the average sailmaker about twenty dollars. The wages for other crew members were miniscule. A skilled able-bodied seaman (rated as an A. B.) received not more than, and often much less than, sixteen dollars a month. Many of the crew were not skilled, but rather were rated as apprentices and as such they paid the owners a premium of about two hundred and fifty dollars for the "privilege" of making a round-trip voyage or for a year on board. Crews were readily available in spite of those low wages or high premiums, because Germany and Scandinavian countries still required sail experience for mariners' licenses.

Maintenance costs, also, were kept low, in part by cannibalism. Every year at least one vessel was laid up or wrecked and its parts of all kinds were salvaged whenever possible for use on the remaining vessels. The *Hougomont* was dismasted south of Australia in 1932 and everything usable from her was shipped back to Finland on the *Herzogin Cecilie*. Four years later, the stranded *Herzogin Cecilie* was similarly stripped. One well-known ship sailed with undersized sails taken from a scrapped smaller vessel. And, of course, the ships were supplied with a minimum of stores such that even food could be in short supply and the sailors hungry on some voyages.

The Cape Horners at the end of the era carried low-value bulk cargoes of little interest to steamers—wheat, coal, timber, and guano fetilizer. They were able to charter for such cargoes because the loading or discharging was often in ports with primitive or nonexistent cargo-handling facilities, which meant long delays that steamers with high overheads could not afford. But windjammers that often carried only one cargo a year were indifferent to the delays. And in such ports, expenses were low, with no "port" fees, no "lights" fees, no pilotage fees. Tugs were rarely used if they could be avoided; three-hundred-foot ships were occasionally sailed alongside or away from docks.

Coal was shipped from Wales or from Newcastle in Australia to the west coast of South America, where it might be unloaded one basket at a time. From South America, the sailers carried guano or nitrate fertilizers to northern Europe. They might spend months loading the fertilizer.

By the 1930s, only the Germans were able to maintain a profitable trade with a handful of sailing ships to the west coast of South America. They shipped general cargo out and nitrates for fertilizers or explosives home. Powerful vessels such as *Peking, Padua,* and *Priwall* had been built especially for the difficult west-bound voyage around Cape Horn—against the strong prevailing winds—and the Germans built efficient cargo handling facilities to speed the turn-around times of the vessels. Their captains were expected to make one and a half round trips around Cape Horn each year, a tough schedule. Those few German vessels were favored with large crews and guaranteed round-trip cargoes and were not typical of the other Cape Horners at the end of the era, although some of them, like the *Pamir* and *Passat,* ended their careers in the grain trade.

Early in the 1900s, ships were chartered to carry grain from Puget Sound or Portland, Oregon, to Great Britain, France, or Germany, but after the mid-1920s, the ships were almost entirely confined to the trade of carrying wheat from small and remote ports in south Australia to Europe. They usually sailed in ballast (that is, with no paying cargo, but with the ship's hold partially filled with stones or other heavy material—ballast—to provide stability) to Australia. Some ships occasionally were able to get a timber charter from Finland or Sweden to South Africa, and then sailed on in ballast to Australia. And it could happen that, after sailing halfway around the world, they might fail to get a grain charter and then were forced to lay idle at anchor for a year in Australia or return to Europe in ballast.

Grain from Australia to Europe was the principal sailing-ship cargo from 1920 until 1949 (except for the years of the Second World War). This annual odyssey of up to thirty great sailing ships came to be known to the general public as the Australian Grain Race, and ships could make money in it. In those years the carrying rates for grain could vary from perhaps four dollars to eight dollars per ton. The owners of the *Parma* bought their vessel in 1932 for about ten thousand dollars and then loaded over 5,200 tons, or 62,650 bags of grain, for a gross income of forty thousand dollars. The ship paid for herself and all her expenses for the year from the income of that one voyage even though she had sailed in ballast halfway around the world. In most of those years, the Cape Horners in the grain trade could clear about five thousand dollars each.

While the public thought of this trade as the Grain Race, there was no compelling economic reason to be first home with a cargo of grain, and the owners severely discouraged racing by their officers (although they did not mind if their ship arrived ahead of another). Racing in the winds and waters around Cape Horn meant straining ships and losing sails and gear, and it meant the expenses of repairing or replacing those damages and losses. Such expenses were not to be endured. Unlike the hell-bent racing captains of the celebrated tea-clippers of the 1860s, there were no gold-headed canes waiting for the winner of a grain race of the 1930s. More likely, the captain of a grain ship who lost gear would loose his job.

The Scandinavian owners operated the last big sailing cargo vessels not from sentimental attachment to sail, but for very sound economic reasons. In the rather poor Scandinavian countries (particularly Norway and Finland) of the 1910s, 1920s, and 1930s, with long traditions of seafaring but with few indigenous natural resources, the price-depreciated sailing vessels were one of the few options to accumulate the capital needed to acquire a modern merchant fleet. That was always their owners' goal. The 1932 voyage of the *Parma* showed it could be done, and indeed Scandinavians did it and now are major owners of very modern ships.

———

You may trace the Cape Horners' trade routes on a map, but a globe will give you a much better impression of the immense journeys those ships of sail carried out. Even a small globe conveys a sense of distance, from Tacoma, Washington, to England, or from Copenhagen to South Australia for wheat, that a flat map cannot. Only on a globe do you get a sense how far south the vessels had to go, deep into subantarctic waters, to find the strong west winds they needed to drive to Australia and then home around Cape Horn. A globe can better reconcile the meaning of three- or four-month voyages with a sense of distance across the vast emptiness of the world's oceans. A hundred-day passage does not seem so long, after all, when you trace a voyage on a globe from New York to Calcutta, nor eighty days from Belfast to Tasmania, around either of the great capes. I suspect that the average steamer of the time, if it had to follow the same tracks as the sailers (which did not use the difficult and expensive routes via the Suez and Panama canals), would not have been much faster over those immense distances.

The mariners of the age of exploration in the fifteenth and six-teenth centuries had painfully discovered the predictable patterns of ocean winds that the last of the windjammers depended upon into the middle of the twentieth century. The patterns are based on a simple symmetry north and south from the equator of climate zones caused by the heating of the earth's surface.

At the equator are the doldrums, the zone of heat, exasperating calms, sudden and short-lived squalls and downpours, and uncertain light winds, all the result of rising hot air. When that air, cooled by its ascent and expansion into the sky, descends again to earth, it tends to flow toward the equator to fill the void left there by the rising hot air. But it is deflected by the rotation of the earth into the northeast and southeast trade winds that blow with a steady force that gives a sailing vessel its finest passages. Beyond the trades are the variables or horse latitudes, also zones of calms and variable winds. Still further from the equator, the higher latitudes of both the northern and southern hemispheres promise the sailing ship the westerlies. In the southern hemisphere they are called the roaring forties, named for the latitudes in which they are found; they are the gale-force winds that are so important to vessels traveling great distances around the world. (Beyond the roaring forties are the howling fifties and the screaming sixties, but vessels went to those latitudes only rarely.)

There are always variations in those patterns of wind, but the shipmaster took advantage of the patterns as best he could in planning his voyage, and, in fact, the ships were designed and built with them in mind. There were unending efforts to find the form of a ship's hull that could slide easily through the calms of the doldrums and also run safely through the mountainous seas of the high latitudes, together with a rig that could stand up to the storms of the westerlies.

The square-rig, not the fore-and-aft rig, was always the most practical for ocean voyaging, and so it prevailed until the end of the era of deepwater commercial sail. The patterns of ocean winds are such that for long voyages the sailing vessel, by good planning and some luck, could run most of its way *with* the winds, the particular virtue of square-riggers. It was found from experimentation and hard experience that over great distances the fore-and-aft rig carried no significant advantages over the square-rigger, and in heavy weather it had substantial disadvantages. Great fore-and-aft sails and their gear were hard to control and could be dangerous in strong gales and rolling seas. Columbus converted the *Nina* from fore-and-aft rig to square-rig before his first transatlantic voyage. A Maine square-rig captain took a large fore-and-aft cargo schooner around the world and swore he would never do it again.

—·—·—

There was a conservatism of design and management in the last of the Cape Horners that in hindsight is both remarkable and deplorable. Frederick William Wallace, a Nova Scotian shipmaster in sail, wrote: "In the designing and building of sailing ships, the humanitarian aspect has generally been neglected. The comfort of the crew was hardly considered, and seemingly very little was done to reduce the peril of their work. . . . Life in the sailing ship may be heroic, but it was often desperately cruel and unnecessarily harsh, and that largely because of the fact that nobody bothered to make it less so. . . . If anything, the latter-day sailers, huge switch-backed cargo tanks, are the worst ever built as far as the sailor's comfort is concerned."[6]

The use of safety harnesses when working aloft is mandatory now on all tall ships. I made sure of mine on my first hesitant climb, when I was hanging seemingly upside down, over the futtock shrouds of a modern and handsome topsail schooner. The value of the harness seems obvious, and its neglect would be stupid, but in spite of falls and frequent near-falls from aloft, safety harnesses are never mentioned in any of the accounts I have seen until the voyage of the *Pamir* in 1952. Were they never thought of? That seems unlikely. The old mariners might have scoffed at them, maintaining, perhaps, that one could not work aloft in such a rig. Sailors were supposed to work with "one hand for the ship and one hand for thyself," but everyone knew that that admonition was a joke; most jobs aloft or on deck took two hands. Alan Villiers fell from aloft in the *Lawhill* and had to leave the ship severely injured. Basil Lubbock, another author of these accounts, fell

6. Frederick William Wallace, *Under Sail in the Last of the Clippers* (Boston: Charles E. Lauriat Co., 1936).

from the mizzen mast in the *Commonwealth*. Falls and near-falls are too frequently noted in these accounts. The short-handed *British Isles* in 1905 under Captain James Barker lost two men from falls. Why safety harnesses were never used until the new generation of tall ships is an unhappy mystery.

Except in the very last German ships and a very few others, deck-houses accommodating the crew and essential gear such as freshwater pumps were located in the low, open midsection of the deck, a very exposed part of ships, guaranteeing misery and hazards for the crews when seas inevitably broke over the rails of deep-laden ships running through the stormy North Atlantic or across the southern ocean. And many of the ships had no stoves or heat for the crew in the forecastle—their accommodations—when there was snow on deck and ice in the rigging. A close friend of mine crossed the North Atlantic in winter as a crew member in the *Brynhilda*, its course just below 60 degrees North (the latitude of Cape Farewell, Greenland) to avoid the legal requirement (and the expense) of providing heat in the forecastle when north of that latitude. Indeed, in some of the last of the windjammers, the forecastle stove had been removed and not replaced, presumably to save the fuel bill.

The *Parma* was nearly lost in the southern ocean in 1932 because her compass lights were primitive and unreliable. During a midnight gale, the helmsmen kept that great ship on course by the compass and from broaching to (swinging out of control) only with the help of a cheap, handheld flashlight—the only one on the ship—when the storm blew out the compass lights.

And the food on most ships remained, until the 1950s, true to the latest in eighteenth-century knowledge and technology. Part of this was for economy in the hard-pressed ships, but part was also parsimony, and part was pure tradition.

Life at sea was surprisingly healthy in spite of the frequently poor diet and primitive working and living conditions. The young first-voyage apprentices generally had grown and matured beyond their parents' expectations after a two-year voyage. They went to sea as boys (age fourteen or fifteen was normal) and returned home robust young men. Sailors rarely got colds in spite of cold weather and wet, cold accommodations and clothing for weeks on end. Salt water and salt air seem to counteract cold infections. But skin boils were a routine curse, as will be noted here, on the long voyages, and all seaman were subject to minor or serious injuries. There was the tragic case of beriberi from an unusually long voyage of the *Olivebank* in 1928 from which two men died. The old seamen, but not the younger, could be quite sentimental and fatalistic about death at sea, as a favorite ballad reveals:

> Our bark was far, far from the land
> When the fairest of our sailor band
> Grew deathly pale and pined away
> Like the fading light of an autumn day.

Perhaps it is not surprising that sailors isolated at sea and with few and primitive medical resources developed a fatalistic response to an unavoidable loss.

Most sailors became immune to seasickness after the first few days of their first voyage, but that initiation could be misery. Seasickness and other such minor ailments evoked little sympathy from overworked and underpaid officers, who had suffered and survived the same trials in their youth, and their remedies were direct and surprisingly effective. James Bisset wrote of his first day at sea as an apprentice in 1898: "Added to my general feeling of misery, I had a terror of being seasick; my imagination probably helped to bring on an attack of the very thing I feared, and soon I was retching my soup up over the rail.... Homesick and seasick and thinking I'd never be missed, I crept into the half deck and threw myself into my bunk, hoping to die; but the Mate came in and, grabbing my feet, hauled me out on deck like a sack of coal.

" 'Seasick?' he growled. 'I'll cure you!' Then, taking a tin pannikin from the galley, he filled it with sea water from the scuppers, as a sea came over the lee rail and washed across the deck. 'Here, drink this!' he ordered, holding me by the scruff of the neck and forcing the pannikin to my lips.

"I drank the lot, hoping it would kill me. The powerful emetic worked. Strangely enough, in about half an hour I was better and actually feeling hungry. I have never been seasick from that day to this; but I have always hesitated to recommend this old-fashioned remedy to passengers in luxury liners."[7]

Even so, whatever may have been the hardships, necessary and unnecessary, the call of those ships was compelling then and is powerful still. "A curse forever, but still a thing of beauty!" cries one of our authors about the last of the windships. John Robert Spurling went to sea at age sixteen and on his first voyage suffered a fall from a fore upper topsail yard that put him in a Singapore hospital for five months. It could have killed him. His recovery was only partial, and the injury could have ended his sea career. But Jack Spurling's near-fatal fall could not extinguish his love of the ships. He spent seven years at sea and went on to paint the finest portraits of ships that we have, pictures that are filled with the grandeur and grace of one of our finest creations, pictures that are faithful to the details of their lines and rigs. Even now pictures—photographs and paintings of the great ships—fill our dreams and lift our spirits with undeniable pleasure. New editions of Spurling's work appear periodically, testifying to the everlasting appeal of those wonderful ships. We can be confident that it will always be so.

7. James Bisset, *Sail Ho* (New York: Criterion Books, 1958).

The Last of the Cape Horners

Getting Under Way

[Basil Lubbock came down from several months of seeking gold in the Klondike to San Francisco. He had intended to ship aboard a South Sea schooner to Australia, but failing to find such a vessel he decided "to ship home round the Horn in one of the magnificent windjammers which lay in the port." He knew little about sailing ships, but he knew enough, he wrote, "not to ship before the mast [to sail as a common sailor] on a ship with 'down-east' [Maine] or 'blue-nose' [Nova Scotian] mates, who, though they are the finest seamen probably in the world, are terrible 'drivers,' and are a bit too free with belaying pins, knuckle-dusters, and six-shooters to please me, —the 'gun-play' on board some 'down-easters' being almost worthy of an Arizona mining camp."

This voyage home before the mast was not Lubbock's only passage under sail. The experiences led him to spend the rest of his life searching for and recording the histories of late-nineteenth- and twentieth-century sailing ships, histories that would otherwise have been lost. He became the most famous of sailing ship historians and wrote over a dozen volumes.

Lubbock called his ship the Royalshire in his book of the voyage, but she was in fact the Ross-shire. He described her in the first volume of his The Last of the Windjammers as "a very handsome and a very powerful ves-

3

*sel with quite a respectable turn of speed; but she was something of a hand-
ful for a watch of ten hands, there being no aids to manpower in the shape of
donkey engines, halliard winches and the like beyond four maindeck capstans. Neither had she any bridges to help her crew get about when the main
deck was flooded, which was generally the case in heavy weather . . . she
knew how to scoop up the sea over either rail."*

Lubbock's ship got under way in 1899.]

FRIDAY, 25TH AUGUST.—Manned the capstan at 4 A.M. The crew
were turned out with some difficulty, and some of them looked very
much the worse for wear, especially those that only came aboard last
night. The German-American bosun soon began to give tongue,
which, with his size, soon brought the loiterers up to the scratch.

The longbars were put into the capstan, and we were soon tramping
drearily round in the raw, misty, morning air. As no one felt equal to a
chanty, we hove her short to occasional "Heave and she comes!"
"Heave and break her out!" "Heave and she must!" "Heave and bust
her!"

Presently the anchor was hove short, and we had to wait a while for
our tug. . . .

. . . as it grew lighter, we made out the tug coming off. We soon had
her hawser aboard, and "Man the capstan!" came the order, and "Break
out the mudhook!"

Then came a struggle; everybody strained with all their might,
slower and slower went the "click" of the pawls, until at last we were
almost at a standstill;—that mudhook refused to leave his pleasant
quarters at the bottom of Frisco Bay, and twenty men did not seem
able to move him.

Puff! goes the tug, and with its help we soon break out the demon,
which presently appears at the rail, with a mass of dark blue clayish
mud clinging to him. A man is sent to the wheel and the tug goes
ahead.

The anchor is soon catted and fished, and we are turned to getting all ready for sea.

Slowly, in the light of early dawn, we leave Frisco, and pass our comrades lying in the bay. One of them, the smart French barque, has a tug alongside her, and will soon be on our heels. . . .

"All hands make sail!" sang out the mate. There was a steady breeze from the north-west.

I went up on to the fore-topsail yards and loosed those sails, and then to the fore-topgallant yards, and finally the royal. We had a busy morning of it setting all sail.

When the royal yards had been mastheaded, I was sent up to the fore-royal to overhaul the leech and buntlines, which are, of course, of chain, and just within reach from the top of the topgallant rigging. *[In this somewhat technical sentence, Lubbock says that after the highest sail on the foremast had been hoisted and set to the wind he climbed up and cleared and tied off the chains that were used to gather the sail up to its yard when not in use.]*

Up I went, without any difficulty as regards the climbing, and luckily for me I have a very good head, so I was soon on the royal foot-ropes overhauling the gear.

What a magnificent lookout one gets from the royal yard of a ship, and what wee specks the people working on deck do look from such an elevation! . . .

When all the gear had been overhauled, and the *Royalshire* was off with the wind on the beam *[at 90 degrees to the ship]*, with everything drawing and the decks cleared up, all hands were called aft, and the watches were picked. . . .

. . . the tug had cast off directly we had got our topsails mastheaded, and with a toot of farewell had turned her head for the Golden Gate; and soon after the beautiful pilot-boat, the schooner *Bonita*, ran down to us, and sent a boat aboard to take off the pilot . . .

The forenoon watch is our watch on deck; the wind is not very strong, and has hauled ahead, so that we are close-hauled on the starboard tack. The French barque soon ran past us, and heading higher, much to our disgust, was soon almost out of sight to windward. . . .

At noon we went about, and no one who has not witnessed the sight of a big ship going about, can imagine the yelling and excitement that goes on.

— ·· — ·· —

[A sailing ship cannot sail directly into the wind. But by "tacking," by sailing in a zigzag pattern with wind first on one side of the bow and then on the other and by thus keeping its sails full and pulling, it can make progress toward the wind. The business of changing directions, or "going about," while tacking a square-rigger required good seamanship.

Holger Thesleff described the technique of tacking a big Cape Horner. Thesleff, a Swede, sailed from Europe as an apprentice on the last voyage of the Passat *and arrived back in Europe in 1949 as third mate, which says something about the problem of manning such ships at midcentury. It also says something about Holger Thesleff. His book is the only record we have of that last voyage of the great tradition.]*

When you turn through the wind with a square-rigged ship you must in the first place be sure that the crew are smart enough. The next most important thing is that the brace-winches, blocks and gear should be well greased. Then all the topgallant and royal braces, that is, those that do not run on winches, must have their by-the-wind hitches at the right place, they must overhaul well and run clear. The mainsail and the crojack are clewed up and the spanker sheeted to windward, or, in other words, is backed up against the wind. The log is hauled in. "Lee oh!" calls the Skipper from the midships-deck, the wheel is put down and the ship begins gently to turn her bow against the wind. Her speed slackens and the square-sails back more and more beginning from windward. At the right moment, which is when only the lee sides are full, the Skipper calls "Mainsail haul!" Then all the mizzen and main yards must be got round at once. One watch is at each brace-winch, and you haul on the wires with all your strength over the winches to give them extra speed. The topgallant and royal braces are cast loose. If you have been quick enough the two riggings will now crash round of themselves. Seen from the deck it is a tremendous spectacle, with a mighty thundering and rattling as the heavy yards move first athwart and then obliquely in the other direction. The mate stands ready by the winch-brake and at times there can be sparks flying from it before the yards halt.

Then it is the turn of the fore-rigging. These sails are now all aback and they have to be hove round. That is a tough job for one watch; the other is meanwhile seeing to the fore-sheet and tack, some shifting over the staysails. The ship is still almost head to the wind and going slowly astern. The wheel is put hard over, and, if all goes as it should, she falls off and the sails fill, first the jibs and staysails, then the square-sails. She is then sailing on the other tack. The whole manoeuvre, including the preparations and the clearing up of ropes afterwards, usually takes something over half an hour, though it is said that with a very expert crew it can be executed in a quarter of an hour.

— · — · —

[But tacking ship was not always carried out in the seaman-like manner we might think, as Paul Eve Stevenson recorded. Stevenson was a wealthy American at the turn of the century and an enthusiastic yachtsman in the era when most yachtsmen had professional crews. Stevenson was also keenly interested in commercial sail and, with his wife (whose name he never mentioned but which must have been prefixed by "Saint"), made two voyages as passengers from New York in square-riggers, one to Calcutta in the British full-rigged ship Mandalore *and one on an American ship around Cape Horn to San Francisco. The American ship was not rightly named nor were the officers, probably because of their behavior. Stevenson published two excellent books based on his daily journals of the voyages. He described the*

maneuver of tacking ship on the American vessel a few days outward bound
from New York.]

In our lives we have witnessed many scenes of great tumult, but
never have I seen any to compare with that on board this ship this
afternoon at four o'clock. Captain Scruggs had been growling and
yapping around the main deck all day, cursing everything, and particularly the light air which came fanning along, whenever it fanned at
all, straight out of the south. Thus far we had not once tacked ship,
though several times the wind had shifted so as to bring it to the other
side. We were crawling along then this afternoon toward the east when
eight bells went and both watches came on deck; while in another
minute, without previous warning, the skipper yapped out, "All hands
'bout ship *[tack ship]*." Paint-brushes and serving mallets were dropped
and tar-pots stowed away, while every one hastened to obey the summons.

Now, there is always more or less confusion the first time that a
square-rigger tacks or wears *[another method of changing direction into*
the wind] on a voyage, though if everybody keeps his head there ought
not to be so very much; and if our skipper had only let Mr. Goggins
attend to the small details there wouldn't have been a tenth of the dis-
order here. From the moment that the helm was put down, however,
until we filled away on the other leg the ship was like a mad-house at
recess. I don't believe that there ever was heard on a vessel's deck such
yelling, or howling, which is a more comprehensive word. Nearly every
order given by either mate the captain at once countermanded, sometimes without knowing it, often on purpose. The main-deck was full
of capstan-bars, lead blocks and braces, which had been cast off when
the order came to 'bout ship; and over and among these encumbrances
eighteen men wrangled, stamped, and swore to an accompaniment of
chattering blocks and thrashing canvas, as the ship came up to the
wind, the mates cuffing and thumping the awkward ones with unflag-
ging diligence, Mr. Goggins lumbering heavily aft to administer a

painful booting to that hapless creature, Neils Brun, who has been in almost continuous trouble since the mate nearly pulled his ear off, a fortnight ago.

And where was the master of the ship all this time? Behold him at the break of the poop raging like the heathen, while at times he shook both fists together above his head and swore like a pirate, as his voice went booming and crashing above the noise of battle. But the full glory of the scene was reached when, a few moments after he had roared out "Maintop-sail, haul!" *[the critical order for shifting sails when tacking]* the main-brace jammed in the brace-block and wouldn't render. His passion was almost fearful as he called upon the blank-blank-blankety who fouled the brace to show himself; while he jumped off the poop and raged away, tearing the braces apart as though he were wringing some one's neck. Even the second mate lost his head once as the old man shouted to his bosun, "I told yer to let go that t'gallant brace, didn't I? Do ye want me to show yer how it's done? I will; but I'll wipe the deck with yer first. Where are ye steerin' the ship to, yer at the wheel? Maybe yer'd like to have her aback?"

Now, if we had never been to sea before, we might have supposed that this was the necessary and proper manner of putting a ship about; but as we had seen the *Mandalore* under similar conditions several times, where there was almost perfect order during such evolutions, this scene was positively astounding, and disgusted us with Captain Scruggs. He is manifestly a fine seaman (American shipmasters are invariably that), but he loses command of himself and every one else as soon as there is anything to be done.

—··—··—

[Getting the anchor and leaving the harbor did not always mean that a ship was thereby free of the land, at sea, and away upon her voyage. Square-rigged ships are not efficient at sailing into adverse winds and particularly in confined waters, where they must tack back and forth frequently, perhaps

even losing some ground with each tack. The Oban Bay *spent six weeks in 1904 thrashing about against headwinds in the Irish Sea, back and forth between England and Ireland, trying to get clear of the land. It was not an uncommon trial. Elis Karlsson, mate of the* Penang, *experienced the difficulties of escaping the land.*

Karlsson was a native of the Åland Islands in Finland, where most of the last of the commercial square-riggers were owned. Like many of his neighbors, he went to sea as a matter of course in the 1920s on the old ships, intending to make a career in sail. After serving in small barks and schooners sailing on the Baltic Sea, he sailed as able seaman on the Herzogin Cecilie, *then as mates on the* Penang, *and finally as chief mate on the* Herzogin Cecilie. *He ended his career in sail in 1936, when the* Herzogin Cecilie *went ashore on a foggy night on the coast of Devon, England, after a fast passage from Australia. He later served briefly as a mate in a steamer and then retired from the sea. Karlsson is apparently the only professional seaman from the last of the Finnish fleet to write about his experiences. He published two books. Here, from* Mother Sea, *he describes the difficulties of getting out of the narrow waters between Denmark and Sweden, when outward bound in November, 1931, to Australia. The* Penang *was caught at night in a blinding snow storm and with a head wind.]*

A shout from above brought me on deck in a hurry. Before I reached the poop, the Captain shouted:

"We must anchor, Styrman *[mate]*! Get the sails off her and let go starboard anchor. Hurry!"

The watch below was tumbling out on deck at that moment, and selecting some of the hands on the way, I ran to the fo'c'slehead. While the hands tore the lashings off the anchors, I explained to the Carpenter, a young Ålander, what to do when the anchor went down. *[The anchor chain in these circumstances would go out with a rush. Since the ship was close to shore, it was important to keep the chain under control and to prevent too much from going down. Karlsson tells the carpenter to slow the rush of chain, if he can, by applying the windlass brake carefully and lightly.*

If applied abruptly or too forcefully, the chain could break the pulling wheel
of the windlass. Karlsson then tells the crew to let the wind out of the sails
but to leave the cleaning up of running rigging until later.]

"Hold what you can, after the first rush of chain, but don't brake too hard, or you'll break the gipsy-wheel." The Carpenter hurried below the fo'c'slehead to his windlass.

"Let go all sheets and lower away everything. Clew and bunt when you get the time. Fore-rigging first!" I shouted to the Second and Third.

"Let go the anchor!" came faintly through the wind and sleet from the poop. It was blowing hard now. I saw the Captain signaling frantically with his hands to let go. God, I thought, she has too much sail on her, she isn't up in the wind; but I hurried to obey. I sensed that we were in shallow water, and I had caught a glimpse of land to leeward in the snow and sleet. How desperate our situation was I had no means of knowing.

I jerked the release-lever upward, and the anchor struck the water. The chain roared out to windward, but far too fast for my liking, and through the speaking tube I shouted:

"Slow it down, Timmerman! Slow it down!" The next moment the Carpenter, covered in rusty chain-dust from head to foot, stood beside me and shouted in my ear:

"I can't hold anything, Styrman! The chain is jumping the gipsy-wheel" *[the chain was going out too fast and could not be controlled with the brake]*.

"All right, as soon as you can, apply a little brake. Release port brake, and if I let go port anchor, you'll have to attend to that as well." The Carpenter was gone as soon as I was finished speaking.

I had kept an eye on the Captain all the time, waiting for a sign to let go port anchor; it should have been in by now, in my opinion. At last the signal came, and the port anchor chain added its roar to the one on starboard.

The starboard chain was slowing down a little, and as I hurried through a barrage of flogging fore-staysail sheets—I had managed to haul the staysails half-way down while up there—and down the ladder to the main deck, I looked aloft. Would we be in time, getting the sails off her, before the masts went over the side? The clews *[lower corners]* of the foresail were flogging; the other sails lay still plastered against the masts and riggings, and exerting enormous pressure on the wrong sides of the masts. Aft, the Captain and the Steward were hauling out the spanker to help the ship up in the wind.

In the dust-filled gloom under the fo'c'slehead, the Carpenter stood at the windlass, easing the brakes in turn amongst ominous clanks and groans from the straining chains. I took over starboard brake. The Carpenter shouted across:

"Starboard hawse-pipe is cracked!" *[by the anchor chain out of control, off the pulling wheel of the windlass, and cutting through the steel of the ship's bow]*.

We had dropped the second anchor none too soon. With the hawse-pipe gone, the anchor chain might have cut through the steel plating and the forward frames along the ship's side; the sails would have filled and the ship gathered way, before there was time to attend to the braces, and the chain would then have to snap.

Both chains were now under control. . . .

We secured the chains and gave a hand at clewing of the sails. The danger to the rigging over, I went aft to find out where we were. What I learned was not very reassuring.

We had anchored on the fringe of a shoal, extending to the north from the island of Lessö, and there was very little water under our keel, as I found out when taking soundings. . . .

For five days we lay there, while the northerly gale blew itself out. . . .

On the fifth day a fair wind . . . carried us to the Skaw.

— · — · — · —

[Only when the ship was well clear of the land would the anchors be taken off the catheads and brought inboard for secure stowage on deck, well lashed to prevent their movement while at sea. Dewar Brown described the procedure. He was one of those Scots who turn their hand to everything and everywhere. At age nineteen he was employed in the British consulate in Fez, Morocco. Brown served in the British army in the First World War. He was in the diplomatic service again in Iraq and in the Norwegian army in the Second World War. Between the wars he was in three square-riggers. His first voyage was in 1933 in the three-masted bark Winterhude, *perhaps the ugliest, and with the hardest reputation, of the last of the windjammers.]*

We of the port watch had reason to regret our inclusion in the mate's crowd in such weather during the first days at sea, for it was part and parcel of the duties of the port watch to secure the anchors inboard to the ring bolts on the fo'c'sle head, under the circumstances a wet and cold job. When a sailing-ship puts to sea on a deep water voyage, the anchors are hoisted inboard by means of a fish tackle set up either to the foretop or, as in our case, to a small anchor crane mounted on the fo'c'sle head, and hove in, in the usual sailing-ship fashion, by treading the capstan.

Such was our occupation on this cold, grey day at the outset of the voyage. Great care had to be taken during the whole operation, particularly when the anchor, weighing many tons, was lifted clear of the fo'c'sle head, to prevent it, while suspended in the tackle, from taking charge by swinging abruptly inward to the roll of the ship. A playful tap from an anchor, so slung, on a plunging ship would mean trouble for the victim.

Having manoeuvred the anchor into position with flukes amidships, the fall of the tackle was slacked away, allowing the anchor to come to rest on the deck. Here it was secured by a steel hawser to the ring-bolts set in the deck, so that nothing short of a catastrophe would start it from its lashings. When both anchors were thus secured, the shackle-pins were knocked from their shackles on the anchor rings and the laborious task of winding in the cable through the hawse pipes began. Round we trudged in the drenching spray, heaving on the hand spikes, while slowly link by link the cable was stowed in the chain-locker. How we looked forward to two bells of the afternoon watch and the change of the watch, when we would go below and the starboard watch would take over—so, at least, I thought, but was soon to learn that making fast anchors is the prerogative of the mate's watch, and to that watch alone belongs the right to perform this duty. . . .

Robert, my American shipmate chum, had just been relieved at the helm by one of the starboard watch. He came forward, reported the ship's course to the mate and turned to go below, when he was checked in his footsteps by August's *[the mate's]* shout, "Hi, you! Where you go?" "Guess I just struck two bells aft there. Going below," answered Robert. "Never on your bloody life! Get a hand spike and heave in." Robert came up on the fo'c'sle head, joined me at my capstan bar and commenced to heave away, commenting loudly the while on all things Finnish. The uneasy August, his wary sidelong eye focused in our direction, stood the chatter, which by this time had become general, until with mounting ire he turned upon us with the usual shout of, "Håll käft . . . Satan" *[very rude Swedish for "Shut up . . . the Devil"]*.

When the two anchor cables were hove short *[pulled all the way]* inboard, the ends of each were shackled together and the hawse-pipes plugged with wooden blocks to prevent the further inrush of water as the ship curtsied to the seas. Hitherto the entire area under the fo'c'sle head had been inundated by sea water spouting up through the open hawse-pipes and there washing about in the alleyway, making every-thing wet and sodden. The place resembled a dank and gloomy cavern from the side of which water dripped and oozed continually.

— · — · —

[Cargo hatches were the most vulnerable parts of the old ships because, unlike steamers, the ships' holds were not subdivided. If a hatch were broken in heavy seas, the ship could flood and sink very rapidly. Extraordinary care was taken to secure and protect the hatches, as Holger Thesleff explained to a passenger on the Passat.*]*

I explained . . . how the hatches were secured and lashed, he listened with growing astonishment. I told him how for the hatches of the holds there were first steel baulks running athwart the ship and covered with caulked wooden hatches. Over these were stretched two layers of the thickest canvas, tarred and oiled. On top of that was a third piece, brand new, its corners turned down and sewn up, and wedged well home. The wedges were nailed two and two together. Over this again was laid a layer of planks running lengthwise and secured athwartships with double baulks screwed to iron rings in the hatch. Lastly thick wires were stretched cris-cross across this and pulled tight with the help of a capstan. It had taken several days to batten down No. 2, 3 and 4 hatches. No. 1 hatch had good canvases but was not battened, for it was partly sheltered by the fo'c'sle and a lot of important material was kept in the 'tween decks, which was free of cargo there.

First Days at Sea

[*Frank Baines, early in the 1930s, sailed in the* Lawhill *from London to South Australia in ninety-one days. He was ordered aloft for the first time as the ship beat to windward down the English Channel.*]

With, I flatter myself, an altogether to be admired imitation of enthusiasm and spontaneity, I leapt into the main weather rigging and began climbing towards the main futtock shrouds. Everybody went about their jobs with the same elaborate assumptions of non-awareness and nonchalance but they didn't deceive me: the solo flight of an apprentice is always a matter of speculation and interest particularly to the ship's officers. As I climbed into the shrouds and made my way up the lower rigging I was conscious of that heightening of tension which always occurs as the orchestra is just obviously about to bring the overture to a conclusion and the curtain to go up. The back-draught from the mains'l was blowing me about in disturbing eddies but I couldn't be certain that it was this and not my apprehension that was crinkling my flesh. The ship was heeled ever so slightly to port and climbing was easy, the ratlines were firm and evenly spaced and with difficulty I suppressed an inclination to run up them in order not to be accused of trying to show off. As the mains'l bellied and emptied the buntlines made a soft drumming upon the canvas like the patter of countless feet. The rigging was full of strange, mute noises as if it were lived in and I became conscious of millions of tensions, and movements as of people going about their business, and the small interaction of everyday things. It was possible to conceive of it as you would a city teeming to the activities of countless draughts and currents drumming along carefully conceived arteries and highways, pressing dumbly upon barriers, surging down corridors designed for it, through flumes and into funnels, as intricately disposed and channelled as the runnels of an irrigation system or a sortie of traffic; musical as a fountain, inevitable as death.

I reached the futtock shrouds and swung up over them without so much as a tremor and stood on the main top. The lower tops'l, sheeted home to the main yard-arms, was as tight as a buttock and just as straining, just surging forward with a suggestion of effort. I couldn't help being reminded of a man on the job. The tight graceful curve of the bunt swept below me, just below eye-level, thrumming with wind like the overactivated, overcharged hum of a dynamo, almost aggressively potent. . . . I started up the topmast shrouds half afraid of it, as if it might pursue me. The topmast shrouds were secured to the top with bottle-screws and the ratlines were of rope and sagged in the middle when you put your foot in them, drawing the shrouds together and sort of pillowing your feet. This didn't give any sense of security. It was more like having to pull your feet out of a trap at each step. The topmast shrouds led to the crosstrees. . . .

Once or twice, when I was tempted to look down, I was overcome with vertigo. The pressure of the wind on the body had increased and was inclined to pluck at clothes with an aggressive and resentful hand like a half-intimidated mob with the intention of lynching you which yet lacks a little of its courage to do so. But there is no mistaking its intent; there was no getting away from the presence of the wind. It had body, was solid. In the topmast rigging the wind was no zephyr but an entity with purpose pouring out of the west as tangible as water from a conduit, and with unimaginable power and gusto, tossing its mane, saying Ha! Ha! stamping like a stallion. I was quite unable to come to any sort of terms with it. The wind pressed me against the rigging and impeded my steps. Unlike the lower shrouds, the topmast shrouds were almost vertical and though not aggressively loose, were loose enough. The sensation of having to pull your feet out of ratlines as though they were bird snares implied a hostility towards effort on the part of the entities who lived there was not encouraging to confidence. . . . The spirit of the rigging, cantankerous and aloof, brooded; it was ready to pounce upon the smallest relaxation, the slightest mitigation of effort, a least error, one's tiniest slip. . . .

I reached the crosstrees and without pausing a moment to look around me or take stock of my position, plunged into the t'gallant shrouds. I had not been in them a second before I realized they were everything the Admiral *[a crewman]* had said. After the massive stability of the tubular steel topmasts and lowerm'sts it was with absolute terror one projected oneself onto the t'gallant mast to feel it whip and quibble. The t'gallant mast was a spar of massive Oregon *[pine]* stepped into *[fastened to]* the topmast below the crosstrees through steel rings. I couldn't make out where or how it was secured and in examining it I suddenly became aware I was gazing down a mast that bent and whipped like a hazel. The whole stupendous gear was leaning to le'ward, away from the wind and swaying with it, as the wind increased or slackened. And sometimes, as the vessel rolled or pitched, the mast whipped backwards and forwards two or three feet, plunging and jerking in the step, with a most unpleasant motion, setting all the shrouds a'tremble and convincing me that the whole damned contraption would tumble to the deck at any moment. As the ship worked and rolled, rolled back against the wind, the t'gallant shrouds set up a shrill screaming in protest, doubly high, doubly intensified, echoing through the mind and giving rise to a sort of horrified attention and setting

afoot all sorts of panic trembling as echoes awoke in sympathy, in harmony, in protest, and the mad jangling goes on echoing ceaselessly in
the jangling, echoing corridors of one's own consciousness. It is of this
I am afraid. . . .

The ship rolled. The t'gallant mast screamed across the sky in arcs
of movement. . . . For a second, appalled at the danger and powerless,
as I felt, to do anything to meet it, I clung to the rigging like a child to
its parent. The t'gallant mast lurched sickeningly away from me—
back; the shrouds suddenly slackened. I was left swinging nerveless.
Then slowly they twisted upon themselves and crossed over and I
found myself facing seawards, away from the mast, two hundred feet
up. It was a moment of pure beauty and terror like coming upon a
precipice—the abyss opening at your feet. I was gazing upon a view of
sky and seascape extensive and grand beyond the wildest dreams of
imagination. . . . I was interrupted by a shout. Wrenching my eyes from
the fabulous prospect in the sky above and before me, I came back to
earth and searched on deck. The Mate was on the poop, gesticulating
and carrying on in a manner that left me in no doubt as to his meaning, namely that I was to get up and get on with it.

I felt doubly angry; with the Mate for his impossible demands and
outrageous orders, and with the ridiculous rigging that had precipi-
tated me inside out two hundred feet up. I looked down on the poop
and if I had dared loosen one I should certainly have shaken it at them,
an impotent fist. The Old Man was aft by the wheel, looking up: could
it be with some sort of apprehension? Were they concerned about me?
I gave the rigging a wild shake like a petulant schoolboy. To my astonishment it shot round and untwisted, almost shooting me off. The
ship had rolled lazily to port, the t'gallant mast whipped over to
le'ward, the weather shrouds were brought up taut with a jerk. The
ship had simply completed one wallow in a sea way. It might have been
a lifetime. Making the most of my opportunity while the ship was still
heeled over, I scrambled hastily up the rest of the way to the upper

t'gallant yard in a great hurry and sat breathless, more from emotion, the strangeness of my position and the slight queasiness of vertigo than from exertion, astride the yard itself. . . . I stopped the buntline that was causing all this trouble and climbed back into the rigging and rather leisurely down. "Vy you take so long?" the Mate barked at me as soon as I put foot on deck. "You go up kwickly, you come down kwickly. No stay. See?" He was right. Once you paused up there to let the beauty and wonder of the scene lay hold of you, gave a place in your mind to aesthetic appreciation, to thoughts of boundlessness, you were done for. God knows what might happen. You would as soon open your fingers and let go.

—··—··—

[*Sailing ships were a lifelong obsession with Alex Hurst. He served in a Baltic Sea bark and then in two four-masted barks out to Australia and back in the 1930s. After the Second World War, he served on the council of the Sail Training Association, but resigned in protest against the kind of "tall ship" it decided to build. He wrote a half dozen books. His* Square-riggers: The Final Epoch *is a history of Cape Horners, enriched with his personal knowledge of many of them and their personnel, from 1921 until the end in 1957, when the* Pamir *was overwhelmed by a hurricane in the Atlantic. Alex Hurst, in* Ghosts on the Sea Line, *described his first trip aloft on the* Moshulu *in 1936 outward bound toward Australia.*]

By the next evening, with the gale blown out, the ship was almost steering herself, gently swaying through the water, her sails a pattern of sun and shadow until the night came, and before long 55,000 square feet of white canvas was gleaming in the bright moon light while the wind scarcely rustled overhead, and the whole silent machinery of the sailing ship passed slowly down the Baltic Sea. After the dawn I was sent up to overhaul the mizzen royal buntlines and was confronted for the first time with the problem of reaching a royal yard when the sail was set, for it is the topmost hoisting sail, and, as the ratlines end at more or less the point where the yard rests when it is lowered, the only way to reach it is by shinning up the royal backstay for the last fifteen-odd feet, reaching out for it a little over 150 feet above the deck. Although the action became automatic in a very few days, that first morning took a certain resolution, not for fear of the height, which never bothered me, but because climbing had never been a strong suit, and that was hardly the place to experiment or make a mistake.

However, the deed was done, and once I had accomplished my mission I stayed up on the yard for a little while drinking in a scene the magnitude of which holds an enchantment beyond the comprehension of anybody who has not seen it for himself, for the tracery of the rigging below seems to culminate in some minute deck with which one feels no connection at all as if it were another world; the sunlit sails belly forth right beneath on all sides, and all around as far as the eye can see is the great curve of the sea's rim. The acreage encompassed from the truck of such a tall ship is enormous, and on this morning, when the horizon was fifteen miles away, I could survey with the utmost clarity over 550 square miles of sea, with all the Baltic shipping dotted over it. Later, I spent the first of many watches below perched out on the tip of her bowsprit, which is the finest vantage point to survey a square-rigged ship: the very sea itself is below with the fine bow cutting it from blue through emerald greens into white; the sails tower above, and the whole beautiful fabric swings gracefully towards the watcher. It was a morning of sheer exultation as Gotland faded away astern, and Öland lay on the starboard beam in the glory of the autumn sun. Scarcely a steamer was to be seen; the sea was full of schooners and barquentines, but we were the finest and tallest of them all, and slowly overhauled all the fleet save only one auxiliary top-gallant-yard schooner whose engines helped her to hang on to our quarter. One by one we passed those splendid landmarks, the churches of Öland, and, as we finally dropped the Long John Lighthouse on its southern tip, one of the onker barques beat up to us and went about, flying light for a timber port, as pretty a picture as one could hope to see.

———·—·—·—

[Elisabeth Jacobsen, Norwegian by birth, spent the first five years of her life at sea in her father's ships. At age seventeen, she was a stenographer in New York and typed Alan Villiers's manuscript Grain Race, *about the 1932 voyage of the* Parma. *She found that she "loved to read the story of these gallant old ships fighting their way against wind and weather on the longest, stormiest ocean voyage it was possible to make." Betty Jacobsen sailed as an apprentice in the* Parma *in 1933. It was on this voyage that the* Parma *arrived in Falmouth, England, eighty-three days from Australia, the fastest sailing-ship voyage since the First World War.]*

The working day here starts at six o'clock in the morning, no matter what the weather may be like, and the first half hour is given up to menial jobs—performed almost entirely by apprentices—such as cleaning out the pigsty and the water closets, and fetching the cook his coal and water for the day. We do not have to bother about cleaning the decks, as the sea always attends to that.

After that the real work of the day begins—chipping the darned rust. There is always rust in a sailing-ship; in fact, some of them, I gather, are nothing but one big piece of rust held together by a little paint.

At eight o'clock the watch which has been on deck since four goes below to eat a breakfast of curry and rice or something equally distasteful . . . and to sleep until twelve-thirty, when we are called to eat the midday meal and come on deck to work again at one, until seven in the evening, more chipping of rust. Then sleep again until midnight, deck until four, sleep until eight, and so on. You sleep four hours one night and eight the next; work nine hours one day and five the next.

"Work" means actually doing things apart from the necessary sailing of the ship; in the night watches the rust can stay where it is, and we do nothing but such jobs as are made necessary by the caprice of the wind or of the mates. The mates keep us busier than the wind does. We are awake fourteen hours one day and ten the next, the watches alternating throughout the whole voyage.

For relief from the gloom of the forepeak there are wheel turns and lookout for ice, when it is foggy. Sometimes we make a sail fast; sometimes we set one. Often the wind changes and we haul the yards around until they are placed in such a position that the sails may make maximum use of the wind.

I do not see anything very romantic in all this, nor anything adventurous either.

It is very discouraging, and I am inclined to look upon this life as one of the least glamorous pursuits of hard labor known to man. The sea is always the same and there is not much beauty to be seen in the sails when they are wet and cold and gray, and you are wet and cold and gray, and they fight you with a malignant ferocity when you go aloft to take them in. You only get them in to set them again, when the wind drops, which it does as promptly as the ship is shortened down *[that is, sail taken in]*. Oh for an engine to go put-put-put astern sometimes I have sighed, appalled at all this labor. But I have sighed in secret, and no one here will ever know.

———

[Neil Campbell was an apprentice for four years just before the First World War in the Elginshire *and* Arctic Stream. *He then served in steam for a number of years and finally became a harbor pilot for Cape Town, South Africa. Campbell early learned, on the* Elginshire *in 1910 or 1911, that officers in sail were skilled at finding or making jobs to keep young apprentices busy.]*

Many little annoying jobs were found for us, particularly in the second dog watches (6 to 8 P.M.), the traditional period of relaxation, should the weather permit, from the stern discipline of the ship. That was the time for a noisy sing-song, a bit of playful wrestling or boxing. But often the officer of the watch would imagine we were enjoying ourselves too much. Spitefully he would roar from the poop, the High Seat of Authority: "Three of you boys—up aloft and overhaul the buntlines from the royals down!"

Buntline overhauling, the bane of our lives, was an important part of the work of a sailing ship, and requires some explanation. Buntlines are those ropes which run aloft from the deck to each and every square sail. Their purpose is to enable the sail to be hauled up close to its yard before the hands go aloft to make it fast. Those buntlines, hanging down on the foreside of each sail, caused considerable friction on the canvas, which would soon chafe through if continual attention were not paid to them. A boy would go up each mast with a few lengths of sail twine, haul up sufficient slack on the rope concerned, and then put a small "stop", or lashing, of twine around the buntline or leechline. By this means the chafe was minimized. If a change of weather necessitated the furling of the sail, a jerk on the rope was sufficient to break the "stop" from the deck.

Sometimes the officers would go down on to the main deck and wilfully and deliberately jerk the buntlines until the stops were all broken and the lines bearing heavily on the sails. Then the voice of authority roared out, and we made a toilsome journey aloft to do the job all over again. In the end we often got so exasperated that we stopped the gear with *rope-yarns*—foolish and dangerous action which usually meant a hurried trip aloft to cut the rope-yarns if a sudden squall struck the ship.

—·—·—

[The Moshulu *was the largest sailing ship in the world in 1938–39 when Eric Newby sailed in her as an apprentice. In this, the last of the so-called*

grain races from Australia, she came home in ninety-one days, the fastest
passage of thirteen ships. Early in the voyage, outward bound from Belfast,
Northern Ireland, Newby discovered one of the realities of life under sail that
the enthusiast who had urged him to go to sea had neglected to mention.]

In the watch below I had been plagued by things running up and
down my legs inside my camel's hair sleeping bag. At first I attributed
the sensation to some condition like nettle rash brought on by eating
too much salt food. Then I attempted an ambush by sticking my head
inside the sack and suddenly switching on an electric torch, like a
hunter after big game at night; but I bagged nothing. Lastly I tried
withdrawing my legs completely from the sack, but this method also
produced nothing—whatever it was had been brushed off in the process. I was reluctant to speak of these matters to the rest of the watch,
for I already had enough to live down. When I saw Hermansonn, who
was clean and above suspicion, searching his blankets by torchlight at
two o'clock one morning and muttering to himself, "Vagglus—bogs,
bogs, bloody bogs," I knew that I was not alone.

On the sixteenth day, with Madeira on the starboard beam, I
opened Captain Jutsum's book on knots and splices and out fell a big
red bedbug, big because he had been feeding on me. I lifted the "Donkey's Breakfast," the lumpy straw mattress I had bought in London.
Underneath it, on the bunk boards was a small piece of canvas folded
in half. I opened it and found it full of them. I lifted the bed boards
and saw that the frames were seething. Far worse, in every crack and
mortice joint in the wood were thousands of eggs. Everyone else was
making similar discoveries. Only Yonny Valker and Holmberg, those
leather-skinned men, seemed unimpressed. Cedarquist borrowed a
blowlamp from Doonkey. . . . Cedarquist went over each bunk with the
blowlamp and I followed with boiling permanganate of potash solution. We should have used caustic soda. The best thing would have
been to throw all the bunks overboard and build new ones. This time
we killed thousands, but the nucleus remained.

This was no new colony; perhaps it had lain dormant for eight years on the West Coast at Seattle; possibly its ancestors had boarded the ship at Port Glasgow in 1904 before she was launched. In a week they were back in force. I threw my bed boards into the sea, drilled some holes in the side of the bunk and made a crisscross netting of wire to support the mattress. Then I found they were inside the straw, so I threw that into the sea too and slept on the wire alone. I spent long happy hours disinfecting my sleeping bag by hand and thinking how lucky it was that I had been unable to buy a caribou skin.

The bugs grew bolder as the weather grew warmer. At the breakfast table they crawled up our legs. Then they started climbing up the table legs. When we built a *chevaux de frise* of tin round the bottom to foil them, one of their number, a born leader, swarmed up the wall, traversed the ceiling, and dropped down to the deck easily negotiating the barrier which it had taken in the rear. Fixed defences were useless against such an enemy. We began to cast round for materials to make hammocks.

————

[*Claude Muncaster, an artist, signed on the* Olivebank *and worked as a seaman because he "wanted to learn about the blue-water sailor's life at first hand, and for the reason that as an artist I might depict one of the last surviving windjammers which will ever be seen." In 1930 the* Olivebank, *outward bound, had encountered very bad weather in the North Sea and North Atlantic and battled with gales north of Scotland for over two months. The trip to Australia had taken 158 days, an extraordinarily long time, and, on arrival, she was leaking. She was too late for a charter for that year and remained in Melbourne until the next year, 1931, when Muncaster joined her. Her passage from Melbourne to Cardiff, Wales, was 122 days, the second longest of the year.*]

During the afternoon I went aft to take my trick at the wheel,

Koskinnen accompanying me to give instructions. We mounted the poop by the lee-side ladder, for this is the custom of the sea. Should a sailor go up by the weather side, he would meet with an unpleasant ticking-off from the Captain or Mate for an unwarrantable breach of sea etiquette.

The steersman stands on a raised platform at the windward side of the wheel, and in front of him is the steering compass, which he watches carefully. But there must be one eye for the sails and another for the ship's head, though if he is steering a compass course he does not need to watch the sails so carefully; he keeps an eye on the needle and does his best to keep the ship steady on that given course. In a vessel with a well-balanced sail plan a steersman should not have much trouble when the wind is on the quarter and the sea moderate: under these circumstances she will almost steer herself; but should the wind be dead aft it is the devil's own job to keep her running true. A man has to keep the wheel turning first to starboard, then to port, and not too hard over, but in time to meet the swinging of the ship's head.

This is where the experienced seaman shows his skill. But with a smart press of canvas, the wind right astern, and a heavy following sea, even he cannot stand his trick at the wheel for more than an hour at a time. This wheel is not the handy little thing you see on the sheltered bridges of steamers, but is a big clumsy six-feet affair calling for the whole of a man's strength to keep it from spinning round out of control. At times it is so obstinate that one can make no impression: it is like trying to move a ton of bricks. There are few more irritatingly helpless situations than to see the compass needle gradually slipping away until it is a whole point, or even a couple of points, off the course, whilst you are uselessly wrestling with a wheel that refuses to yield. Everything wrong seems to happen forthwith. The sails, which have been kept asleep, suddenly flap violently, and the noise brings the "Old Man" out of his chart house like the flash coming out of a gun.

"Vat de hell you doing? You vill have de whole ship dismasted. Hard over dere—hard over! For Heaven's sake!"

In his anxiety he would even run to the lee side of the wheel and lend a hand. Inch by inch, spoke by spoke, the great circle would yield, the sails would draw and go back to slumber, and once more the ship was on her course.

"Dere, now," he would say. "Keep her dere."

For some time he would remain standing, and giving an occasional direction with his hand. The physical exertion and and nervous antic- ipation of all this made one furiously hot, but during the next few minutes she would run steadily and allow one to breathe freely. It gave one opportunity to glance at the sky; enjoy the colour of the sea, the changing shadows of the sails; even to feel a little more confidence in oneself as steersman. But such moments would be short-lived. Almost before one could realise, the ship began to take charge again. The compass proved it. One point—point and a half—two whole points! Slipping badly! Oh! Damn the thing, and *Olivebank,* for being such a perverse devil!

One heaved and heaved with all one's might and reserve strength, and then I began to understand the practical meaning of the phrase: "Put your shoulder to the wheel." It was a matter of putting not merely shoulder, but legs, arms, thighs, and one's whole body. The spokes pulled out fingers from joints, broke the blisters, and tore the skin. If for a moment control of the wheel was lost, it kicked, flew round with such terrific velocity, that it would have broken a limb had any part of one's body got in the way.

As I learned my job and became more practised, however, these incidents of bad steering rarely occurred. I began to know how much helm she needed, that it was useless to try moving the wheel when it was too heavy; but that the tip was to wait the right opportunity, and at the proper time the wheel would slip round of its own accord. All this education took time and involved many mistakes, yet I cannot remember having been once sent down from the wheel in disgrace. There even came a time when I took turns for Jim and Frank, whom the Captain could not trust in heavy weather.

The *Olivebank* has a wheel-house, and we used to say this was the best part of the ship. In the early days of big sail, such ships never had such protection, but as a result of accidents continually happening to ships and sailors these houses were added. They exist quite as much for their moral security as for their shielding against physical forces. Let me explain. Any reader who has never been afloat in really heavy weather can scarcely imagine the immensity of big seas rising sixty feet. Until he sees for himself, it is impossible to appreciate the mighty force at the back of those Southern Ocean rollers. In unbroken power the wind has driven these green mountains over vast spaces for thousands of miles. They rear themselves up astern in terrifying grandeur, and whilst the ship seems doomed she avoids being swamped to death because she lifts and lets the danger sweep under her.

But the moral effect on the steersman is something too serious for expression. Many a sound, normal sailor at the approach of these terrible rollers has suddenly lost his nerve, forsaken the wheel, and fled for'ard for safety, thus gravely endangering the ship, which might broach-to. Should one of these following waves leap upon the stern and poop the vessel, irreparable damage may ensue; and it is merely repeating ancient history to state that over and over again have wheels been smashed to tiny pieces, and the helmsman washed to the fore part of the ship even though he had been lashed to the wheel. Chart-houses, too, have been swept overboard, and the poop left a complete wreck.

Some captains therefore used to rig a canvas weather dodger abaft the steersman to prevent him from seeing an oncoming wave, thereby preserving his nerve. But a wheel-house is a more efficient shelter and, in shielding the man from the wind as well as the sun, affords a welcome comfort. To turn out of a warm bunk in the middle of the night, and stand for a couple of hours at the wheel, bitter wind, sleet and snow driving over you, is not exactly amusing. After a while, when oil-skins and clothes have ceased to keep your body dry, and you stand shivering; or the rain trickles down the back of your neck despite a good "sou'wester," finding its way down to wrists and boots; or your fingers and limbs seem so stiff that they must be frozen, you begin to want some shelter badly. It is now that a wheel-house proves its defen-siveness in most weathers, and we who at times called the *Olivebank* every name that we could lay tongue to, were no little thankful that she at least was a ship with a wheel-house.

But it was not always bad weather, and personally I rather wel-comed a spell of steering. There was more variation and less monotony than in certain other jobs, and assuredly it was a great relief from the eternal paint-chipping, or washing out the fo'c'sle with strong caustic soda. Get some of the latter into a cut or blister after you have been hauling ropes, and you don't feel too pleased with the cleansing duties! I used to like the steersman's job, because it demanded one's intelli-gence to learn her little tricks that she continually kept altering; for seldom did she steer alike for two consecutive watches. At times, when we were sailing "by the wind," it was necessary to turn the wheel not more than a couple of spokes during a whole hour.

Happiest were those days in the Trades, when the only difficult thing about one's trick at the wheel was how to keep awake. At night steering under these conditions could not be anything else than enjoy-able, whilst one watched the stars peep through the sails. Often it was possible to steer as much by stars as by compass, having chosen some bright star and then keeping it in line with the cro'jack yard or the main royal. During the warm, Trade Wind nights, one could stand at the wheel in a shirt and trousers only, watching the moonlight playing on the canvas, the ship steering so easily and, so long as the weather leach of the main-royal was just lifting *[meaning the ship was sailing as close to the wind as possible without spilling the wind out of the sail]*, it was certain she was on her course. At night there is something beautiful, romantic, picturesque, about a sailing ship, with her great spread of canvas dimly silhouetted against the starlit dome of heaven; and all the nautical noises make a strange symphony. The flickering yellow light of the binnacle, the warm glare from the chart-house door, and perhaps the dark form of the Mate leaning on the rail at the break of the poop, are the features of many a picture I remember still. It makes me restless to see and hear all these items once again before they shall disappear from the ocean for ever.

———

[In the last days of sail, perhaps every other passage was in ballast. Such passages gave the mates, ever alert for ways to shelter the crews from the evils of idle time, opportunities for cleaning the holds. Dewar Brown cleaned the hold of the Winterhude.*]*

A more sheltered occupation, although possibly a more unpleasant one than aloft in the rigging, continued daily in the vast and gloomy hold. The hatches were removed, then, armed with brooms and shovels, we descended the iron ladders into the hold to clean up the mess left from the last cargo of grain. Down here it was incredibly dirty, everything powdered by a heavy red pungent dust. Here were old tatters of rotten dunnage, broken side battens, baulks of heavy timber and grain—grain everywhere, heavily impregnated with rats' droppings. Out of all this chaos we had to bring some sort of order. The heavy timber was hoisted into the 'tween deck and there lashed to the midships stanchions so that it would not break adrift in a heavy sea. The side battens were set up anew and lashed to the frame members of the ship, which in turn were brushed clean of all grain and dust. All the sweepings were sent up on deck in a barrel on the end of a draw rope, which was hauled up by one of our number, and the gash tipped over the lee gunwale into the sea. After a short time, the dust and the stench in the hold were almost sufficient to choke and blind one, while the amount of vermin we managed to collect on our clothes in carrying out these duties was reminiscent of trench warfare in the First World War.

All this activity progressed slowly, if not quietly, over a considerable period, for in usual shipboard style nobody made the slightest effort to accelerate their movements; the work was certainly more deliberate than frenzied. During this time there was also far too much motion of the ship for safety, while handling heavy and awkward timber in the semi-dark hold, without our adding to the danger unnecessarily.

The 'tween deck was such in name only, for with the exception of the small area around the hatchways which was decked with timber, the rest was merely a network of girders running longitudinally and athwartships within the hull. Moving about from one point to another on this skeleton 'tween deck presented considerable difficulties and was attended with far more danger than any work aloft in the rigging. Except for the shaft of light, which penetrated like a ray from a magic lantern, where a few of the hatches had been removed, the rest of the hold was as black as the inside of a cow. This, together with the constant motion of the vessel, made it a very simple matter to over-balance and pitch to the bottom of the hold some thirty feet below. More accidents probably occur in holds of ships than anywhere else at sea.

With the hold swept and cleared of debris to the satisfaction of the mate, who viewed the proceedings from time to time from the hatchway coamings, we now started operations on the limbers. With the sealing boards removed, there was exposed the foulest and most evil-smelling mixture of decomposed grain and bilge water, all of which had to be shovelled out and sent up on deck to be dumped overboard. The stench from this noisome mess was nauseating, and, as so often happened, through carelessness on the part of the individual hauling up the bucket, those below would receive a liberal libation splashed over them. Consequently, until the work of cleaning the limbers was completed, the odour in the fo'c'sle during our watch below was as repellent as the hold itself. The only relaxation on the job was the hour spent at the wheel standing one's trick, and the time one could enjoy "dodging Pompey" sitting in the heads smoking a cigarette. . . .

While at work all conversation, being forbidden, had to be carried on *sotto voce* and smoking was entirely out of the question. Anybody cheerful enough to sing was immediately suppressed by the ever ready: *"Håll käft, Satan!"* of the mate. Whistling was, of course, taboo always.

— · — · —

[Every account of sailing ships expounds about food, and only very rarely favorably. Dewar Brown's is no exception.]

The food on the whole, considering the conditions, was by no means unreasonable, although I doubt whether any British merchant seaman would tolerate such fare. Twice a day, apart from the recognised meal times, coffee was served to all hands: once at three bells of the morning watch and again at seven bells of the afternoon watch during which the watch on deck was allowed a clear half hour knock-off. The watch below could choose between sleep or coffee, although sleep was usually an easy winner. Nevertheless, coffee was invariably brought for'ard for both watches. All meals were eaten in one's own time, that is to say during one's watch below, either immediately before going on watch or on completion of a watch on deck before turning-in, thus leaving the entire watch on deck free for uninterrupted work. Breakfast, dinner and tea were all meat meals. Coffee was served again with breakfast, but tea was brewed at tea-time while water only was taken at dinner. The usual breakfast consisted of meat stew, which was tinned beef or mutton mixed with sliced onion and known to all as *cabel jarn*—why, I never discovered, since *cabel jarn* is Swedish for "spun yarn", another matter altogether.

Another breakfast dish served regularly once a week was curry and rice which, although palatable and well-prepared, was not popular with the majority of the crew. There was always enough and to spare of this dish. On Sundays we invariably had *pulsa,* a sort of sausage meat that, although new to me then, has since become a universal but somewhat unpleasant item of diet both at sea and on land. Dinner consisted of either more *cabel jarn* or sometimes slabs of *buffelkott* covered with some thick pasty sauce of indeterminate flavour, while again once a week we were served with stockfish which had to be broken into pieces with an axe before setting to soak before cooking. This stockfish varied considerably, sometimes being almost palatable whilst at other times it was well-nigh inedible.

Potatoes in progressive degrees of decomposition, as the voyage lengthened, were served with all these delicacies. Soup at dinner was usually either tomato or macaroni, but at times it would be sweet soup, a savoury concoction of barley, raisins, prunes and apricots boiled together and served hot as one would a soup, but usually eaten last like a sweet. This definitely was one of the better dishes.

Cabel jarn was generally served again for tea or alternatively, *labskois,* a dish of meat, cabbage and potatoes cooked together in a solid mass. This dish, however, could only be served while the fresh vegetables lasted, which was not long. Tinned fish-balls, a not very satisfying and entirely tasteless form of food, was another dish served sometimes for tea. White bread and margarine was always available, since it was whacked out once a day by the steward and kept in the fo'c'sle locker. Exactly the same food was served for'ard, midships and aft—not that this had any relative significance, since the majority of those for'ard were far more fastidious than those aft.

By far the most repulsive article of diet was the salt beef which really has to be seen and smelt to be believed; it was incredible stuff. Only sheer necessity and hunger induced one to eat it, even then the nauseous smell was only surpassed by its choking salt petre fumes. August *[the mate],* however, was quite partial to this form of food and consumed large quantities with avidity.

The apprentices took weekly turns at making *backschaft* for the entire crew, port and starboard watch combined. [Backschaft] entailed the duties of a general servant *[for the crew]* for a week and included, as well as washing up the 'tinnies' afterwards, fetching and carrying food from the galley to the fo'c'sle and the midships house, an extremely tricky business in heavy weather. It was an unenviable job trying to wash the greasy dishes in a bucket of lukewarm water—largely salt water at that—drying them with totally inadequate bits of filthy rag, which served as dish-cloths, and stowing them in the locker so that they would not beat themselves to pieces with the first show of bad weather. *Backschaft* could be made the excuse for a first-class fight and often was.

— · — · —

[Eric Newby was equally eloquent and less charitable about the food on the Moshulu.*]*

After little more than a week [the cook's] repertoire of dishes was exhausted and except for the crossing of significant lines of latitude and longitude and days of rejoicing, when he always produced something good and new, he permutated remorselessly on a few basic dishes. Indeed he had no choice, and we sometimes wondered what would have happened to us if the kock *[cook]* had been a bad kock.

There were two kinds of meat: salt pork and salt beef. There were unlimited supplies of both. Salt pork, which appeared in various disguises at least once a day, was like theatrical property, produced to create an atmosphere and then whisked away uneaten. In its worst form it was fried and smothered with a metallic-flavoured bean stew. Only Yonny Valker attempted to eat this, and he eventually complained of pains in the head. Sometimes the pork arrived floating in a thick heroic kind of pea soup as solid as porridge, which was eaten laced with the same sulphurous-looking pickle that had been part of the night watchman's perquisites in Belfast. The pea soup was my favourite dish; the pork could be thrown away—its function was only decorative. It is said that old sailors still remember the pea soups of fifty years ago with nostalgia. I shall always remember the pea soup in *Moshulu*.

The beef was unboned and awaited our pleasure in casks of brine. Boiled, it became "buffelo"; hashed with potatoes and pounded ship's biscuit, it became "lobscouse," a famous old-fashioned sea dish; and stewed with potatoes, "kabelgarn," or rope yarns, which it resembled. Kabelgarn was either good or very nasty. We never discovered the reason why it was such a temperamental dish. Sometimes buffelo was given a short spell in the oven and emerged as "rosbif", which invited derisive comments from Cedarquist and Hermansonn on the decline of the British Empire. Potatoes appeared at every meal and were a godsend. After the first week there were no more fresh vegetables. It was not age that made the contents of the beef and pork barrels so unpalatable, but the liquids in which they were embalmed. Yonny Valker and I had been down into the after peak to fill the potato bins and had seen them. Each barrel had a red seal on the rim stating that it had been packed and tested under the supervision of the Board of Trade Marine Department on August 22, 1938. . . .

For afters there was sometimes a pallid sweetish kind of macaroni which the boys rightly called "angelskit" and a gooey kind of soup made with dried fruit that looked rather like frog spawn. With a lot of sugar it was very sustaining and perhaps more than any other food helped to keep us healthy and free from scurvy. The nickname for this was absolutely revolting. Occasionally angelskit appeared with kabelgarn, but this was never successful, for the two dishes were in some way hostile to one another. Sometimes there were pancakes. Usually they were as heavy as lead. It was best to cut them into small squares and dissect each one separately, to avoid damaging one's insides. There was good porridge and rice too, served with watered-down jam.

The officers aft had some little extra luxuries, but they were not of a very exalted kind. Things like tinned salmon, tinned fishballs from

Norway, and jam. But I think that during the voyage we tasted most of the cabin stores in the fo'c'sle, for the Captain was not a mean man.

There was always plenty of fresh bread because the cook baked twice a week. At coffeetime on Saturdays he produced a special loaf with an elaborate design on top sprinkled with sugar and sometimes with fruit in it. The arrival of the special loaf marked the end of the working week and always put us in a good temper.

For the watch on deck from 4 to 8 in the morning, there was coffee at 5.30 A.M., coffee for everyone at breakfast time, and at the break at half-past three. There was enough for everyone, but it was advisable to be early. The pot—a large enamel bath jug—was not often washed out; as there was tea at dinner and supper, there were alternating layers of tea leaves and coffee grounds below the drink of the moment. The tea bore no resemblance at all to English tea, civil or military. There were two tins of unsweetened condensed milk to last the entire watch for a week. Inevitably this was all consumed by Monday, or at the latest coffeetime on Tuesday.

In addition to the communal food, each one of us had a pound of margarine each week and a pound of sugar which he kept privately. Both the sugar and the margarine were issued in bulk, but by common consent they were divided up. This came about after an awful week in which we tried to live like civilized human beings who are only civilized because they know that they can replace any commodity they may run short of by going down to the local shop. The sugar and margarine were left on the table and after two days nothing remained.

The rations were issued on Saturday mornings. Sometimes a collective frenzy of hunger would overcome us and we would finish all our sugar and margarine by Thursday and then endure two sugarless, margarineless days. Once it was Wednesday. Two lean days before Saturday made it more difficult to start the next week in a proper economical frame of mind. To those who have suffered real hunger we cannot appear as proper objects of sympathy. It must be remembered that most of us were still growing and we were all working like Trojans. The eating capacity of the fo'c'sles *[the crews]* was immense but they rarely had the opportunity to indulge it. One Saturday afternoon our fo'c'sle was given an eight-pound canister of Flett's plum and apple jam. By suppertime on Sunday the eight of us had eaten it.

———·—·———

[A very few food concoctions were the sailors' own, unique to the sea, and in fact a pleasure. Basil Lubbock describes one he first met on the Ross-shire.*]*

Spent part of the afternoon busy with needle and thread, putting patches on my overalls and oilskins.

As I sat sewing, Loring came up to me and proposed that we should make some dandyfunk for tea. I was always ready for anything in the eating line and at once seconded the proposal; but what dandyfunk was I had no more idea than the man in the moon.

"What do you make it of?" I asked.

"Well, first we must have a canvas bag," he answered.

"What, to put it in?"

"No, to smash it up in, of course."

"Smash it up in?" I asked; this was truly curious. What could be the dish, that to start making it you have to smash it up in a canvas bag? At last I struck it.

"You are not going to make us a pudding out of brick-dust and oyster-shells, like the hen's food, are you? because, if so, I'm off."

"You'll eat it quick enough when I've made it," Loring answered. "I'll make the dandyfunk if you will make the bag."

Well, curiosity and greed got the better of me, and borrowing a palm and needle from the third mate, I soon had a small canvas bag made.

This Loring proceeded to fill with hard tack, and then went forward with it; I followed.

He took it to the rail forward of the galley, and then looked about him for something.

"Get me an iron belaying pin, will you?" he asked.

"Certainly, if you swear not to use it on me."

I gave him the belaying pin, with which he proceeded to pound the bag of biscuits until it was so much fine dust.

He put this dust into my plate (as it was the largest in the half-deck), and then proceeded to put water to it, and mixed it up until it was a thick paste. Then he added molasses and some jam (Don and I still had a pot or two left). This compound, after being thoroughly mixed up, was taken to the cook, who put it in the oven.

At tea time we were all curious to see the result of the dandyfunk. Loring went to the galley for it, and brought it aft steaming hot, a mixture between a cake and a pudding.

I thought it extremely good, and it had another excellent quality, it was exceedingly stodgy, and filled up the chinks nicely.

—·—·—

[Paul Stevenson, the wealthy yachtsman, maintained his enthusiasm for the big ships in spite of realities of life at sea under sail—even for passengers. Stevenson comments on food storage on the Mandalore *(which was perhaps not her real name—I can find no reference to her elsewhere).]*

The harness-casks were cleaned out to-day for the first time . . . an occasion always dreaded by us. The harness-casks are large square boxes into which the salt meat is dumped when a fresh barrel has been broken out of the lazarette and broached. The harness-casks on the *Mandalore* are made of teak, beautifully varnished, and lined with big slabs of slate, one single piece forming each side and one on the bottom. But if the casks are pleasing to the eye they are most horribly offensive to the nose; for so vile an odor is diffused throughout the ship when one is opened even for a moment, that a bone-boiling establishment would have to take a back seat in the presence of a ship's harness-cask.

A few minutes before the casks are opened warning is given to us, and we close the ports and companion-way so as to exclude as much as we can of the terrible smell. I never had sufficient strength of will to witness the cleansing operation, but it is done by removing the pieces of old, decayed meat, with as much of the brine as can be conveniently baled out; then, when the process has been performed to the satisfaction of the mate, the fresh barrel of meat is rolled over to the cask, the head stove, and two men with stout iron hooks lift the hideous, ragged chunks of beef or pork, as the case may be, into the cask, rejecting those pieces that are the most tainted. Sometimes half a barrel of meat has to be thrown over the side; indeed, we had to heave seventy or eighty pounds of pork over board to-day. This generally smells much worse than the beef; and as the great, dripping, reeking hunks of fat are lifted out of the barrel, I cannot but marvel how the men can bring themselves to eat it. No wonder lime-juice plays so important a part in the life of the man before the mast. This sort of food accounts, perhaps, for the small appetites of sailors as a class; for, contrary to general opinion, they eat but little.

— · — · —

[Alex Hurst, based on his experience on three windjammers, had this to say, in Ghosts on the Sea Line, about food and what might have been.]

The food in a sailing ship was seldom anything to look forward to, even when a man was hungry. It varied a certain amount between the ships, some being relatively good in quality and poor in quantity, whilst others were the opposite way round. Some ships were bad both in quantity and quality, but I never heard of one that was good in both respects. In the old days there was little help for the type of food which was necessarily all dried or salted but, although the sailing ship rarely carried any form of refrigerating plant, the advance of the canning industry might have led to a much more appetizing diet. As it was, owing to the exigencies of economy, canned foods merely served to alleviate the monotony of the menu on high days and feast days, and one of the few additions to the age-old fare of salt beef and pork, fruit soup and stockfish, potatoes, biscuit and tinned salmon and curry were white bread and, very occasionally, tinned fish-balls on a Sunday. One ship in my experience, and one only, provided fresh eggs twice a week for the first seven weeks at sea one voyage.

Whatever the need for economy, science had made such strides in preserving foods that there should never have been any need to see scurvy or beri-beri in the ships, but see it we did sometimes, and not always on the exceptionally long passages. Beri-beri was the more common, usually affecting a man's knees first so that they become spongy, but a few days on proper food soon put it to right if it had not advanced too far. Afterwards, when I saw a good deal of this sort of thing in the prison camps of Japan, I realized how near those Cape Horners sometimes came to disaster.

The Ways of a Ship
and the Sailor's Life

[There has always been speculation about the nature of men who would commit themselves to the isolation, hardships, and dangers of ships far from dry land. Judgments on the character of seafarers have not always been charitable. Dr. Johnson observed that he who would go to sea for pleasure would go to hell for a pastime, and if there were a choice between ships and jail, the sailor would be better advised to go to jail. Alex Hurst offered some views on the question in his Ghosts on the Sea Line.*]*

Most of the Scandinavian boys with whom I sailed were in sail as a means to an end, for square-rigged time was still necessary as a means of promotion in their countries, which maintained the better traditions of the sea to the bitter end. Some of them actively revelled in the life, the majority merely tolerated it and enjoyed the highlights, whilst very few of them really disliked it. Amongst the foreigners in the ships, however, there were very mixed impressions. Relatively few of them made more than one voyage, the majority having come for some sort of experience which many disliked, when they had got it, for a variety of reasons. There were those who came to sea dreaming of starlit nights and swelling sails and who never associated themselves with the hard realities of life. There were those who came to sea too late, having forgotten such humility as they may have once experienced, with the result that their mental revolt at such jobs as cleaning out the lavatories more than transcended any good or happiness which they might otherwise have gained. Many had never been aboard a sailing ship before they signed on, but in my experience these lads either loved the ships or loathed them whole-heartedly. . . .

In order to understand the outlook of a man in a sailing ship it is necessary to understand the conditions under which he is living. It is, in a sense, a very lonely life; not because there is no one to talk to as there obviously is (and oddly enough there is never any lack of topic for conversation), but lonely in the sense that the ship is almost completely isolated from the world of man, a state of affairs which became progressively more marked as the numbers of the square-riggers dwindled, because they seldom crossed the steamer lanes, they carried no radio and, due to their very rarity, they met each other at sea very infrequently. This spirit of being so self-contained together with the very nature of the work, the hauling of ropes and handling of the sails, demanded a close teamwork which usually led to such an excellent spirit of give and take that it was generally possible to keep rationed foods like butter (though never, sugar) in a common container. A sea-chest was never locked and would have been kicked open in protest had it ever been, for this was an ancient tradition of the sea which has probably gone before the cardboard suitcase of the sea-toiler of today. The sailing ship fo'c'sle usually brought out the best or worst in a man and, in the rarer cases where it was the worst, one could be pretty sure that the man would not last long.

Latterly the crews were almost all young, for'ard and aft, which led to a good deal less of sea-lawyering and morale-breaking on the whole. A high standard was generally set and everyone was expected to conform to the accepted codes of conduct which were generally termed "Style". A bunk in a steamer is often a soulless framework affair, but in a sailing ship it became its owner's home as it was generally arranged in such a way to make him detached from his fellows when he was in it. It was, of course, wooden, and contained the bedding which belonged to the occupant and generally consisted of a donkey's breakfast (or straw mattress), a selection of blankets, and sometimes a pillow. Then there was a bunk curtain which was the one and only way a man could obtain privacy and shut out the fo'c'sle light. Inside the bunk some men had photos of their family, particularly on their first voyage, some had past ships and, very seldom, there were "pin-up" girls. Perhaps there would be some books on a shelf, and always a small hurricane lamp, which was one of the essential requisites to comfort as the central oil lamp was seldom adequate to allow a man to read in his bunk, particularly as the oil lamp was all too often diluted with kerosene. Often one would enter the fo'c'sle to find all the curtains drawn and the chintzes gay with the lights behind them. Most bunks had a shelf at some point on which, apart from his books, would be an embryo model or some precious possession reflecting the individual taste of the owner.

The bunks were round the side of the fo'c'sle and next to them, on the deck, the sea-chests, then a couple of long forms, one on each side, and a table in the middle. Sometimes the oilskins hung in the fo'c'sle, sometimes in a thwartship alleyway outside, depending on the ship. There would be a locker for bread, a water tank, and a locker for cutlery. Very few deep-water ships had their accommodations under the fo'c'sle head in the last days and, for the rest, the open-decked ships generally berthed in a deck-house abaft the foremast, and the three island ships housed their crews in the Liverpool section.

The insularity of a sailing ship was felt at its most extreme when the stand-by came in off a wet deck to call the watch. When he turned the light up the gloom of the loose water could be seen swishing under the bunks and about the lashed chests; there was a faint aroma of the oilskins and the stertorous breathing of the watch below, punctuated by the crash of the deck-ports and the breaking seas outside. It all seemed very remote from the world. The modern apprentice—nay, the modern seaman—may find it all a bit primitive, for I have sailed as A.B. in a tanker with my own four-poster bed, my own wardrobe and carpets on the deck of my two-berth air-conditioned cabin with mess-rooms and washrooms, but in my experience there were few apprentices in the big screw ships who would not willingly have changed berths and exchanged their "Iron Mike" for four men at a kicking wheel. Even if the ships had all but gone it was good to see that the will had not died with them.

Sometimes a well-meaning mission would present a ship with a gramophone, probably not realizing that no other article could cause such strife and dissension in an otherwise happy community. Often the records would be Swedish folksongs which would bear plenty of re-playing and which had a pleasant melody; but all too often the records would emanate from the British Empire and be of a type that crams the greatest cacophony into the fewest grooves as possible. . . . Chess was a favourite game with the Finns who were usually quite good and, on a fine Sunday morning, every man would be on deck, bent over their boards, fore-and-aft. It was not only a very fine game but it provided a good exercise for the mind on these long voyages and later, when in British ships, I was staggered to find how few men even understood the game, let alone possessed the ability to play it competently.

— - — -

[The only concession to Betty Jacobsen, apprentice on the Parma *in 1933, was that she lived aft in a cabin of her own. She took her typically clear-eyed view of things forward when allowed to visit the forecastle.]*

Blue sky and sunshine, with intermittent rain squalls. We are running along under all sail, at about eleven or twelve knots, with the wind from SW.

Today being a holiday, the captain took Ruby *[captain's daughter]* and me for'ard to see the boys' quarters. Gee, what a lot of human misery and discomfort there is on a sailing ship. These boys have not many clothes. They are paid scant wages, if any at all, so that they have to suffer with what they have. Even the highest paid gets only about four dollars a month, as able seaman, and that will not go very far with a Cape Horn outfit. I have better clothes myself than many of them.

In the big focs'l the last dry shirt had long been used, and the boys are always in wet clothes. Their quarters are hung with wet garments; their bunks are wet and the deckhead leaks; their oilskins are useless, and their hands are torn and bleeding.

In the half-deck it is worse. So many seas break there in the waist of the ship that the door is caulked fast, and the only means of getting in or out is by way of a ladder from the table through a skylight. The place is surely one of the poorest abodes for human beings on earth, with the sea swishing across the floor, full of debris, water oozing down the steel bulkheads—wet clothes, and wet boys and gloominess everywhere. Is that what they have paid for? Is this the "sail training" in a four-masted barque at sea? I do not see much training in it, although it might be good for character. But the boys here seem to be pretty good charactered anyway, and do not need such training to make them go straight. The boys who do need it do not come.

Yet I think the boys here like it well enough. They joke of their misfortunes, make light of their worries, put up with the dirt and the wet and the misery, and talk to me always of the Trade Winds and sunshine and peace. What a place those Trade Winds must be! . . . certainly these boys learn how to be sailors. They have to, because there isn't anyone else.

—————

[Ken Attiwill was a young Australian journalist who shipped in the Archibald Russell in 1929, not for the sake of the voyage, but just to get to England. "In my seabag I carry 8 pounds 10 shillings and plenty of good letters of introduction. This is not heroic, it is merely just damned silly. A man *only does these things when he is young. I want to see the world, and have no money." Archibald Russell was the last square-rigger built in England, in 1905. She carried apprentices in 1929 as did most of the last of the wind-ships even though few saw much of a future career in sail. The ships carried apprentices because some countries still required several years in sail to be eligible for certain merchant marine licenses and because the apprentices paid the shipowners a premium, which helped pay the ships' bills.]*

One of the boys here has given me a document embracing an extra-ordinary set of rules by which apprentices in Finnish ships are governed. He also gave me a few appropriate comments thrown in:

> ### Apprentices Must
> 1. Do all the work with the rest of the crew.
> 2. Help load and unload ship in port.
> 3. Be keen to learn in practical work, and receive theoretical instructions from the Captain. ("All he tell me is, 'V'ere de bloody hell you are taking my shep now?'")
> 4. Be clean.
> 5. Not smoke, except with Officers' permission. ("De boys don't vant to smoke dat stuff de peeg stooard give us.")
> 6. Not drink. ("Hell! He don't no give us any to drink.")
> 7. Take all medical requirements, together with doctor's certificate that they have such requirements. When joining the ship must deliver them to steward. ("Stooard take medikin, and don't give us v'en *sjuk*, dat beeg peeg!").
> 8. Join in serious prayer with the Captain. ("Dat ole bawsted don't know how to pray. All he say are, 'By —! Can't you steer straight yet?'")
> 9. Take plenty of fresh water baths. ("Plenty vater bath v'en come bloody vater here on deck.")
> 10. Take plenty of gymnastics during the voyage. ("Goddam gymnastics all day up in rig.")

11.   Receive instructions from the Captain in:
Swedish
English
Grammar
Writing
Mathematics
Algebra
Geometry
Trigonometry
Navigation
Meteorology
Deck work
Shipbuilding (construction)
Rigging
Ship terminology
Signalling (morse and lamp)
Port declarations
World geography
Coastography

(N.B.—Apprentices must abide by these rules. The Captain may, at his discretion, alter any rule or rules, if the necessity arises.)

— — · — · —

[At the end of the nineteenth century, discipline, especially on American sailing ships, could be brutal, often unnecessarily so. As the end of the windjammer era drew near, by the 1930s, such tactics had pretty much disappeared in the Finnish ships if not in the few remaining German ships. But even the Finns occasionally enforced discipline with their fists, as Elis Karlsson, first mate on the Herzogin Cecilie, *explained in* Mother Sea. *Those officers, after all, were responsible for sailing the largest sailing ships the world had ever known with minimal crews of largely inexperienced youths for thousands of miles through the stormiest of the oceans. Instant obedience to orders was essential.]*

One morning shortly after four A.M. I decided, after having had a good look at the weather, that we ought to set the fore-staysails, as the wind showed a tendency to come in from our quarter instead of from dead aft. The staysails had been hauled down because they had been slatting and chafing against the stays; with the wind more on the beam they would draw again. I sent the Third to blow for the watch and set the staysails, while I was admiring the morning and thinking of the day's work ahead.

When the Third came aft he was a little annoyed; one of the ordinary seamen had voiced his opinion to his mates that it was silly to set the sails; he had obviously meant the Third to hear. I told him not to do anything about it; I would deal with the fellow myself.

At six o'clock, when the watch assembled on the fore deck below the break of the poop, waiting to be detailed for work, I went down on the fore deck and up to the chap concerned. I asked what he meant by questioning a plain order. I hit him and he split his lips against a bulwark-stanchion. Staggering to his feet and spitting blood he was mouthing curses and threats; I put my foot on his stern and sent him sprawling, then told him to get forrard and clean the pigsty, or if he had anything more to say I would put him in his bunk for a while.

This on the face of it brutal treatment served two purposes. The fellow knew that he had done wrong, and he had been punished for it. Although he did not like me for what I had done, he would not have liked me any better if I had taken the matter to the Captain and had him logged *[recorded for bad conduct in the ship's official record of the voyage]*. As far as I was concerned the matter was closed, and afterwards he got his job back as top hand in the fore-rigging, as he showed promise of becoming a good seaman. To the rest of the watch the fact was brought home that nobody could argue against an order and get away with it, and that I was prepared to go to any length in enforcing that rule. Maybe a lecture to the hands would have had the same effect, but that would have wasted precious working time, and in any case would have left the less sensible members unimpressed.

Fortunately, physical violence was very rarely needed to enforce discipline, and discipline for discipline's sake had no place in our ships as a rule; a man's energies were expended in things worth while, and the pulling of forelocks does not assist in furling a flogging sail in a gale. Perhaps the relationship between officers and men was more free and easy in our ships than in ships of other nationalities: I have been told that. For instance, if I found myself alongside some of our hands in a bar I would shout them a drink, and if the company was good I would stay on for the evening. If somebody had suggested that such behaviour was detrimental to discipline, I would have put his remark down to silly ignorance; I would have considered myself a dud if I could not afford to meet my shipmates on equal terms when the occasion arose.

With all this I am not trying to maintain that our ways were better than anybody else's. Each maritime nation has a tradition as regards shipboard customs, developed through the ages to suit its circumstances, and so had ours.

[But crews did not always accept Karlsson's rationalization for his manner of discipline. Two seamen who were on the Herzogin Cecilie *when she was wrecked in 1936 were quoted by Basil Greenhill and John Hackman in their biography of that great ship. Per Hjelt: "We who left were so angry and fed-up with the captain and the first mate that we did not give a damn about the ship. There was too much damn discipline on board that ship. Both the captain and the first mate were slave-drivers." And Erkki Koskivaara, later a master mariner: "second mate Leman was a pleasant person but Elis Karlsson was somehow odd. I did not understand him, he attacked one now and then. Is it not a sign of weakness when you have to use force? And Sven Eriksen* [the captain] *was of the same kind. When I sailed in the* Archibald Russell *it was altogether much better. There everything was more peaceful and no 'hurry up' like in the* Herzogin*."[8]]*

––·––·––

8. Basil Greenhill and John Hackman, *The Herzogin Cecilie: The Life and Times of a Four-Masted Barque* (London: Conway Maritime Press, 1991), 168–69.

[Richard Sheridan, a nephew of Winston Churchill, was born in England and as a child had lived in America, Mexico, East Prussia, England, Constantinople, North Africa, Switzerland, Algiers, and Paris. In the fall of 1933, at age eighteen, he shipped on the Lawhill *from London to Australia as an alternative to attending university in France. The* Lawhill *came home around the Cape of Good Hope in 1934 in 122 days, which was the average of all her voyages from Australia. Alex Hurst's history,* Square-riggers: The Final Epoch, *recorded it as a voyage of little incident, but it made an impression on Sheridan.]*

Once every five years the bilges have to be chipped. Rust accumulates in such thickness that if it were not removed, the ship's life would not be more than quarter of the number of years that some of these sailing ships attain.

Although the rust is at times very deep, it eats away comparatively little of the ship's plates, and therefore after some forty years of chipping, during which time tons of rust have been removed, there is little enough to show for it in the actual appearance of the plates.

One is puzzled after seeing the accumulation of rust from hours' chipping that there is anything left of the ship.

Once the bilges have been thoroughly cleaned they are painted with a cement wash which is apparently more resisting than red lead or paint.

The general principle of chipping is simple enough.

Holding in either hand a hammer, V shaped at both ends, you strike the rusty plate smartly, causing the rust to flake or (when it is close-packed) fly off like shrapnel in all directions.

. . . the correct chipping rate is 60 hits a minute, 3,600 hits an hour, or something just under 18,000 hits a watch.

This, of course, fluctuates somewhat according to the presence or absence of the superintending officer. So much for the origin, general principle, and timing of the subject. Now the torture chamber outward bound is the ship's bilges. "Bilge" in its technical definition means the curvature of the ship's bottom, but Mayfair uses it as a shortened form of "bilgewater," an unpleasant odoriferous liquid, black in colour, and very often thick and sticky. It consists for the most part of rotten wheat, stale salt water, and dead rats in various stages of decomposition.

Its stench cannot be overrated. The bilge-water lies not unnaturally in the bilges. These are formed by frames that run athwartships or from side to side, dividing the ship's bottom into compartments spaced about three feet apart.

In the middle of the ship's bottom, running her whole length, is a huge girder called the keelson, which is the *inside* keel. This forms the backbone of the ship. Now these compartments or bilges are about three feet deep at the keelson and get as shallow as six inches where the bottom turns into the side.

It is these frames that run from side to side that are rusty and need chipping. Not unnaturally at the bottom of the hold it is very dark. The small main hatch lets comparatively little light in, and therefore that you may see where to chip you are given a small mining lamp. These are crude in design and inefficient in illumination. They look very like diminutive tin teapots, the spout of which contains the wick. They burn paraffin and smoke assiduously. If you push the wick sufficiently far in to prevent them smoking, they go out. If you let them smoke you are blinded by it, and it gets in your throat and makes it sore.

Whenever the Mate turned his back we turned our hammers on the lamps to express our feelings. It can hardly be wondered that they soon lost their first bloom of youth. The discomforts are considerable. Having lifted up the floorboards which rest on the top of these frames, you are assailed by the stench of the bilge-water.

This muck is baled out with an ex-Uruguayan corned beef tin and placed in a barrel. (The barrel remains in the ship's hold.)

When we started chipping it was December in the North Atlantic.

Everything was almost freezing. The rust, indeed, where damp, was frosted, and the bilges had turned into frigidaires.

As soon as the corned beef tins had done their work you squatted on the ship's bottom and got on with the chipping. The bottom, however, was slightly swilling, and the wet steel plates cooled by the North Atlantic on the outside were excessively cold. You cannot squat on your haunches for five hours so you finally sit. The next day you wish you hadn't. After a quarter of an hour face, hands, and all other exposed parts of the body resemble a brown coal-heaver's.

At every other stroke rust gets you in the eye; when you rub it with your hand a lot more gets in. It stings like acid and makes them stream. You inhale this cloud of rust and paraffin smoke which finally inflames the tonsils. The progress is so slow that you realize that there is no end to the work, and so long as the officers choose to keep you at it you will keep at it.

Five hours is a long time to work under such conditions without a break, and very soon one understood how easy it would be to go mad.

Day after day as regularly as clockwork I went down to prison and stayed there till the end of the watch, except for an occasional wheel or a call to the braces. (There is, of course, no look-out or police during the day.)

When the bitter North Atlantic gave way to the tropics I chipped rust; when the hold turned from a frigidaire into an oven I chipped rust; through the Doldrums down the South Atlantic I chipped rust; running the Easting down to Australia, when it was once more bitter cold, I went on chipping rust.

There was nothing to look forward to, no hope of a break in the routine. After the first week the other members of the watch got jobs on deck, and so I remained in solitary confinement still chipping rust.

When we were nine the inferno of noise was frightful, but at least we were all together and made the best of a bad job. We laughed, joked, cheated the Mate whenever we could, and all groused. But when

I was alone I used to go off my head at times. I would listen to the noise of one solitary hammer re-echoing the length of her huge hold, chip-chip-chip, in the darkness, 60 times a minute, 3,600 times an hour, 18,000 times a watch. My brain used to work with the hammer in a monotone keeping time, thinking the same thing over and over again. To-morrow-you-will-chip-next-week-you-will-chip-next-month-you-will-chip-chip-chip-until-you-go-mad-stark-staring-mad. . . .

When we got into the Tropics I used to look up through the main hatch and see a patch of blue sky, a swelling straining sail, and then once or twice I did go mad. I jumped up, seized a sledge hammer, and hit the ship's side, the frames, stanchions, and then hurled it from me and screamed. I would dash the lamp on the ship's bottom, and yell, laugh hysterically, and cry.

Then quite suddenly one word rang out, barked at me from the 'tweendecks above. I would look up, and there was one of the mates standing quite still, looking down at me from a height of twenty feet.

"Sheridan!"

I would drop back into my bilge cowed and sobbing, and go on chipping-chipping-chipping.

It broke your spirit, that game. You felt like committing murder, but when you saw the person you were going to murder you just collapsed like a pricked balloon.

There was plenty of time to think, plenty of time to dream, and nothing of course to distract the attention, but I never thought of anything down there except how to try and get out of my prison, how to get the officers to let me do something else, how to try and keep my reason, how to try and stop my wrists from feeling they were broken. It was a lonely life too. When I got back on deck there was nobody to talk to, nobody to confide in. I would walk into my mess hungry, tired, and half blinded by the light, and sit down ignored by the Finns and the object of the Donkeyman's remarks. "Why couldn't the god-damned Englishman wash before he came into the mess?" etc. It was a wretched enough existence during those early days, the cold, the lack of sleep, the misery, depression, loneliness of it all. The feeling that they were always watching to see if I would give in. Those strange mechanical supermen, that felt neither pain, emotion nor misery.

I remember the third day at sea, when we were all chipping together, the Third Mate came up to me when I was doing my best.

"Cheep faster. . . ."

"Can't, sir."

"Moost, moost!"

"Yessir."

"Sheridan, do you ever vash?"

"Vash?"

"Yas, vash."

"Do you mean wash, sir?"

"Yas."

"Every evening, sir."

"No-not."

"I'm not a liar, sir."

"Donkeyman say you never vash."

"Donkeyman's a bastard, sir."

"You vash tomorrow, or we take you forward and scrub you with deck broom." (Howls of delight from the rest of the watch.)

"Yessir."

"Horry up, cheep faster."

"Chip faster, sir."

It must be explained that we had just over a quart of water each to drink and wash in per twenty-four hours. The only place to wash was the foredeck. Try being a coal-heaver, and then wash naked on a ship's deck in a hailstorm with a quart of water, and see if you can get clean. It took me some time to learn the trick of it.

I thought them intolerant at the time, and yet months later, when a freshly joined Australian was going through all the symptoms of my first days, I had little enough tolerance. "Each one for himself and God for us all" is the motto of sailing ships.

It makes you or breaks you, and if I didn't give in and throw up the sponge in the North Atlantic, it was because a dear old English stevedore had said to me just before sailing, "They'll give you hell at first to see what you're made of. Don't let them break you. Don't get beaten by a bunch of bloody squareheads."

And after all, I reflected, I knew what I was in for before I started, and it was my own choice.

——·—·——

[On every circumnavigation, every ship's crew changed the suit of sails four times. Outward bound, as a ship approached the zones of trade winds and doldrums, the crew sent down the best, heavy-weather canvas and replaced it with old, worn sails that were good enough for light winds and fair-weather sailing. When the ship left those zones behind, the crew sent aloft again the best sails that could stand the terrible strain of the gales and hurricane winds of the roaring forties, the high latitudes where the ships made their easting or westing around the world. Similarly, as the ships made their way home, the crews went through the same process of sail changes as they passed from one wind zone to another. The ships always returned to their North Atlantic or North Pacific ports with their best canvas aloft, for even in summer they could encounter gales in those latitudes. The Winterhude left Europe in October with its heavy sails aloft. With better weather as she approached the trade winds, as Dewar Brown wrote, the captain ordered the customary sail change.]

Accordingly, on the morning of the third of November in latitude approximately 25° N., work was put in hand to shift sail. Willi was sent aloft to the fore-truck, bearing with him a large block which he made fast to the pole, by slipping the strop over the mast head, thus setting it up well clear of all standing and running rigging. Through this the girt line was to be rove off, by means of which the sails, once unbent from their spars, were to be lowered to the deck and the new ones roused aloft to be bent in their place.

We started with the topgallants and worked downwards to the forecourse. The girt line was secured around the sail at the bunt or middle part, then the bunt lines and leech lines were unshipped from the roach and leech of the sail and shackled to the jackstay so as to prevent them, once cast loose, from running freely through the blocks to rush with an ominous whistling sound through the air and finally to land a tangled mass of wire at August's feet. While such things did accidentally happen, by taking thought they could be, and usually were, avoided.

We next unshackled the *gigtag* and *skot* (clew garnet and sheet), also taking care to shackle the ends of these two together for the same reason as in the case of the clewlines. This was a tricky business indeed, calling for considerable manoeuvring of heavy gear before it was completed. The sheets consisted of lengths of heavy chain, which passed through sheaves at each end of the yard arms and thence to the deck, where for easier working they were fitted with purchases shackled to eye-bolts in the deck. It was by means of these lines that the sail was actually set and sheeted home. If these chains, once unshackled from the sail, were allowed to escape, through not being first properly secured by a rope end, they would run clattering—to the accompaniment of a shower of sparks—through the iron sheaves to the deck where they were capable of doing considerable damage.

Such a thing was unthinkable, but I have, on occasion, hung with my belly jammed over a yard arm, holding on to the end of one of the chain-sheets for dear life to prevent it crashing to the deck, while my shipmate was struggling to pass a rope end through one of the links to make it fast to the spar, and when, to cap it all, August, the mate on deck below, was cursing and shouting to know why we had cast off the shackle before securing the sheet by a gasket. All very true and to the point, but not helpful at such a critical moment, when one's chief concern was whether one's arms were about to be wrenched from their sockets or whether one would be bodily and inexorably pulled off the yard arm by the sheer weight. The whole operation was rendered more difficult by the fact that in order to reach the shackles it was necessary to sit on the footropes suspended below the yard, a position in which one had little or no stability and next to no scope for exerting the force necessary to start the shackle-pins.

But to get back to our sail shifting, the next thing we did was to cast off the lashings of the head earings from the eye-bolts at the yard arms and finally cut adrift the robands by which the sail was held to the jack-stay along the top of the yard. As each one was severed, the sail dropped away clear of the spar until finally, with the severing of the last rope yarn, it hung suspended by the girt line. On the signal of all clear from aloft, it was slacked away and the sail lowered to the deck.

We followed by way of the backstays. There existed among us friendly competition as to who should gain the deck first, and, although they were not timed by stopwatch, some amazing records were made, the drop of over one hundred feet from truck to deck being completed within seconds. This proved highly destructive to boots and trousers, the friction wearing holes in our garments, particularly our boots which were used as brakes in the final stages of the rapid descent. But our hands, which were unbelievably hard and horny, suffered no ill effects whatever.

Having gained the deck, we started rolling up the sail which had just been sent down, great care being taken in folding the canvas before stowing. Sails were made up into long cylinders of tightly rolled canvas, carried aft to the poop deck and there left until we had completed the entire change, when they were stowed below in the sail-locker.

It was hot work down there, heaving and struggling with the various sails that we required in exchange for those sent below. Exhausting work, too, in manhandling them up on to the poop deck through the relatively small hole of the sail-locker hatchway, which measured only some three feet by two. Especially was this so in the case of the large and heavy forecourse and maincourse, which measured some ninety feet in length by forty feet in depth, or approximately the size of the average suburban garden.

Having selected the sail—the sailmaker did this—we carried it for'ard, borne high on our shoulders, and hitched it to the girt line in the same fashion as the one just sent down. Then began the labour of treading the capstan until we had hoisted the sail to a point level with the yard where we were going to bend it.

Long and laborious work this proved to be. The sail crept scarcely perceptibly up the mast in response to what seemed to be endless miles tramped round in a circle, throwing one's weight on a capstan bar. Eventually, however, it was raised to the required position, and August, who had been watching its ascent with varying degrees of impatience, shouted, *"Avast"*, and before anyone had time to draw breath, we were ordered aloft to bend it.

This procedure was much the same as before, but considerably heavier work as, in order to centre the sail, the head earings had to be hauled out to the yard arms and there made fast after the bunt had first been bent to the jack-stay. We worked three to a yard arm usually, except in the case of the heavier sails, while all hands were engaged in shifting the forecourse and the maincourse, a job, like so many others, that cut heavily into our watch below. It was unbelievably difficult to sit astride the extreme end of a yard arm and exert sufficient strength to stretch a somewhat heavy roll of canvas to its full extent so that, when finally set, it lay tight and flush along its spar with no undue sagging. There were also many little snags for the unwary, one of which was the discovery, after the earings had been drawn out and lashed to the eye-bolts, that the whole sail had a turn in it, in other words that the sail was twisted longitudinally with a kink in the centre. This had repercussions in the form of heated arguments as to who were going to cast off their *nock bansel* (head earing) in order to take the turn out of the sail.

For convenience in handling while being bent, the sails were loosely seized along their lengths at intervals with rope yarn to prevent the wind filling them and thereby rendering them unmanageable before they were ready for setting. On this particular sail shifting we had scarcely hauled out the weather earing of the lower-topsail yard and taken one turn around the eye-bolt, when the rope yarns, by which the sail was made up, parted, and it went up like a balloon. It was wrenched from our grasp, and for a moment the whole weight and strain was thrown on Nils, who, to prevent his fingers becoming jammed in the eye-bolt, was forced to release his grip on the rope. In so doing he lost his balance and, to the consternation of all, he somersaulted backwards off the yard into space. Miraculously he was lucky in grasping the foot-rope in his fall and the next moment he was swinging in mid-air, from where, assisted by the helping hands of his watch mates, he was hauled up on the yard arm again, rather breathless and very shaken. The only comment that floated up from the deck at this little episode was to the effect that we were just so many farmers and should be handling hoes, not marline spikes. Amongst the Finns it was considered the greatest insult to refer to sailors as farmers, in spite of the fact that the great majority of them were originally farmers and indeed many still returned to their farms between voyages.

This sail shifting went on for two days, by the end of which time the ship presented the appearance of having been clothed in rags, so old and patched were these tropical suits. In the days of the "Iron men in the wooden ships", sails were changed much more expeditiously by the simple practice of dividing the watch into two squads: one working in the rigging to unbend and bend sail, while the second group was on deck, employed solely in sending up the sails and stowing away those which were sent down from aloft. In these times when crews are small, no such division of labour is possible, and it is often only by the united efforts of the entire crew applied to one particular piece of heavy work that anything is achieved at all.

During the last half hour of our watch on deck, while the sail-shifting period was upon us, we were occupied in stowing the sails away in the sail-locker where the heat was terrific and the atmosphere heavily charged with suffocating dust. Almost dropping with exhaustion, our streaming, sweating bodies stripped to the waist, we heaved and pulled at the stiff and obstinate canvas until each roll found its appointed place. No haphazard packing here, for space was limited, and there were many suits of sails to be stowed. Furthermore, the sailmaker had to know, in the event of a sail blowing to ribbons in a sudden squall, just where to put his hand amongst all this collection for an identical replacement. Nevertheless, in accordance with the perverse nature of things generally in sailing ships, it was usually the bottom-most sail of all that was required in just such an emergency. Nobody's fault; no one to blame. It was just one of those things that happened. Another thing that just happened fortuitously, although of no consequence, but naturally observed and commented upon in a small community such as ours: Theo's trick at the wheel would coincide with the hour during which the rest of us were toiling and straining in that stuffy sail-locker.

All hands on knocking off at two bells received a tot of punch diluted with water in recognition of truly strenuous task completed.

— · — · — · —

[Changing sail was a single-minded business; nothing was allowed to interfere with it once it started, and the work went on without rest so that the best sails could be sent down and stowed dry before rain should come. Basil Lubbock, at the wheel of the Ross-shire, *was forgotten as the mates kept the watches at the work of changing sails.]*

At six bells I relieved the wheel, and for the next few hours stood there, the only man in the after-part of the ship, for everybody was forward shifting sail on the foremast.

In solitude I leant against the wheel and meditated, gazing over the foam-flecked sea and drinking in the unspeakable grandeur of the great deep.

Before me rose the bellying sails, and from forward the sounds of toil and sweat came floating aft, sharp commands, the chorus of a chanty, cries from aloft, the rattle of blocks, the stamp of many feet, the flapping, cracking sound of a sail being sheeted home; whilst around me, but for the swirl of the water alongside, all was silent. Whilst they worked, the ship was in my hands; I steered her, I showed her the way to go, I kept her from prancing away to one side or the other, with inexorable hand grasping the spokes I held her on her course, ever and anon casting an eye to windward.

No bells were struck; time passed; amidst pillows of pink and yellow clouds and a counterpane of deep, purple shading to mauve and lilac, his majesty the sun went to bed; still they worked forward, and aft I steered and steered. The black pall of night began to descend upon the sea; there is no twilight in these latitudes, and whilst yet the afterglow lit up the west, the stars were beginning to peep forth in the east.

It was evidently long past eight bells, still they toiled; the welcome shout of "Sidelights out, hand on the lookout!" remained unheard, and I began to wonder if they were going to work all night. It was so dark now that I had to strain my eyes to see the compass card.

I could see them at work bending the staysails; all the square canvas was bent, and some hands were putting the discarded sails below.

At last came the welcome voice of the mate,

"Clear up the decks, sidelights out, binnacles, hand on the lookout."

Don brought me up a couple of binnacles and then went forward.

Both watches went to their tea after the decks were cleaned up; the mate, who walked the poop whilst the second mate was at his tea, came and had a look to see that I was on my course, but said nothing, so I steered on in silence.

I had relieved the wheel expecting only to be at the helm an hour, and here I was still, running into five hours.

I was awfully hungry, and Loring had promised us some meat balls out of the remains of our salt junk. I began to speculate whether some hungry person would eat my share or not, and to wish that I carried about a piece of hard-tack in my pocket like Don does; at any rate, I thought, it's my watch below at 8 P.M., and it must be pretty close on that now.

Presently the second mate came on deck from his tea and relieved the mate.

"Who's at the wheel?" I heard him ask.

"Lubbock," answered the mate.

"Why he's been at the wheel since three o'clock; hasn't he been relieved yet?"

"No; I thought he relieved the wheel when we knocked off."

So the second mate called Mac out, and sent him forward to find out whose proper wheel it was, and at last I was relieved, and went below quite stiff from standing at the wheel so long, and not in the best of tempers. But I soon cheered up when I found that good old Mac had put two meat balls on my plate, though there was no hot tea left.

———·—··—

[Even the first voyager soon became practiced at working aloft and often felt quite at home high amidst the rigging. A common way of descending to the deck was to slide down the back stays at great speed. Basil Lubbock recorded another way of getting around aloft.]

We are busy working aloft today, sending down all old gear and sending up new rope; several of the braces have been renewed, besides leech and buntlines.

I nearly had a fall from aloft. We had sent up a new crossjack leech-line, and the second mate asked me whether I could clinch it by going down the leech of the sail. This is not easy to do, as you have only the sail to hang on to, but it is not anything out of the way: some men brag that they have come down from the royal-yard by the leeches of the sails.

I went on my old motto, "What one man has done I can do," so I said I would try.

I slipped off the yardarm, and gripping with hands, knees, and feet, proceeded to slide slowly down the sail, tearing my nails, and skinning my legs.

The sail did its best to shake me off; there was not much wind, and it kept flapping, each flap swinging me violently from one side to the other.

I found it was all I could do to hold on, and on trying to leave go with one hand to clinch the leech-line, I all but fell, just saving myself by gripping the bolt-rope with all my strength. Again and again I tried; my muscles groaned and crackled under the tremendous strain, the whole weight of my body falling on the ends of my fingers, which were but slightly assisted by my knees and feet, owing to the flapping of the sail. I ground my teeth, as I hated to be beaten; how I did strain, until the muscles felt as if they would break, my veins stood out like cords on my forehead, from which great drops of sweat were falling. I crooked my fingers, and tore my nails as I dug them into the sail; but it was impossible, I could not hold on to the flapping sail by means of the tips of five fingers, whilst I clinched the leech-line by means of my teeth and my other hand. At last I had to give it up and slide down. I was quite blown when I got to the deck, and had ripped the skin clean off one shin, which, by the way, took over two months to heal, so bad does one's skin get at sea.

No one else would tackle the job, so finally I was lowered from the yardarm in a bowline, and so clinched the leech-line. Clinching the leech-line simply means making it fast to the leech of the sail about half-way down.

Trade Winds and Beyond

[*C. Ray Wilmore escaped from "four years grinding away at uninteresting clerical work in a dingy mill office" in California and took a working vacation in Hawaii in 1911. At age twenty, he signed on the American four-masted bark* John Ena *to return to the East Coast. He was, he said, lured by "Dame Adventure . . . under the shadows of tall masts with stout yards towering above the gleaming, polished decks of a sharp-prowed clipper. Once enmeshed in the snares of that wily siren, there is no argument, no line of reasoning or persuasion that can effectively rescue a victim from her clutches until all desire is satisfied."*

The ship had taken fertilizer to the islands and carried sugar back to Philadelphia. The John Ena *was a very handsome, lofty vessel, perhaps one of the most beautiful ships ever launched. Wilmore described her "extremely graceful, yacht-like lines." Basil Lubbock noted in* The Down Easters *that many seamen considered her to be the fastest vessel in the Hawaiian trade. The previous year she had sailed from Hawaii to the East Coast in eighty-four days, a record exceeded only by the extreme clipper* Sovereign of the Seas *in 1853. The* John Ena *was also known to be a wet ship, quite capable of taking a lot of water on deck. Wilmore adapted well to the life and became a proficient seaman, interested in everything that happened and everything he saw. This was his only voyage under sail and he recorded it well.*]

Shortly after I took over the wheel, still steering full-and-by, a faint line of grayish light began to appear along the eastern horizon, soon turning to a faint shell pink, then to deeper shades, and finally to brilliant orange or burnished gold. I was fascinated by this spectacle of the most gorgeous dawn I have ever seen, and at the same time had to remember to keep the slightest flutter in the mizzen royal weather leech—all peaceful, serene and thrilled—when, without warning of any kind, came a terrific swoo-o-o-sh, a snort and a splash, right close at hand. It all but startled me out of my dungarees. While the curtain of darkness was gradually lifting, at the moment I could not see far beyond the taffrail and could only guess what was going on. Other swooshes and snorts and more splashes followed and soon it was light enough to confirm my guess as to the cause: whales. A school of forty to fifty whales, big ones and little ones, were disporting themselves like a group of kids in the old swimming hole. Such splashing, snorting and blowing as went on! Sometimes a group of them would swim along quietly on the surface, bodies about half submerged. Suddenly there would be a blow and a splash and the whole school would disappear, diving straight down toward Davy Jones' locker. For a few minutes all would be quiet, then with a roar the leader would come to the surface, pop clear out of the water—such was his upward speed—and land with a resounding "belly-flopper" splash, followed in rapid succession by all the rest of his gang. This round of follow-the-leader took place over and over, now and again interrupted by a general free-for-all battle royal, churning literally acres of the glassy sea into froth.

—·—·—

[*Rex Clements served his apprenticeship on a small Scotch bark, the* Arethusa, *about which he gave almost no information in the book he wrote of the voyage and which does not appear in Basil Lubbock's histories. Clements later became a master mariner and wrote another book called* A Stately Southerner, *by which name a vessel bound to ports in the southern hemi-*

sphere was known. On Clements's first voyage in 1903, the Arethusa *took general cargo to South Australia, coal to the west coast of South America, and guano to Antwerp, a typical round in the early 1900s. Clements recorded his first experience with the trade winds.]*

All this time the fresh breeze blew and slowly hauled into the nor-east. On the 24th of January we entered the tropics, with the wind a steady whole-sail breeze and the horizon piled with fleecy masses of white cloud. There was little doubt that we had got the "trades" at last. Two days later when we were in the latitude of the Cape de Verde islands, having run 500 miles in the forty-eight hours, there wasn't a doubt of it. The steady, singing breeze, true to a handsbreadth; the tumbled whites and blues of the sea all a-sparkle in the sunshine; the untroubled rim of the far horizon—these were signs unmistakable of the authentic Trades, the glorious winds that make seafaring a pleasure cruise.

No need to touch tack or sheet now; the ship sailed herself and the helmsman had an easy time, a spoke or two now and then was all she needed. The days began to be a sheer delight. Most of the time we were employed aloft—serving, parcelling, repairing, renewing, attending to the hundred and one jobs that a sailing-ship is constantly in need of and that suggest comparison of her with a lady's watch—always out of repair. There is nothing more delightful imaginable than sitting astride a gently-swaying yard, high above ship and ocean, with a pot of tar and a ball of spunyarn, for long hours on end, casting an occasional glance at the acre of foam under the bows or the long white wake astern that tells of a good passage to be made.

Running the Trades down in a sailing-ship is an experience worth having—a taste of sea-life at its best. No words can well convey the beauty, the freedom, the glorious exhilaration of it all. The long halcyon hours wing by, with blue sea beneath and blue sky above and unending glitter of spray and sunshine. The ocean is all one's own or shared with a white seabird or two. The day seems twice as long as usual, and when the western sky floods with rainbow hues and the day's glory of gold turns to the silver splendour of the night, there comes never an abatement or alteration in the steady onrush of the wind.

It would be hard to find a more beautiful sight than that of a sailing-ship running through the Trades as she appears, when viewed on a moon light night, from the end of her own bowsprit.

Perched out there one seems alone in space, projected into a world of emptiness and utter beauty. Ahead the shoreless sea stretches dimly out into a mysterious eternity. The dark vault of the sky is powdered with stars, save where the sailing moon rides high and pours on the quiet sea a river of white radiance, a pathway to unimaginable realms of faerie.

And how lovely the swaying vision of the ship herself! In grace of outline and harmony with the sea and sky she seems none other than the winged Spirit of the Night. Beneath one's perch the sharp stem snores unendingly on through the dark tumbling water, smashing it into a splinter of white foam; while aloft, rising tier on tier in contours of unmatchable symmetry, a mighty cone of canvas, carved in rigid ivory or blackest ebony, sways silently amid the stars.

— · — · —

[Alan Villiers went to sea from Australia when he was fifteen and served in more square-riggers—two three-masted barks, one full-rigged ship, and four four-masted barks—than any other author of these extracts except Captain James Learmont. Villiers became part owner of the four-masted bark Parma, *in which he made two voyages. He later owned and circum-navigated the small full-rigger* Joseph Conrad, *now at Mystic Seaport in Connecticut. All these voyages were recounted in his* The Set of the Sails. *Villiers wrote prolifically to the end of his life about all aspects of life at sea. He became best known for his books about voyages in the grain ships* Her-zogin Cecilie, Grace Harwar, *and* Parma. *These books were largely*

responsible for the surge of public interest in the ships in the 1930s. Alan Villiers's account of making sails on the Parma *in 1932 no doubt was part of that appeal.]*

The Old Man bends his white trousers (pretty well covered with tar) and begins his sailmaking activities daily before the sun is above the horizon, while the sailmaking gang sews on steadily on the seams of the new fores'l. This is an ideal existence, to sit on a sailmaker's bench in the sun with one's beeswax and twine by one's side, steadily stitching away at the sail. It may sound dull to those who have not tried it; in a sail loft ashore it would be dull, but here in the shadows of the masts and sails it is the best job in the ship. Now and again you raise your eyes and take in the sweep of her as she goes: how beautiful and graceful she is! How peacefully she sails! Here is the poetry of motion; she lifts gently and rolls quietly as she goes, undisturbed by engines, unmarred by smoke. Over the rail one sees the blueness of the tropic sea with flying fish skimming from crest to crest, harried silver streaks in the sun; aloft is the symmetry of the sails, swelling out white and noble one above the other into the sky. There is no noise, no vibration. There are no extraneous elements, no passengers. There is no contact with the outside world, no daily receipts of sensational happenings chronicled in newspapers. The spray breaks and the wind blows, the sun shines and the trucks circle slowly below the whiteness of the cumulus clouds. Stitch, stitch, stitch—how quickly a seam is done! Is this the real joy of human existence, then, this working with the hands upon congenial work amid congenial conditions? . . .

The Old Man . . . sews all day at his sail. While he was ashore in the interval between the *Herzogin Cecilie* and the *Plus*—while he was "retired"—an automobile crank acting the wrong way gave him a thwack on the left thumb which put it out of joint for a year, and now he finds this a serious impediment to his sailmaking activities. But he always stitches on.

It is a big job, sewing a sail. Everything is done by hand; even when we come to the eyelets for the robands along the head of the sail, we make the small rings to be sewn in by hand, first taking some old yarns of hemp rope and rolling them by hand into spunyarn. When it is spunyarn we lay it into a circular piece of three-stranded rope of the requisite size, working only with the fingers. The whole operation, from picking the strands of hemp to delivering the finished ring—grommet is its seafaring title, in English—takes about two minutes. There seems to be nothing that cannot be done by hand around a sailing-ship's decks; that is why they make such an ideal training-ground for boys.

I look aloft and calculate how many million stitches there are in a suit of *Parma*'s sails. Into this fores'l that we sew now we stitch 10,000 metres of twine to hold the canvas together; the canvas is about as tough as the tarred tarpaulins which are used to cover open railroad trucks ashore. Nearly ten miles of twine! How many stitches is that? The stitches average about two to a centimetre; that makes 200 to a metre, and in a whole sail, about *two million*—two million stitches that four of us sew in by hand, using a steel-shielded palm and steel needles. The twine is tarred and copiously beeswaxed to run better; but the needle takes an almighty lot of shoving through some of the seams where the stiff new canvas is four thicknesses. Half a million stitches each, with lots of other work besides—sewing in the eye-holes for the robands, splicing in the bull's-eyes for the buntlines and the cringles for the leechlines and reef-tackle, roping the wire boltrope, sewing the foot with new leather. Each thrust of the needle, on such a job, is an accomplishment: there is plenty of blood on the sail before ever it is bent.

Parma has eighteen square sails altogether. We are thankful—I am, at any rate,—that after this there is only time to sew one more before England and we have only canvas for one more, anyway.

The Mate recalls a thirty-eight-month stretch he served in the bark *Vidylia*, during which he sewed an entire new suit of sails alone in addition to doing a great deal of other work. The older masters and officers in these ships are good men because they have had all this kind of experience. They have been sailmakers and able seamen, bos'ns and even cooks (as small boys); they have rigged ships, cut sails, argued with towboat masters all over the world. The Mate has been ten years in command himself, in the Baltic and North Sea, and would be a capable officer of anything that floats. I do not believe he has ever been in a power-driven vessel; if he has he never talks about it.

— · — · —

[Felix Riesenberg first went to sea in 1897 from New York to Honolulu by way of Cape Horn on the American ship A. J. Fuller, *one of only two wooden ships written about in this collection. He followed the sea for a career and became a master mariner in sail and steam. Later in life he wrote a number of books, including a history of Cape Horn.*

American ships were always known for their smart appearance and well-cut, well-set sails. Riesenberg described the details of sails and sailmaking on the A. J. Fuller.]

During these days of the voyage we overhauled our best suit of sails preparatory to bending them for the heavy weather off the Cape *[Horn]*. I had by then become fairly proficient in the use of the palm and needle and could sew a presentable flat seam, or round seam, as occasion demanded. . . . We had our benches in the most comfortable part of the deck and of a morning, after the washdown, while we were getting the canvas out, the rest of the crowd would wipe the deck dry with pieces of old sugar bags, getting right down on their shin bones and rubbing the planks. We put in new tabling, renewed lining cloths, sewed on new leather at the clews, wetting it so that when dry the leather would shrink tight, gripping the bolt ropes so that the strands would show through. In some of the older sails we sewed an extra line of stitching down the middle of the double flat seam where the cloths join.

I learned to properly work the reef and head holes. The canvas was cut with a "stabber" and a small fish line grommet laid over the edge, the hole then being finished off with a fencing of heavy waxed and double laid twine. In these later degenerate days, a brass eyelet ring is often crimped around the hole, a much quicker job and about one-third as strong.

In all of the lore of cutting canvas for sails, and we made a set of skysails on the voyage, the mate was past master. The "roaching," the proper way to allow for gores in the cloths, the fact that "square" sails are anything but square; all such old-time knowledge was handed down and eagerly assimilated. We talked of the "hoist" of this sail, meaning sails that spread by hoisting the yard; and the drop of that sail, referring to the courses and lower tops'ls.

On the *Fuller* the mains'l and crojik were fitted with "cross leeches" and a "midship rope." These were stout hemp ropes sewed to tabling clothes on the forward side of the sail, the cross leeches running from the head earings to the middle of the foot, and the "midship rope" from the head of the sail to the foot of the sail also on the forward side. This left the after side of the sail smooth so as to draw best when flattened on a wind. At the foot of the sail, and hooked into a stout thimble where the cross leeches and midship rope joined, the "slap line" led aft, and the "midship tack" led forward. With wind a point or two on the quarter, the weather clew garnets of the main and crojik would be hauled up and these sails set perfectly by the midship tack and the weather cross leech, in this way allowing a good share of the breeze to distend the great foresail for all it was worth.

One thing Mr. Zerk *[the mate]* always harped upon was the necessity of making canvas set flat, whether on the wind or before it.

A large sail, the main course, for instance, is fitted with what at first blush appears to be a useless amount of gear. The sail being bent to the yard by means of the *head earings* and *robands* is handled by use of the following ropes: the *tacks* leading forward from the clews, the *sheets* leading aft. When before the wind the sail is held to the deck by the two *sheets*, the *tacks* being idle. When on a wind, that is, closed hauled, the weather *tack* is boarded and the lee sheet hauled aft. To reef, the tacks and sheets are started and the reef band hauled up on the yard by the *reef tackles*. To furl, the clews are hauled up to the quarter of the yard by means of the *clew garnets* while the body of the sail is gathered in by the *leechlines* and the *buntlines*. Add to this *bowline bridles* for steadying out the weather leech when on a wind, *slap line* for keeping the foot of the sail away from the mast in light winds and calm, the *midship tack* used when sailing with the weather leech hauled up, and we have a very respectable lot of rigging on our sail. Upper tops'ls are almost as bad. Now this means nothing to the landsman, but a lot of queer names, yet the gear has come down through long ages of elimination and represents the utmost efficiency in handling sailing canvas. A main sail is a mighty spread on a large modern ship and may show to the wind as much as four thousand square feet of surface. Our mainsail on the *Fuller* was approximately of this size. Given a heavy press of wind, say twenty pounds to the square foot, and we have the sail urging our ship along to some purpose.

— · — · —

[Riesenberg went on to describe tools of the trade.]

The bo'sun's locker contained everything necessary for carrying on the marline-spike work of the ship, fids, serving mallets, iron spikes, and the like. The tar pots were strung along a beam in the top of the locker and the shelves at the sides held the deck stores of small stuff, *marline, spun yarn, rope yarn, houseline, hanbroline, roundline, ratline stuff*, etc. Several new coils of various sizes of rope, untarred hemp and manila were always carried in the bo'sun's locker against an emergency. Another compartment of the locker held the deck tackles, the "handy billys" and all emergency gear. This locker also carried the *straps*, rope circles use in attaching tackles to spars and rigging. Of such straps we had hundreds, always in apple-pie order. Small *"salvages"* for clapping a fall onto a stay, large three-inch rope straps for hooking the rolling tackles onto the mast doublings. The compartment for blocks was also kept in fine shape, so we could lay our hands on things in the darkest night. Great *snatch blocks* for carrying a tack or sheet to the main or fo'c'sle head capstan, or for taking the fore or main tops'l halyards to the same; *secret blocks* for *bunt jiggers,* a small round block about the size of a soup plate, with the sheave completely covered, the whip, for it is a single block, reeving through small holes in the edge of the shell to prevent the canvas fouling between the rope and the sheave as is possible in an ordinary block. *Clump blocks,* small and "clumpy" like a roly-poly baker's loaf. These are very strong blocks and are used at the ends of the staysail and jib sheets for the reeving of the whips. These sheets, as sailors know, are always in two branches and the clump block makes it easy to haul the weather sheet, block and whip over the stay without catching, as the lee sheet is hauled aft. There are others called *sister blocks, double* and *treble blocks, fiddle blocks,* great *jeer blocks* for sending up and down heavy spars, stepping masts, etc. Many of the blocks aboard ship take their names from the particular use to which they may be put, such as *quarter blocks, brace blocks, hanging blocks, clew-line blocks.*

— · — · —

[The sailors of sail saw things that the crews of steamers would never see. The creatures of the sea were not alarmed by the quiet motions of windships and went about their affairs indifferent to the presence of the old sailing vessels. Ray Wilmore on the John Ena *in 1911 saw and expanded upon phenomena that others may have merely mentioned.]*

I was fascinated today watching a school of porpoises playing about the ship. They ride in perfect military formation, in squads of eight, twelve, sixteen or so, usually four abreast and in two, three, four or more rows, with sometimes an odd "soldier" or two bringing up the rear. They would rise to the surface with a sort of rolling, undulating motion, sometimes shooting up entirely clear of the water, front line and each succeeding line in perfect unison; then dive deep and come up again a few seconds later twenty to thirty yards ahead. There were twelve to fifteen such squads. Occasionally they would all break ranks, apparently at some signal from a leader, and for a few minutes there would be the wildest thrashing about, churning the water into a veritable sea of suds. Whether this was just a part of a well-organized drill, a free-for-all fight, or a playful bit of rough-house during recess from drill, I don't know, but it was all done with such precision and regularity that it seemed planned. The recess would last but a few minutes and then, just as quickly as the playing started, it would cease, and the uniform squads would again line up and go through another session of drill work, unbelievably smooth, graceful and rhythmic. So fascinating it was that I spent practically my entire watch below on deck watching the performance. I should have washed some clothes and had a little sleep.

— · — · —

[*Between the northeast and southeast trade winds in all oceans are the doldrums, the zones of calms, heat, drenching rains, and baffling airs most frustrating to sailors. Dewar Brown described them.*]

We found ourselves towards the middle of November in the latitude of the Doldrums. Heavy banks of leaden cloud suffused the sky, through which at dusk and dawn the shafts of russet light cast weird shadows about the ship. The sea, a vast expanse of purple black, lay oily and placid, save where a distant squall lashed the surface into a mist of seething torrential rain. The wind dropped away and all about was deathly still: the atmosphere oppressive and overpowering, no sound except the occasional creaking of a block aloft and the sucking slat of canvas as it fell in against the mast when the ship rose to a periodic swell. This oily undulation came rolling like the fold in a carpet across the limpid ocean, a lone symptom of a troubled sea many hundreds of miles from this region of perpetual calm.

Although the mood was peace and quietness, we were nevertheless kept busy as a crew, attending to the ship and taking advantage of the slightest puff which happened along. We spent long hours standing by the braces, shifting the trim to meet each little waft, often only to find that by the time all sail was trimmed to its requirements the fitful breeze had died away. More often, the calm was rudely broken by a squall of wind and rain of tropical intensity which, bearing down upon the ship, sent her smoking through the spume like a mad thing, every stitch of canvas straining at the bolt-ropes until, left behind by this impetuous fiend, she slowly recovered her dignity and poise to float motionless as before on a glassy sea. Sometimes if we were unlucky we did not weather these sudden violent squalls without loss of sails, and, as those we had bent were old and worn, it was a matter of cutting adrift and saving what was possible of the tattered remains and getting another sail bent and set in its place as soon as all hands could manage it. . . .

These Doldrum squalls never seemed to come twice from the same direction; often four or more could be observed on the horizon at different points of the compass at the same time, yet none would overtake us. They were so exceptionally local in effect, that the line of demarcation between the storm centres and the atmosphere through which they moved was sharply defined, so much so that a squall might pass within fifty yards of the ship without ruffling a sail leech or wetting a plank. Constant care had to be exercised, however, in case the ship was caught aback by one of these squalls, and a watchful eye kept lifting aloft to judge where the next one was coming from and whether it was likely to hit or miss the ship. Thus a considerable time was spent standing by the braces waiting for what might never happen. One's entire passage through the Doldrums seemed to be employed expectantly grouped around the brace-winches. . . .

Every opportunity was taken during these brief but heavy down-pours to collect fresh water. All available receptacles were brought out and placed in strategic positions about the decks where rain water, cas-cading from the deck house and other superstructures and even from the sails themselves, could be saved from escaping through the scup-per ports and thus lost. Fresh water is very precious in a windjammer at sea, so that every opportunity was taken to replenish the tanks dur-ing these Doldrum squalls. Failure to take advantage of this bounty from the heavens would entail serious hardship, so there was always a wild scramble to collect all that was going while the going was good. A large tank, to which everybody in the ship had free access so long as the water lasted, was lashed to the deck at the break of the poop under the orlop deck. From this tank, we obtained all the water for our per-sonal use such as for washing ourselves and our clothes. There was, in addition to this, a deep tank from which the water was obtained by pump, but this was kept locked and the key was held by the mate. Water from this source was strictly rationed and drawn only by the hand making *backschaft*, our quota in the forecastle, two buckets per day, being kept in the breakers lashed to the fo'c'sle bulkhead. The gal-ley used some four or five buckets and a proportion went aft. This water was normally used entirely for cooking and drinking. When, however, the tank aft had run entirely dry, the two buckets of water per day for twelve men (six per fo'c'sle) had to serve every purpose. Hence the scramble to collect every available drop of rain water.

Although overcast and dull, the weather was hot and oppressive and one would have welcomed the sun again, and skies with fleecy white clouds. Under existing conditions it was not difficult to decide between oilskins or bathing costumes as working rig. The former were too hot and heavy, causing the wearer exceeding discomfort through sweating, and ordinary clothes became rain-soaked within a few minutes and it was a constant problem to get them dry again. The latter were both cool and dried quickly. The ideal was found in the naked flesh: nature's own oilskin, impervious to water, and soon and easily dried. We invariably worked naked at night in the tropics, that is to say so long as we were within the zone of the equatorial downpours, but during the day some inherent modesty impelled us to don some form of light attire, if only a loin cloth. . . .

Tempers became frayed and everyone hated each other's guts during these long windless spells. Over a period of some ten days, we logged an average *per diem* of only about thirty miles, much of this distance run in either an easterly or a westerly direction, since what little wind there was came from the south.

With the continuation of this insufferable heat and consequent stuffiness below, we took our bedding up on the fo'c'sle head and lay there during our watch below. Lying on our backs, staring up at the towers of idle canvas, we speculated when we were likely to cross the Line. Some of us had made hammocks in which to laze away our leisure hours, basking in the glorious tropical sunshine which had now taken the place of the overcast skies of a week or two before. The sun shone with such intensity that it caused the pitch in the deck seams to bubble and boil, while the deck planks were too hot to tread with the naked feet. From exposure to the fierce rays of the sun, our skin had assumed a copper hue; our hair, bleached by the salt air and the sun, was streaked with tawny yellow. Our bodies, in fact, made us look more like Arabs than representatives of the Nordic race. . . .

These Doldrums days dragged wearily on, each in its turn bringing the usual round of toil, while our bodies reflected the varying nature of our work. One day we looked like resplendent savages, our bodies always naked to the waist, smothered with paint from the masts and spars which we had been repainting. Next day we resembled coal miners, our skin smeared and begrimed with Stockholm tar from the rigging which we had been tarring down whilst suspended aloft in bosun's chairs. We always contrived to stow away pieces of cotton wastes saturated with turpentine to remove the paint from our torsos at the end of the day's work. Otherwise we might have remained daubed for months, as indeed some of the more careless actually were. . . .

After nine days of unrelieved calm, during which we had nevertheless managed somehow to log about thirty miles a day, we picked up a southerly wind which proved to be the earnest of the S.E. Trades. A more cheerful spirit prevailed in the ship at the prospect of leaving behind us those latitudes of dull depression and weeping skies, where our nights were made hideous by the constant summons on deck to shift the trim of the yards, although by day this continual manoeuvering of the gear did relieve us to some extent of the soul-destroying monotony of chipping rust in the dark and gloomy hold. Hot and oppressive though the weather was, the rain struck chilly on our naked bodies when we were roused in the middle of the night to do a job of bracing and to stand around waiting afterwards for the next twenty minutes while the mate, eyes lifted to the sails, decided whether to complete the operation. In the light and fickle airs which played around the ship, we often found that having braced the yards, the little williwaws of wind passing over the surface of the sea had died away by the time we came to brace up the fore yards. Then ensued a long and weary wait, grouped around the brace-winches, while the relentless tropical rain chilled our glistening naked bodies. Not so, however, Henri, who had adopted another comic outfit of his own invention, consisting of a sou'wester (worn back to front), a short oilskin jacket, below which protruded a pair of Aertex underpants, and, while the legs were bare, the feet were thrust into a pair of outrageous French button-boots! A more incongruous picture of a sailor it would be hard to envisage, as he stood there disconsolate and dejected in his panto-mimic attire.

Falls, Fatalities, a Rescue, and Fires

[Safety aloft depended not only on the agility and luck of the seamen in the rigging, but also on the care of those on deck who controlled the myriad of lines leading aloft. In those great ships, with their maze of rigging, yards, and sails overhead, it was at times not possible to see the men aloft or perhaps even be aware of men aloft. Alex Hurst recorded such a time in his The Call of High Canvas.*]*

I recall a day . . . when, after the weather had eased a little, a couple of us went aloft to reeve off a new clewline for the mizzen upper topgallantsail since the old one had carried away on three separate occasions, for no reason that we could divine. We were still on the job when the watch was relieved at two bells and the mate's watch came on deck. It had started to rain and, since we were wearing no oilskins and were both very cold, neither of us were in the best of tempers. The ship was rolling along at a shade over twelve knots with her surging wake growing away fine on the weather quarter to be lost in a white-crested following sea and, as the starboard watch had started to square the ship in a little before the change of the watch, the port watch took over the operation but we, because we had not finished, carried on to complete our job.

Kahila was above me, sitting on the end of the horse under the upper yard, whilst I was sitting astride the lower yard in the very act of shackling the end of the clewline into the spectacle as he overhauled it down to me. With the ship rolling heavily, our positions were no sinecure at the best of times, for my job took both hands—another occasion when 'one hand for the ship' became an empty phrase!—but, without any warning, the mate slacked the topgallant braces right off and the two yards jerked about like mad things, and I felt as though I were riding some unbroken bronco! The clewline was jumping in my hand, and it was all I could do to hold it. It was a really bad moment—one of those when a man is temporarily balanced on the abyss—for it was a few seconds before those on deck, who had been unaware that we were aloft, realized the source of the imprecations that coloured the air. Certainly we were sufficiently forthright in our opinions of the mate and made them so abundantly clear to him that he was quite subdued for several days!

—·—·—

[P. A. Eaddy was a New Zealander who had sailed in small barks and barkentines among the South Sea islands and across the Tasman Sea to Australia. He had "a great longing to ship deep-water and gain some experience in large sailing-ships, and also with the object of seeing more of the world." He shipped in 1908 from the coal port of Newcastle, New South Wales, on a vessel he identified only as a large, black-painted, full-rigged ship, hailing from Liverpool. He called her Cambrian Lass *in his book "though that was not her real name." The ship took coal to Valparaiso, then went in ballast to Portland, Oregon, where it loaded wheat for Hamburg. Eaddy's partner in the voyage fell from the rigging.]*

We were busily employed painting the yards and masts while the weather was favourable, and one day whilst hauling the yards around in our watch, someone had left a foot-rope on the main upper-topsail yard, stopped to the topmast rigging with a spun-yarn seizing.

"Up aloft there, someone with a good sharp knife, and cut that stop," said the Mate, pointing aloft at the foot-rope on the main upper-topsail yard, which was stretched bar-tight with the pull of the braces against it.

My mate jumped into the rigging, and was soon aloft at the scene of the trouble.

Whipping out his sheath knife, he reached out from the main top-mast rigging, and drew the sharp blade across the spun-yarn seizing.

"Ping!" went the seizing, and the released rigging, flying back into place like the string of a bow, threw Bill from the rigging like a stone from a catapult, and sent him hurtling down through space.

We all saw him falling, and all we could do in those few seconds was to pray that he would not hit the deck, but go clean over the side.

He struck the main-top, just above the futtock-rigging, a glancing blow and then hit the main lower rigging about half-way down, tearing off two or three round rod-iron ratlines in his rapid descent.

This last obstacle was the saving of Bill, for the spring of the main rigging when he hit it sent him with a rebound right over the side. The huddled-up shape of him saved him also, as he seemed to fall like a round ball, arms, legs and body all doubled up together.

He hit the water with a splash, like a shell landing into the ocean from a heavy cannon, after his eighty-foot fall, and down he went like a stone, to reappear a few minutes after, about half a dozen yards from the ship, with a red stain of blood all round him from a huge gash on his head.

As he rose to the surface the Second Mate, who had rushed out of his room at the commotion, threw a line over the side, and calling on me to get another and follow him, went over the side after Bill.

I followed with another line, and both of us getting hold of the injured man, we passed a bowline round him under his arms, and sang out to the people on deck to haul him up.

They quickly had him up over the rail, and when the Second Mate and I reached the deck Bill was laid out on the deck under the break of the poop, with the Old Man shaving the top of his head in readiness for sewing the wound together.

The steward was here, there and everywhere, and after shaving and bathing the injured head, the Old Man got to work with his surgical needle and catgut thread from the medicine chest, and put seventeen stitches into Bill's thick cranium.

"He has a hide like a bullock, look you," said the Old Man to the Mate, as he pushed the stitches through, but Bill, being only in a semi-conscious state, didn't seem to feel it much, and save for an occasional groan, took no notice of the operation.

After bandaging him up and feeling him all over for any broken bones, we got him into the spare cabin, and laid him in a comfortable bunk.

The heat worried him, and he began to get delirious, so the Old Man sent for me as we were from the same place, and had been ship-mates before joining this ship.

"You stop aft while he is like this, Avery, and watch him. Don't let him get up, and humour him a bit when he gets talking to himself, we must keep him quiet for a few days."

"Aye, aye, sir," I replied, and so was duly installed as Bill's nurse until he got over the worst of his fall.

Bill, however, was young and hardy, and had the constitution of an ox, and within a week or so he was convalescent, and sitting out on deck in one of the big wicker chairs from the cabin, and after about three weeks he insisted on coming for'ard to his own bunk among the rest of us.

Though he had a bad fall, and had been pretty badly knocked about, still he had a lot of luck. If he had not hit the main rigging, he might have fallen on the deck and been killed at once. Then again, had the ship been moving quickly through the water (at the time she was only just holding steerage way) we would have been longer getting him aboard, and most probably he would have sunk with his injuries, before we could have reached him.

Lastly, had we not caught an eight-foot shark just before Bill fell from aloft, the shark would probably have got him when he hit the water, especially as he was bleeding like a pig with its throat cut.

When they hauled him back on deck, the shark and Bill lay side by side for a few minutes, and the thought came to many a mind that it was a very lucky thing Mr. Shark had been caught when he was.

— · —— · · · —— ·

[Accidents were not uncommon aloft, on deck, or, when in ballast, in the holds. More than a few caused serious injury if they were not fatal. It was said that, on average, each ship killed one sailor a voyage. Alan Villiers's friend and filming partner was killed aloft in the Grace Harwar. *Some ships were relatively trouble free, but others injured more than their share. The* Archibald Russell *lost two sailors, swept from her bowsprit, the year before Ken Attiwill joined her. Basil Greenhill and John Hackman in* The Grain Races: The Baltic Background *wrote: "The risk of industrial accident on board sailing vessels, especially square-rigged vessels, has always been very high. The Grain Racers overall, excluding disasters in which many men were lost as in the sinking of* Melbourne *and the loss of the* Admiral Karpfanger, *lost perhaps one or two percent of their crews through fatal accident every year. The working conditions on board late nineteenth century merchant sailing ships—and by definition on board the Grain Racers—would not be acceptable, or indeed legal, today in any Western country, nor would unions tolerate them for one moment." Betty Jacobsen wrote of the loss of life in the ships.]*

Looking around these clean decks in the shadow of the lovely sails, there does not seem to be much tragedy associated with this life. But there is. Many boys have died in these ships; many boys die every year.

This year *[1933]* five died, at least. I know only about these five; there may have been more. In the school-ship *Herzogin Cecilie,* so called because the crew pay to work but are not taught anything except what fools they were, an apprentice boy fell down from the rigging when the ship was only one day out of Mariehamn, and was killed. His mother had come with him to be a passenger to Australia, and the boy fell almost at her feet. He was sent aloft to get some sail in, with some other boys; they got it in, and he looked down to wave to his mother, far below, looking up at him. He waved. Then he slipped and fell, and was killed.

It is almost too horrible a tragedy to have happened. But it happened, all right.

The boy and the demented mother were put ashore in Visby, and the ship continued on her voyage.

Another apprentice lost his life in a strange way. He was sent to pull up water from the seas, in a bucket; he threw the bucket in and when it was full it just pulled him from the rail overboard, and he was drowned. The ship was making fair speed, and he had not estimated the effect of the ship's speed plus the weight of the bucket of water on his arms. Once he was over the side he was dead. There was no chance of saving him, although it may have taken hours for him to drown.

In a German school-ship a boy fell down from aloft in Port Victoria and was buried there. In the *Pamir* another boy fell; in the *Pommern* one fell down the forepeak and broke his skull.

Those five tragedies are just from ships that happened to be in Port Victoria. We do not know anything of the others; they tell me that usually there is a five percent loss of life each voyage. Some ships are always losing somebody; others kill but rarely. But they all kill, sooner or later. . . .

I yarn with Old Red *[the mate]* in the afternoon sun, and he tells me that some of these old sailing-ships are so unsafe they ought not to be allowed to sail. One of them the boys call "the floating coffin"—an appropriate name for a ship that kills two or three boys every voyage. One of the mates sailed in that ship once. Their sailmaker died; another boy was killed in the rigging; a third was washed overboard; one of the officers went out of his mind; a cargo worker fell down the hold and was killed; and the captain slipped on the poop one night and broke his leg.

— ·— · —

[The First World War created a huge demand for shipping, and sailing ships earned great profits while the conflict lasted. A number of German square-riggers in U.S. ports were confiscated by the United States government when it declared war on Germany in 1917. Mrs. Woodrow Wilson, the wife of the president, was requested to suggest appropriate American names for the con-fiscated vessels. She chose native American names. The Steinbeck, *a steel full-rigged ship, was renamed* Arapahoe. *Another, the* Kurt, *was renamed* Moshulu. *The U.S. Shipping Board created a merchant marine cadet corps, composed mostly of very young men, to supplement the short supply of expe-rienced sailing-ship hands. Lou Schmitt was eighteen years old, and straight out of a small town in Oregon, when he joined the* Arapahoe *in San Fran-cisco for a round-trip voyage to the Philippines. The voyage across the Pacific to Manila was uneventful except for an encounter with a typhoon, which the* Arapahoe *successfully weathered. During the night, its crew sighted a distant and intermittent light and, surmising it to be a distress signal, hove to. The light disappeared during the darkness.* Arapahoe's *crew awaited the dawn not knowing what if anything they would find with the first light.]*

It was Lofty who sighted the wreck. Clinging to the slender main topmast, and seated in a precarious position on the topgallant yard, his eagle eyes caught the movement of a dark object as it rose to the top of a swell. His hail, heard indistinctly above the roar of the wind, brought the mate rushing back up the rigging. On deck we could see white faces upturned. The Captain, who stood by the starboard lifeboat with hands cupped around his mouth was shouting, but his words were snatched away by the gale.

As the mate reached the crosstree, we could hear him calling up to

Lofty who, extending his arm, pointed off to port. Looking in the direction he indicated, we scanned the sea closely, at first seeing nothing but the great waste of water. Suddenly I saw it. Far away, much farther than we had been concentrating our gaze, something that looked like tiny match sticks pointing upward. It appeared only for an instant and even as I grasped Johnny's arm it was gone.

Our attention was diverted to the deck where Brodie and the Finn were beckoning all hands down from aloft. Eight bells was striking as we hurried down to find both watches gathered at the break of the poop.

Throughout the ship excitement prevailed as the order was given to square the main yards and get the ship under way. With the main topsails filled, *Arapahoe,* close hauled began to rush through the water, the gale heeling her over to port and mountainous seas smashing into the weather bulwark.

The mate had returned to the poop and was talking to the Captain; at times he gestured toward the south and soon the Captain climbed to the mizzen top. For some time he remained in the rigging, steadying himself against the roll as he pointed his glass southward.

Lofty had also returned to the deck and was quickly surrounded and eagerly questioned about what he had seen.

"Looked like a dismasted ship," he said in answer to our queries.

"See any sign of life?"

"Nope, too far away."

At eight-thirty the mate's shrill whistle sounded and as the morning murk gave way to the sullen light of a stormy day, we went back on the port tack. With the yards braced around hard against the starboard backstays, the port was the weather side over which green seas came pouring aboard. At the first opportunity, as the ship plunged ahead through the morning gloom, we climbed into the rigging. In a minute someone again spotted the wreck, now off our starboard bow but too far away to be seen clearly.

Bearing down rapidly, *Arapahoe* gradually closed the distance and by nine o'clock we could make out broken stumps of masts with several small dark objects in the rigging. At first what was left of the masts appeared to protrude right out of the water. As we drew closer and the wreck was lifted to the top of a swell, we saw a dark hull, which except for the stern, was flush with the sea and covered by breaking combers. Often it would drop out of sight as the hulk slid down into great valleys, each time to reappear.

When first sighted, the figures in the rigging had been nothing more than specks against a background of raging water. Suddenly, horrified, I realized they were men. We attempted to count them as the fury of the gale pressed us hard against the shrouds and *Arapahoe* reeled and pitched. Unable to agree on the number, some said there were four, some said six. Most of us just hung on and stared, wondering what was going to happen.

The Finn, climbing up beside me, gazed toward the tragic scene, his long hair whipping in the wind. Suddenly, nudging my arm, he pointed aft. Turning, I saw the carpenter and Brodie removing the cover from the starboard lifeboat. In spite of the heavy wind and wild sea, it was evident that Captain was going to attempt a rescue.

At the mate's whistle we fell aft to assemble at the break of the poop where we stood by gravely and looked up at the Captain. For a moment he stood gazing down, his hands resting on the teak railing, before he started to speak.

"Dot wreck you see out dere vas a four-masted schooner. She's been dismasted an' is a vater logged hulk. She may break op any minute. Dere's men on her an' ve're going to tak' dem off. All right, Mr. Peterson, you hev' de vatch, pick your boat crew."

The second mate's face had a half grin as he turned to the assembled crew. "Enybody don' hev' to go if dey don' vant to. Pape—Bergstrom—Craig—" for an instant his eyes travelled over the silent group before centering on the husky figure of the carpenter. "Chips, how about you?" He turned to the Captain. "Boat crew's ready, Sir."

The Captain's voice was brisk and sharp as he said, "Mr. Knudsen, heave de ship to an' launch de starboard boat!"

With the main yards backed, *Arapahoe* again lay in the terrific seas, her decks awash with snarling water.

Launching a boat in the angry foam-streaked waves was an undertaking fraught with the greatest danger. There were no smiles on any faces as the grim-featured seamen, each wearing a cork-block life jacket, stood by as the boat was hoisted at the davits. Like watching a drama unfold on the screen, thrilling and unreal, these five brave men climbed into the swinging boat: first, Peterson, the second mate, middle-aged, bony and angular with high cheek bones and a bristly mustache; Pape, able-seaman, young, husky, a giant of a man; Bergstrom, also an A.B., around thirty, short, thick-set, and good-natured; Joe Craig, ordinary seaman, an ex-coast guardsman, about twenty-two, tall slender, and of quiet demeanor; and lastly, Bauma, the ship's carpenter, a Dutchman, sturdy as an oak, a man with a cheerful disposition, a round face, and eyes that twinkled when he laughed.

The handling of lifeboats in heavy seas calls for a particular brand of seamanship but little appreciated by those who have never experienced it. Getting a boat over the side successfully and effecting a rescue, was indeed, the ultimate test in bravery and skill.

Arapahoe lay hove to, nearly broadside, rolling heavily in tremendous seas. The starboard boat was on the lee side; in order to understand the difficulties of launching, one must visualize the great seas, towering high above our decks one moment and dropping away to form deep chasms of dark yawning water the next.

The boat was lowered from davits by tackle hooked into rings at the bow and stern. The hooks had to be released at the proper moment; failure to disengage one hook, or the slightest error in judgement could have resulted in the boat's occupants being thrown to their deaths in the sea. As the boat was lowered slowly under the direction of the mate, an attempt was made to hold it steady by lines at bow and stern. At the same time it was fended off from being smashed against our steel sides by boat hooks in the hands of Bauma and Craig.

There came a breath-taking moment as the wooden craft was raised high by a sea and, at a shout from the mate, cast off. Seconds later, with men pulling desperately on the oars, it cleared the ship and was lost to our view as a wave came aboard in a smother of flying water.

The sharp whistle of the mate again rang out as the command was given to square the yards and get the ship under way. This procedure aroused the curiosity of both watches and, as the ship gathered speed and drew away from the scene, we clustered together and discussed its meaning. By this time our boat could no longer be seen in the haze and heavy seas. The action was made clear when the Finn was asked, "Hey, bos'n, does the Old Man know what the Christ he's doing? What's he running away for?"

"He no run avay," answered the Finn. "Our boat no can row against vind an' sea, so ve gon' tack to lee of wreck and vait dem dere."

Any misgivings we might have had as to the Captain's running away were dispelled during the next couple of hours; during that period we worked furiously, tacking the ship several times. To me it all became a blurred confusion as we cranked on winches and hauled at braces, ducking and hanging on tight as seas came roaring aboard to cover the deck and slosh around hatches in knee-deep foaming water.

Presently, as we beat up into the wind close hauled, I was called aft by the mate. As I reached the poop, Stavanger at the weather wheel with Sanbert at the lee gave me a quick wink as they battled to hold the plunging ship as close to the wind as possible.

The mate, visibly nervous, was standing at the starboard rail talking rapidly to the Captain. Turning, he ordered me to stand by atop the aft fo'c'sle to act as police and carry messages forward.

Taking my position, I gazed long and carefully for some sign of our boat but could see nothing other than the heaving ocean. Remembering the mate's obvious concern, I experienced a sickening sensation as I wondered if the boat had capsized.

Suddenly I saw the wreck again off our port bow. It was still some distance away and the stubs of its masts rocked dizzily as they rose with the giant waves. Plunging her bows into the seas, *Arapahoe* was rapidly drawing nearer.

I watched the Captain as calm, cool, apparently not the slightest bit flustered, he gave his orders to the mate. Standing at the standard compass and occasionally glancing aloft, he held up his hand and, without turning his head, motioned gently to Stavanger. Something about him reminded me of a maestro standing on a podium conducting an unseen orchestra. The music was the high thin whine of the wind blowing through miles of taught rigging in counterpoint to the booming of seas breaking over our bows.

In another thirty minutes we had drawn abeam of the wreck on the lee side. At a command from the Captain the main yards were backed and the ship again hove to. We now lay with our port side to the weather so as to give the boat the benefit of our lee when she came alongside to be taken aboard.

The Captain's strategy was now apparent. Originally, we had hove to on the weather side of the wreck; the boat had been launched at nine o'clock, the Captain depending on the wind and seas to carry it down to the hulk. After getting the boat over the side, he had, by a masterpiece of seamanship in the teeth of a howling gale and gigantic seas, tacked the ship around until now, at eleven o'clock, we were hove to about two miles to the lee of the wreck, waiting for our boat to arrive.

Minutes were like hours as men peered out over the churning ocean from perches in the rigging. At first nothing could be seen but great waves, their tops blown off into flying scud, their very size beaten down and flattened by the force of the wind. Occasionally we would catch glimpses of the wreck as stumps of masts appeared momentarily before being lost in the deep troughs.

Finally there came a hail from aloft and I looked up to see an arm pointing excitedly. Soon I saw it too; at first, far away, an object that bobbed on the crest of a huge swell and disappeared only to appear again, each time drawing closer.

Gradually the distance lessened. Often the boat would disappear for long, agonizing moments while we held our breaths in suspense. After what seemed like an eternity, it was sweeping around our stern, and I had a fleeting glimpse of a scene that was to be fixed in my memory forever. Four stalwart men, their faces pale and drawn, were straining at the oars; in the stern, one hand grasping the tiller, the other resting on the gunwale, his eyes gazing stolidly ahead, sat the second mate; near him, bareheaded, sitting erect and straight, was an old man; he had snow-white hair and a long grey beard that blew in the wind. Huddled in the bottom of the boat were several dark figures, their eyes hollow and vacant as they stared at the plunging ship.

Moments later they were off our lee with death at their elbows as the monstrous waves threatened to dash the frail craft against *Arapahoe*'s side. As the lunging boat sank far below the level of our bulwark, I hurriedly counted its occupants—fourteen in all.

To get the survivors and our crew safely on board was a tremendous task which at first seemed almost impossible. Cargo netting and a boarding ladder were already hung over the side, while ropes were coiled down nearby and heaving lines placed in handy positions.

As the boat surged dangerously close, the second mate shouted up through cupped hands, the only word intelligible above the gale was "line". At the same time, he gestured in pantomime by holding his hands under his armpits.

Quickly a large loop was formed in a rope end and tied with a bowline knot. This was bent to a heaving line which was thrown to the boat. Minutes later, with the loop under his armpits, we were hauling a limp, pallid figure aboard who babbled incoherently as he fell into the mate's powerful arms before being carried aft.

Next came the old man with the white beard who staggered as he reached the deck and was held up by two of our men. In spite of his weakened condition and being on the verge of collapse, he introduced himself to our skipper as Captain Charles Backus of the schooner *Ethel Zane,* and asked that aid be given his crew.

"Vas your men all saved?" asked our Captain.

"Yes, thank God! They were all taken off by your boat," replied the old man as, swaying unsteadily, he also was helped aft.

We worked rapidly, seriously hampered by seas that continued to come crashing aboard, threatening the life boat, flooding the deck, and causing the ship to roll badly. One by one, however, the dazed men were hauled aboard until all nine were accounted for. Only then did Peterson and Bauma come scrambling up the ladder, leaving Bergstrom, Craig and Pape to fend off the boat and hook on the tackle.

Bringing the lifeboat back on board was an operation equally as difficult and dangerous as launching it. It called for extreme cool headedness on the part of both the men in the boat and those on *Arapahoe's* deck. In such a sea it was essential that both falls be hooked on at precisely the right moment and the boat hauled clear of the water. After a mighty struggle with the raging seas it was back on the skids and made fast. Twelve o'clock noon, eight bells were striking as Pape, Bergstrom, and Craig crawled wearily out of the boat to be surrounded by an admiring crew. Questions were flung at them from all sides but the questioners were quickly dispersed by the mate's whistle calling the watches to square the main yards and get the ship under way.

—·—·—·—

[The seaman's worst fear was fire at sea. Paul Stevenson witnessed a fire on the Mandalore.*]*

Last night the most dreaded catastrophe that can happen to a vessel at sea befell us: fire broke out forward. As near as I can learn, it was the carpenter's fault. We were going smoothly along with everything set, the night being fine and clear. The wheel had just been relieved at four bells in the first-watch, and Mr. Ryan and I were walking the poop, calculating how much longer we would probably be at sea, when one of the men came aft . . . and, mounting the poop-ladder, said very quietly, without the least show of excitement, "Mr. Ryan, the ship's afire forward." Not deeming it necessary to awake the skipper, who had turned in, the mate jumped off the poop and ran forward as hard as he could go, I following immediately after; and a sight greeted me, when I had passed the galley, that I'll never forget. Both watches stood grouped about the fore-hatch, those who had turned out being almost naked, gazing, with fear in their eyes, at the port light house, the interior of which was a mass of flames, that cast a deep-red glow over the whole forward part of the ship.

A fire at sea takes the heart right out of a foremast hand. He will witness without flinching the approach of a tropical cyclone, or sleep peacefully though a howling Cape Horn gale, surrounded by a fleet of icebergs. But fire seems to sap his courage, and I actually saw a couple of hands blubbering a little.

When we had approached as close as we could, we saw that the great port light, almost three times as large and powerful as Lloyd calls for, had exploded from being filled too full, and the burning oil was scattered over everything, not only in the light-house, which was iron, but also over the paint-shop under the lighthouse. Things looked very bad, and I own to a dominant sense of uneasiness and dread until I thought of the iron deck under the wooden one between us and the oil below. After this I was somewhat reassured and could survey the proceedings with calmness. We had not been forward more than a minute or two before the wooden ladder by which access to the light-house was obtained from the paint-room caught fire, and the whole of that apartment was then a mass of flames. Mr. Ryan looked around and, picking out two of the coolest hands . . . ordered them to bring some strips of canvas and wads of oakum, wet them down under the head-pump, and then together they would see what could be done in the way of smothering the fire. The canvas, etc., was brought up in a few moments, pending which it was difficult to prevent the rest of the men from throwing water on the flames,—a fatal proceeding, as it would have splashed everything in the vicinity with the blazing kerosene.

Then the mate and three seamen did some really heroic work, entering right into the burning paint-shop and fighting the fierce blaze with great, dripping oakum wads. While this was going on a stream of oil ran out through a little scupper-hole in the paint-shop and into the iron water-ways, down which it flowed, a tiny rivulet of flame. I looked to see the running gear coiled over the pins catch fire, in which case the top-hamper would have caught in an instant, for nothing scarcely is so flammable as dry manila and hemp; while the top-gallant-, royal-, and sky-sail yards being all of wood, we would have had a terrible fight of it if the halliards, etc., had caught. But the men, with more sense than I had credited them with, ran along and lifted big coils off the pins, placing them lengthwise on the pin-rail, and the little rill of oil burned itself out before any damage was done. Meanwhile the mate had fought valiantly, scorching himself badly, but extinguishing the flames so successfully that in fifteen minutes nothing remained of the fire save that here and there a charred ember glowed in the darkness like a big fire-fly. When things had cooled off sufficiently, I went into the paint-shop, which I found a complete ruin, together with all its contents, paints, varnishes, and brushes all being totally destroyed. A great deal of paint had been freshly mixed for repainting the inside of the bulwarks, preparing for port, and this was in open kegs, which had been overturned, thus wasting an immense quantity.

I can assure those who have never been similarly placed that the sight I saw when I rounded the forward house would whiten the face of the sturdiest of men, and no one on board dared breath scarcely till the last spark had been stamped out; and after it was all over I saw more than one brown fist tremble as some of the men lit their pipes. Never shall I forget the picture of the ship's company as they huddled in a bunch about the fore-hatch, the crimson light outlining with singular fierceness their rugged, bearded faces.

— · — · —

[The year 1905 was notorious for the damage ships suffered off Cape Horn. Alan Villiers wrote of it as "the dreadful winter of 1905." Claude Woollard noted that "Out of one hundred and thirty vessels which sailed from European ports to round Cape Horn, only fifty-two appeared to have reached their destination without mishap. Four were wrecked, twenty-two put into harbour to make good their damage, and forty-nine had not arrived or were not accounted for by the end of July 1905."9 W. H. S. Jones was an apprentice at the time on the ship British Isles. *Jones later became second mate on the ship and left her in 1909. He in time became a master mariner. Jones described fighting fire in the cargo of the* British Isles *off the coast of Patagonia in 1905, only the beginning of their troubles in that difficult year.]*

Routine thermometer readings had disclosed that the temperature of the coal in the main hold had risen above normal during our passage through the Tropics. The Mate was of the opinion that the coal would catch fire, by spontaneous combustion, before we could reach Cape Horn. He urged the Captain to put into Rio de Janiero, to investigate and if necessary discharge, cool, and re-stow the cargo.

The procedure would have involved the owners in expense. The Captain was fully aware of the possible danger of fire. A cargo of coal catching alight at sea in the High Latitudes might mean not only the destruction of the ship but also the death of every person on board—

9. C. L. A. Woollard, *The Last of the Cape Horners* (Ilfracomb, U. K.: A. H. Stockwell, Ltd., 1967).

and that included his wife and children—as lifeboats could not live in the mountainous seas of a Cape Horn full gale. Such disasters had occurred, as every mariner well knew; but Captain Barker also knew what his orders were from the owners, to make a smart passage if possible, and that necessitated "keeping the seas" *[avoiding time-consuming harbor stops]*.

It was for him, and not the Mate, to decide what to do, and he did not hesitate to remind the Mate of that fact.

Instead of accepting the position, the Mate very foolishly began talking to some of the fo'c'sle hands, telling them of his fears that the cargo would catch fire, and his opinion that the Captain should put into Rio.

We boys knew nothing of this undercurrent of discontent. The first we knew of the danger was a commotion one morning—the 24th of July—when I happened to be in the watch below, and was roused from slumber by the excited voice of someone yelling:

"Fire! Fire! All hands on deck!"

In a couple of minutes we were all there, on the run, and saw wisps of smoke coming from under the tarpaulins covering the main hatch.

The Captain, the officers and the carpenter were standing on the hatch, in earnest talk, while the crew stood around, silent and sullen. The danger was obvious to all. It was only too apparent the cargo was on fire.

In a sailing-ship there are no steam-injections or fire hoses and pressure-pumps. The only alternatives was either to close all ventilation in the hope of smothering the fire, or to open the hatch and dig the hot coal out.

This latter method could be extremely risky, as the inrush of air could fan a smouldering fire to flame.

The Captain took the decision to open the hatch.

Investigations, and probings with a thermometer, soon revealed that, though the coal was very hot and steaming—it had been taken on board at Port Talbot damp from rain—the main centre of heat was confined to a relatively small area, deep down in the hold.

"Dig it out, Mister Mate!" the Captain ordered, "and pile it along the deck, free of the belaying pins. Rig a gyn over the hatch, and get some baskets. Eight men will go below to shovel, six will tail on the gantline, four will build a heap along the deck with the hand-truck, and two will draw water from over-side to souse it. Not one lump of this coal must be allowed to go overboard. Keep the men moving, this weather may not last too long!"

Whatever the Mate's mutinous feelings may have been, he was an excellent mariner in everything referring to handling the ship's gear, and quickly had the crew told off for the emergency duties.

The Captain gave no orders to alter course to make the nearest port, perhaps only a day's sail away, somewhere on the South American coast. It was lucky that the north-west breeze remained steady, requiring very little work aloft or trimming of sails.

All hands, including the apprentices, set to work with a will as coal-heavers. We worked as though our lives depended on digging out that hot coal, and to a considerable extent that motive was real enough in our minds. The officers knew the ship's position, but no one else had any means of knowing whether we were a hundred or a thousand miles from land, or from the possibility of rescue, if the fire got worse.

To the average sailor, navigation was a mystery. It was always a surprise when land came up over the horizon after the ship had been weeks or even months in the wide waters of the ocean. The discipline of the ship was maintained partly by the respect felt by the fo'c'sle hands for the navigating ability of the officers, which enabled them to bring the vessel to her port of destination by invisible routes over the pathless seas. On that knowledge the safety of all depended. The Captain's word was law and had to be so. When he gave orders for the coal to be dug out, all doubts were at an end. There were no committee meetings at sea to debate what might be best for the safety of the vessel. "The Old Man knows best" was the argument to settle all arguments. His decisions had to be taken, and obeyed, instantly, on the basis of his superior knowledge of all the circumstances of the case and his ability to weigh the pros and cons, and to anticipate contingencies that could occur.

In this case, the calculated risk he took was that the weather would hold, with a steady north-west breeze, for several days, long enough to dig out the hot coal, souse it, and re-stow it, cooled to normal, in the hold. If heavy weather had come up when the operation was only partly completed, and the coal heaped along the deck and the hatch opened, management of the ship would have become very difficult with our small crew. It was for this reason that the Mate had urged him to bear up for Rio or one of the smaller ports to the south of Rio; but the Captain decided that the work could be done while the ship continued under sail, without any variation of her set course southward; and that was the end of the argument, whether the Mate liked it or not.

On deck a cargo gyn was rigged over the hatch by shackling it to the mainstay, and hoisting it up the wire to the height necessary to swing the baskets of coal clear. A 2½-inch gantline was rove through, with a hook on one end, and the hauling part rove through a lead-block beside the hatch-coaming.

The labour of six men was required to operate this hoist. There was a perfectly good donkey-engine, within four feet of the forward end of the main hatch, where the fire was. It may seem incredible to a later generation of seafarers, but Captain Barker decided not to use this engine and winch to hoist the baskets. The reason was that a fire under the donkey-boiler would have consumed a few tons of the owners' uninsured cargo of best-quality, double-screened Cardiff coal!

We had 3,600 tons of coal on board, but the conscientious Captain would not use any of it to ease the heavy labour of the over-worked crew in this emergency. The coal had been bought at the pit-mouth in South Wales for about 10s. 6d. per ton, but its value in the South

Atlantic was considerably in excess of that figure, as it would be sold in the Chilean ports at £4 10s. per ton—if we could live to deliver it there.

The use of a ton of coal under the donkey-boiler would therefore have entailed a financial loss upon the owners of about £4, or in proportion to the amount that might be used.

This sacrifice of the owners' profits could not be endured simply to save the sailors some hard work. What did they receive £3 per month and meager rations for, if not to work?

Men work better with vacuums in their stomachs. Overfed and underworked men become fat and lazy. Such was the logic of the "good old days".

A part of the hatch was uncovered, and eight hands went below, to shovel the coal into the baskets. They formed four two-men gangs, disposed at the corners of a square, above the point where the heating was greatest.

Stripped to the waists, they set to with a will, and were soon in a lather of sweat, half-suffocated by the smoke and fumes, and blackened by dust; but they were working for their lives—their own hides were at stake—and they filled those baskets with a rapidity which would gladden the heart of a stevedoring supervisor of today, if he ever had the opportunity of seeing such zeal displayed.

As each basket was hooked on, it was hoisted up by the six men tailing on the gantline—doing the work of the idle donkey-engine—and encouraged by the shout of "Stamp and go!" rendered in stentorian tones by the redoubtable Paddy Furlong.

When hoisted high enough the basket was swung across and dumped on the deck. There it was trundled along on the handtruck and tipped out, the coal being then shovelled up on to the heap which was being built along the deck by four men, and soused with water drawn from overside in a canvas bucket by the Second Mate and two apprentices.

This water when pulled up was emptied into tubs for wetting down the hot coal, on deck and also in the hold. We boys—being members of the Afterguard, and the future generation of officers—were expected at all times to set an example to the rank and file, so two of us were sent below into the hold to shovel coal with the men at work in that steaming, fuming, choking, half-dark atmosphere, a preview of Purgatory's pleasures. We worked there, turn and turn about with the other two, who were pulling up water from overside with the Second Mate.

The ordeal by fire continued for four days, from 24th to 28th July, getting worse for the men in the Pit of Purgatory as we neared the seat of the combustion.

Progressive thermometer readings showed temperatures increasing steadily from 170 degrees F. to 200 degrees F., as we dug further and further in. Coal-shovelling is hard enough work without being half-suffocated at the same time and having one's boots shrivelled by standing on a hot bed while working. The heat scorched the soles of our feet, as we frantically hopped from one foot to the other to obtain a moment's relief, and kept hopping up for hours on end. The appalling conditions under which we worked might well have earned us some sympathy instead of the goading abuse with which we were spurred on to greater efforts.

The fire-walking fakirs of India might have felt at home in that hold, but to us it was hell. Work went on until midnight the first day, with brief respites of half an hour to enjoy the "dinner" and "tea" viands—for which ten minutes would have been enough, as far as the menu was concerned.

At midnight, the hands were incapable of further effort, and were sent below after the hatch was closed, to turn in as they were, sweat-streaked and blackened, ready for an instant call on deck if the smouldering coal should burst into flame, or if the wind changed or freshened unduly to require trimming yards or handling sails.

Fortunately the breeze remained steady. Next morning, at the first streaks of daylight, all hands turned to, and continued the purgatorial task again until midnight. Now, as the shovellers neared the seat of the combustion, the heat became almost intolerable. Hundreds of buckets of water were poured down into the hold, giving temporary relief, but soon evaporating to steam which made the humidity intense. By this time a great quantity of coal was heaped along the decks, which would have been very inconvenient if a squall or storm had blown up to make the decks awash, but the Captain's luck—and the weather—held good.

On the fourth day, we reached the seat of the fire, where the coal was smouldering and smoking. Some of it burst into flame while being hoisted in the baskets. It was dumped over board, presumably to the sorrow of the owners. To shovel these glowing embers was a task to break the stoutest hearts, and changes of the gangs below were made frequently. At midnight, scarcely able to stand from weariness, we had the satisfaction of knowing that the fire was beaten, and the last of the glowing embers thrown overboard.

The occasion was celebrated with a liberal tot of proof rum—for the men, but not for the apprentices—which for the moment erased all thoughts of the hardships so recently endured.

The loose coal on deck would have to be shovelled back into the hold, before the weather broke, but that would be a less painful and anxious task than heaving it out had been.

To get it back would be a pleasure we could look forward to on the morrow.

Running the Easting Down

[*The last windships were built strong and powerful in hull and rigging to enable them to run for thousands of miles eastward around the world, from the Cape of Good Hope toward Australia or thence toward Cape Horn, before the gales—the westerlies—of the far southern hemisphere. This was known as "running the easting (or eastern) down." The* Herzogin Cecilie *was one of the best and one of the fastest of the twentieth-century sailing ships. Elis Karlsson wrote in* Mother Sea *of his first voyage in the westerlies as able seaman in 1926 in the "Duchess" (the English translation of "Herzogin").*]

On one of the last sunny and calm days before the westerlies we shifted sail, and soon we were running eastern down, after the usual damp work in the variables. The weather we encountered in the westerlies was of a kind I was to get to know well from then onwards. Strong winds blowing steadily from the west for days on end, with the sun shining sometimes, but more often with hard, grey skies overhead; at other times the same strong, driving wind with foggy weather. Another common variety of the roaring forties is a strong, westerly wind blowing, with hail and sleet squalls and wind of gale force during the squalls, the wind changing direction as the squall passes. Sometimes a short period of calm occurs, with the big swell causing a lot of wear and tear of sails and gear. Albatross sail silently over the lonely wastes, sometimes settling on heaving water around the ship. The sullen, grey skies admit no ray of sun and very little light; a dismal, ominous scene, and somehow unnatural in these regions of strong winds and turbulent skies. It is the proverbial calm before the storm, for the winds do not rest for long in these latitudes. A sudden and vicious gale from the eastern half of the compass sometimes supersedes one of these calms, but more often the common west-wind system follows the calm. A light breeze springs up from the north-east, and everybody on board heaves a sigh of relief; the sails are quiet again, and the signs indicate the return of normal westerlies weather. Slowly freshening, the wind as slowly backs through north to north-west with drizzle, which changes to heavy rain as the wind backs into the west and reaches gale force. After a period, lasting perhaps an hour, or sometimes a couple of days, the rain changes into a violent downpour, obliterating all visibility, until a faint paling of the murk in the south-west gives its warning. Immediately the mate on watch sees the sign in the south-west, he tells the helmsman to get the wheel hard over to port smartly; he also blows his whistle for the watch, and he shouts "Port fore-braces!" as soon as he gets the whistle from his lips, for that warning is followed immediately by a fierce wind from the south-west, which clears the skies swiftly. After the first onslaught, the south-wester eases, and sails that perhaps were taken in previously are set again. By this time the seas run really big, and the wind-shift to south-west has created an ugly cross-sea. This was the time when seas would climb on board and do damage. I have seen one of these seas, looking quite innocent, with no noisy, breaking crest to make it look formidable, climb almost leisurely up the ship's side and equally quietly on to the ship's deck with hardly a gurgle coming from it. After floating off the deck, it left behind it twelve feet of nine-by-three-inch broken rail of Burma teak, and one and a half-inch-diameter steel stanchions that the rail had been bolted to, bent and loosened.

In these storm-swept regions the sea is never still, and after prolonged periods with winds of gale or hurricane force the seas sometimes reach gigantic proportions. Exactly how big they are I cannot tell, but I have seen *Herzogin Cecilie,* 337 feet long, her bows in the trough between two seas, and her stern lifted high by a sea licking her taffrail. As to the speed these seas travel, again I must admit that I do not know, but a ship making a speed of sixteen to seventeen knots is constantly overtaken by such seas.

This region of forty to fifty degrees south latitude was to me awe-inspiring, but also fascinating; those immeasurable masses of tumbling seas, reaching right around the globe; this lonely sea, grander there than anywhere else, somehow never made me feel lonely. Small and insignificant, yes, but never lonely. Where the fascination lay, I cannot tell; maybe a sense of utter—if illusory—freedom was produced by an awareness of this vast, untamed sea around one; I do not know. I do know that I felt happy and at peace there.

— — · — · —

[Upon occasion a ship might run all the way from Europe through the North and South Atlantics to the high latitudes of the southern hemisphere without reducing sail, as did the Cimba *in 1904. Shipmasters then drove their vessels hard when running the easting down to make their best speed in favoring gales. This meant much sail-handling for the crew, taking in sail when necessary and immediately setting sail again at the least slackening of the gale. The 1949 voyage of the* Passat, *as fine a ship as ever sailed that route, gave the very last Cape Horn crew a full measure of experience with sail handling, as Holger Thesleff reported.]*

Some were already on their way aloft when No. 1 ordered all hands to the mainsail. It too was to be taken in. We rushed up on the midships deck by the mainmast and swigged on the bunt-lines of the mainsail. I heard someone say that the mainsail was a harder sail, and we noticed that in the stiff bunt-lines. And still more so, when the Skipper himself came and hauled with us. Not till we had his giant's pull did the bunt-lines begin to come, foot by foot. The mess-boy was tugging with us somewhere at the tail end and he kept chattering away till Charlie told him to go to hell.

When the mainsail was clewed up, both watches were sent aloft to furl the crojack. Heinz took command of us up there and Charlie and the other old hands had to submit. Heinz knew his job. First, we divided at the middle of the yard to loose the gaskets, then in time to Heinz's shouts we gathered the hard wet sail under our stomachs until we had reached the bolt rope on the foot and leach. Near the mast the foot rope was so low that it was difficult to work, and so we trusted to the others to take the weight and let the bolt rope stay where it was. But that wouldn't do for Heinz, and with a joint supreme effort on the part of the strongest the bolt rope was got high enough for us to be able to hold it, while we sought to make a suitable fold at the bottom of the great mass of the sail to tuck the canvas in. Charlie got hold of a fold and led it on to the next man. Heinz was still not satisfied, but led another, Len a third.

"We need a lot of slack, otherwise we'll never get the brute up," he said.

Eventually we agreed on a fold, shoved sail and bolt rope in between the yard and the fold and laid hold of the resultant huge roll with both arms.

"Now we'll take her", called Heinz. "All ready? Hi!—Hej!—Ho!" And the roll rose up on to the middle of the yard, where it was furled. Then out to the starboard yard-arm. When sail and bolt rope were impressed under our stomachs, we again had to decide which fold would cover the sail best, how best to make a "skin" to tuck the wet, heavy canvas in. Heinz made the decision and chose one too near the clew line. The sail there would not reach up on to the yard, but went into a hard roll and stopped half way. The heap of sail was too large where the leach-line pulled the leach in towards the mast. We made several attempts, but in the end we had to throw the gaskets provisionally round the roll and furl the remaining part nearer the mast; only then did the whole of the starboard side of the sail lie folded on top of the yard. While we were working away I heard many wondering aloud what was the use of having the sail on top of the yard; but when it lay there well covered by one of its own even folds and well lashed between the double jackstays, it looked so fine and secure that no other answer was needed.

The performance was then repeated on the lee yard-arm. Heinz wanted to have the roll tight and thin before he chose the fold, but that was asking too much of our strength and we had to shift our grip before it would go. Then we found that there were not enough gaskets and the man nearest the mast climbed down for a couple of extra ones, Charlie refusing to let him "borrow" from the next yard above us. That is just how gaskets disappear from the yards, and perhaps we would soon have to take in the mizzen lower topsail. "It's taken in only in a storm and then I imagine you have other things to think of than a couple of rotten gaskets", muttered Pinocchio, who knew everything. For some minutes we hung there holding tight to the sail and to ourselves, then the gaskets arrived and we were able to furl the sail. And so, one after the other, we dropped down to the deck.

— · — · —

[Neil Campbell was one of those smitten with love of ships at an early age. His first voyage on the Elginshire *in 1910 only reinforced his passion.]*

The flight of the ship to the eastward as she shouldered the grey, foaming seas; the song of the great west wind aloft; the goodly company of those grand white birds; the endless dangerous work on the wildly swinging yards—these things filled me with a strange elation.

Climbing out to the tip of the jib-boom one dog watch, I took my place with legs jammed inside the backropes, one hand upon the royal stay. Behind me the big shark's tail, nailed, as was the custom *[for luck]*, to the spar-end, touched my back as I faced aft. Frank Bullen had gone many times to this vantage point in the ships in which he served—and now I found myself there too.

The sight before me was truly magnificent. It was as if I were on a moving stage outside the ship, watching her striving to run me down, yet never doing so. The barque was storming along under fores'l and six topsails, the wind slightly quartering, so that every sail was bladder-hard and pulling its full weight.

An enormous following sea was sweeping up from the westward, and the ship rolled and pitched heavily in her stride. One minute I soared swiftly upwards on the cold steel tip of that finger-spar; the next found me plunged seaward so steeply that it seemed the mad-dened water beneath was about to engulf me.

The thunder of the bow-wave was almost deafening as she lifted aft and hurled her stem into the boiling water till it surged, clutching upwards, to the figurehead. And then her bows went flying skywards again till the dripping forefoot showed many feet below. At such times the roar of the broken water decreased and another sound was heard—the deep boom of the gale as it threw itself exultingly against the rain-darkened topsails and great, bellying foresail. . . .

One of the men was standing at the heel of the bowsprit beckoning to me, his lips moving while no words reached me. I made my way back to the foc's'le head. "Go aft," he said, "the old man wants to see you."

The skipper was waiting for me in one of his severest moods. "Do you know you were in the most dangerous part of the ship in bad weather?" he remarked, his keen blue eyes boring into me from under the thatch of his sou'wester. "How long would you have lasted if you had gone overboard? Not five seconds! If you must go out there for pleasure—go in fine weather!"

He turned from me to continue the watching of his ship as she drove along. For hours in such weather he would stand like that, hardly speaking to the officer of the watch unless it were to give some curt order for the safety of the barque. He was a fine sailor, his life having been spent in square-rigged ships and no others. If we thought him hard at times, he was hard for our own good.

— · — · —

[Elis Karlsson, A.B., found great satisfaction, according to his Mother Sea, *in the work that went on constantly in the rigging of the* Herzogin Cecilie *in 1926. The traditional work of able-bodied seamen was to keep the complex structure of canvas, rope, chain, and wire in repair and good order, upon which depended the lives of the seamen and the progress of the ship. The skills of able-bodied seamen were too valuable to be wasted cleaning bilges or chipping rust.]*

While running eastern down, Mattson and I, in our respective watches, were almost constantly aloft, repairing chafed sails, and sewing up any seam that threatened to burst. It saved a lot of sail-changing, and with the steady west winds the sails wore quickly, in spite of chafing gear; especially the main- and fore-rigging, being partly blanketed by the mizzen rigging at times.

It was cold work up there, but it had its compensations. Up there one was one's own boss—almost—with plenty of fresh air, as compared with the stuffiness and gloom of the sail-loft, or in the holds where the hands were chipping rust. Hauling of braces and the taking in of any of the smaller sails one ignored; only a special signal from the mate on watch brought us down. When a hail squall hit the ship, it was worth it being up there, with the drum-tight sails all around one, watching the ship racing along with the hail and the wind, her bow-waves and narrow wake whiter than the hail-whipped sea. Her rolling almost ceased while she was in the grip of a squall; once the squall had passed she commenced it again.

And how she rolled! Standing on a footrope, or perhaps sitting on a topgallant yard-arm, I was perched above the ship only for a short moment; the rest of the time I was soaring over the Indian Ocean. I never ceased to marvel at the ship's ability to come back again from her mad rolls.

When a job was finished, I hailed the deck. Standing near a ventilator, which led down into the hold, the Second Mate blew two blasts on his whistle. When the watch appeared, the sail I had repaired was set, and perhaps another sail lowered or clewed up and bunted for me. . . .

Monotonous? Maybe our life would have driven some people I know crazy. Personally, I have never felt better, both mentally and physically. I was not aware of having any nerves, in the sense we talk about nerves today. There was perfect coordination between brain and muscle; I could think and act quickly, without an effort of will, which I think is a sign of a healthy balance of mental and physical powers.

You lived like animals and were similar to monkeys, eating and sleeping and climbing about the rigging, instead of trees, somebody might say in disgust. This argument contains some truth, I suppose, for our life in the westerlies was spent sleeping, eating, and working hard, with no opportunities of "widening our outlook" through social intercourse with our fellow men. In lieu of this, we had the contemplation of the vast ocean around us and the ship sailing across it, for one hour at a time when on lookout; a lonely walk on the fore deck, or a walk with a shipmate, with conversation if one felt like it. Not much in the way of compensation for the things a landsman enjoys in his spare time.

Yet I do know that this life of ours gave me complete peace of mind, a rare commodity ashore, and surely to be preferred to the turmoil of doubts, known and unknown fears, and more often than not a lack of faith in anything, which all seem to torment the minds of landsmen.

We had, as I understand it, by sailing our ships, taken a step back into the primitive world, a world where spiritual peace reigned. We sailed our ship with the assistance of the elements, unlike the landsman, who in his everyday life is a victim of capricious forces, created and controlled by men.

Looking back on those days, I am puzzled by one thing: the feeling of being free that I experienced on board a sailing-ship, and especially in high latitudes. One knows that there is no such thing as absolute freedom, and we on board the Duchess were certainly not free; on the contrary. With implacable discipline, and by the fact that we were on board, we were tied to the service of the ship; our bondage was absolute. As an employee and as a member of the armed forces I was constantly aware of being bound, unfree. This was a paradox which I cannot attempt to explain.

Yet I must mention a parallel. A man sets sail in a dinghy. If the day is calm, he drifts out into the open water, but it is not the same as on a windy day; the feeling that he came out sailing for is largely absent. If the wind blows, he finds what he looked for: a feeling of release, of being on top of the world, a truly free man. And yet he is no more free than we were, for he is the servant and the master at the same time of his dinghy. It is something that nobody has yet been able to analyse and satisfactorily explain: man's craving to sail the sea.

— · — · —

[*The fastest daily runs that sailing ships ever made were made in the westerlies of the southern ocean. Claims of daily runs in excess of four hundred miles were defended and disputed. It is an ongoing controversy: just how fast could a sailing ship sail? W. H. S. Jones considered the question.*]

The Captain had decided to "make a passage". . . For about three weeks, we carried on under a heavy press of sail, making daily runs of over 300 miles, for several days in succession. The highest day's run was 342 miles, which I noted in my diary.

I record this now as testimony of the greatest speed the *British Isles* attained during my four years of service in her. I believe it was near the limit of possibility for a deep-laden steel ship under sail, with a small crew, driving on in a following gale. As we were in 50 degrees S. Latitude, this gives an average speed of 14.6 knots in a day of 23 hours 24 minutes elapsed time, implying that for short periods we attained speeds of 15 and 16 knots in the heavy squalls.

Nautical readers of this book will be aware that there is often cause for controversy in claims made for high speeds attained by sailing-ships when "running the Easting down".

These fast runs were usually made in the high latitudes of the southern oceans, between the Cape of Good Hope and Australia, or between Australia and Cape Horn, on an eastward course.

To assess the merits of these passages I have always felt that many factors must be taken into consideration.

What was the nature of the cargo carried? Was it light general merchandise, making the ship ride high in the water, while the holds were packed tight and the cargo immovable? Was it a cargo of wool from Australia, screwed tight and immovable into the hold with jacks? If so, the greatest deterrent to carrying sail which the latter-day Master had to contend with, the fear of a bulk cargo shifting, was never present.

Navigation in these high latitudes was sometimes difficult, although, with thousands of miles of open water on all sides, the ship's exact position was not of serious consequence until nearing the land. It was not unusual to run for several days with the sun, moon or stars obscured by dense masses of cloud; heavy squalls of wind with sleet, rain or snow at frequent intervals; the visible horizon, where sea and sky meet, anybody's guess, perhaps four, perhaps five miles distant; and frequent casts of a water-soaked and shrunken log-line the only means of estimating the day's run.

In these conditions, the position at noon from day to day, and the runs made good, were recorded in all good faith by the only means available, and an accurate position and the aggregate distance run obtained when astronomical sights were again possible.

Average runs for a succession of days could therefore be determined with reasonable accuracy, and from day to day when observations were possible; but I find it hard to believe that, in these latitudes, with enough wind blowing to drive a sailing-ship through the stormy seas at 20 knots, accurate astronomical observations were possible, day after day.

In the *British Isles,* as in many other sailing-ships, there was only one chronometer. It was a standing order to compare chronometers with any ship met, the very first flag-signal, after the ship's numbers (name) were made, being, "What is your longitude?"

With severe shocks, jerks, and changes of temperature, which a chronometer receives on a long ocean passage of several months, and without any means of ascertaining the error, it is not surprising that on one occasion within my experience, when we were making the coast of Chile, though the instrument told us the coast should be in sight, we sailed on to the eastward for another 80 miles before it was visible.

The *British Isles* seldom exceeded 12 or 13 knots in the trade-winds at their strongest. When she attained 15 or 16 knots, in the Roaring Forties, with a following gale, she was being driven to her limit, and risks were being taken of dismasting her.

This speed, for a wind-driven ship with a total dead-weight of nearly 6,000 tons, hurtling along in the mountainous seas with her decks full of water, adding another two or three hundred tons of weight to sink her yet deeper in the water, meant that a tremendous force was exerted by the wind on her canvas, cordage, spars, and rigging generally, but especially on her masts, which, though of steel, were hollow shells.

Being only too familiar, after our months of laborious overhauling of the top-hamper at Callao, with the condition of every wire, rope seizing and splice aloft, we boys, perhaps in our ignorance and inexperience, had ten thousand expectations that something, sooner or later, would have to part under the continuous strain that was being put on all gear.

Yet, even with this anxiety, there was a feeling of exultation, a wild and reckless sense of freedom and of victory over the challenging forces of nature, as, from aloft, a hundred or more feet above the deck, we saw below us the long, sleek and glistening body of the ship cleaving a path through the roaring waters, driving on, driving on, cracking on to breaking-point, to "make a passage", to arrive in port a few days, or even a few hours, earlier than might have been expected.

This was the ambition of every Master in Sail, and few, if any of them, could control the impulse to excel, to win the approbation of people interested in shipping news, or to earn the envy of other Masters. Above all there was the inherent pride of the sail-bred man, to whom a ship under full sail and a beautiful woman were the summit of perfection. To him both were invincible.

Day after day, week after week, the *British Isles* stormed along on her solitary way across the waste of tumbling waters, checking the yards in as the wind shifted a point or two, or hauling them around, as a gale died away for a space, to blow up again with renewed fury from the other quarter.

— · — · —

[The ship bound from Europe toward Australia or New Zealand would normally see no land at all from her departure to her destination. After ninety or a hundred days at sea, landfall was a special event. Richard Sheridan wrote of the arrival of the Lawhill *in 1934 at the entrance to Spencer Gulf in South Australia.]*

Two hundred and eighty miles from Neptune Island we struck a calm which lasted two days. It was desperate being only thirty hours' sailing with a decent breeze and still to be held up. We knew we had got a long way north by the difference of temperature, for it was now divinely warm again, and we all slipped back into trade winds shirts and trousers.

When the breeze returned, although fresh, it had backed more easterly and kept us just off our course. We expected to raise the land within forty-eight hours.

At midnight I turned out into a glorious, warm moonlit night, but, alas, the breeze had shifted even more ahead and the old ship was heading more to the southward than ever.

Nevertheless, with a spanking breeze abeam, she was making 8 knots in a calm sea. We mustered on the maindeck, our tempers perhaps a little soured.

"Relieve the wheel and lookout!"

"Relieve the wheel and lookout," we acknowledged sulkily.

Moving forward, I glanced away on the port bow.

"Flash!" I jumped, then shivered with excitement. Was it just a low planet . . . ? Flash . . . pause . . . flash.

I clutched Johnnie fiercely by the elbow.

"Australia!" I yelled. It was the only word that came to my lips. The scene was intensely theatrical and perfectly genuine.

The watch was incredulous, and even laughed at me. Neptune Island light has a very long pause between the flashes, and suddenly I felt that I must have been mistaken. But then it came again, much clearer.

"Flash! Flash! Flash!" The news spread like wildfire.

I hurried away and looked quietly to leeward. The last light we had seen was the Lizard *[an English lighthouse]* eighty-six nights before.

What a different scene! That wild easterly gale, with ice on deck, when I had kept my frozen look-out on the fo'c'sle head, feeling sleepy, sick, and shivering with cold. I didn't understand anything then, I didn't realize anything.

My faculties registered two things—misery and cold.

Now the warm breeze brought off the smell of the land. It was the smell of the desert, of oases. It was utterly incongruous.

We were, unfortunately, leaving the light too far to windward, and hardly had the starboard watch turned in than three blasts on the whistle summoned all hands on deck to wear ship. The light had been fine on the port bow, but after turning it was rapidly disappearing on the starboard quarter. I spent a depressing hour on the look-out, seeing the land so near and yet knowing that we might have to wait a week for the wind to change before we could come up with it.

At about 1:45 A.M., however, Boiler came forward to say we were again going about. The unfortunate starboard watch were once more turned out, and half an hour later we were again raising the light, this time rather more ahead, for the breeze had shifted back half a point. When the freewatch had finally turned in, they were again dragged on deck to splice the mainbrace, and it was interesting to see those boys, whose rightful four hours of rest had twice been broken into, come on deck with grins of delight to toss off an eggcup full of Hollands gin.

Dawn!

Land!

Broad on the port beam, distant some 3 miles, lay a low, flat, windswept, sun-scorched rock, Neptune Island. I was examining it through Wilson's binoculars when a cry of "Sail ho!" directed our gaze up the Gulf, where, hull down, could be seen the grey-blue blur of a four mast barque's sails.

"That's *Herzogin Cecilie*," a know-all assured us. She may or may not have been. It was impossible to tell at that distance. In any case she had a better wind than us, and was slipping up the Gulf while we beat off and on, off and on, till we were sick and weary.

The sun rose, a withering, blazing mass that was hotter than when we had passed under it in the South Atlantic.

In the afternoon the breeze shifted, and we headed up the Gulf. Excitement rose to fever pitch.

"We're going course!"

"Port Vic. tonight!"

But I firmly believe that to prophesy times of arrival under sail brings bad luck, so I just grunted sourly: "If you say that, we'll be in hell before morning."

Inwardly, however, I was as excited as the others.

The breeze shifted more and more aft, and the strangest part of the whole performance was our speed. We were doing 9 knots, but the sea was a sheet of glass. On deck there was not a breath of air, but an upper current kept the t'gallant sails and top sails filled as though we were running before a fresh wind. This was just the weather the old lady liked, and she went up the Gulf like a knife ripping silk.

We passed barren islet after barren islet.

The mainland was barren, sun-scorched, sandy.

We spent the afternoon, which happened to be our free watch, lounging about in the shade trying to keep cool, scanning the god-forsaken coast with glasses to see a tree. In vain.

Australia changes, however, with evening, and the sun sank in one of the most sublime glows I have ever watched. The breeze died a little, but the t'gallants remained full. . . .

The huge barque ghosted up the mirrored sea at 5 knots in utter and complete silence. Not a block creaked, not a sail stirred. For the first time in the voyage I heard the noise that one hears in one's head in extreme stillness. Even the boys lowered their voices.

The sails turned orange and then blue-grey. The breeze died. We slipped on. The slightest sound was intensified. When the Mate spat on to the maindeck from the poop it sounded like the cracking of a whip.

Night crept down. Ashore, huge straw fires made a red glow in the sky; the land breeze brought off the smell of it.

There was a feeling of drowsy contentment in the air. The officers in their shirt sleeves leant over the rail gazing at the coast, dreaming I suppose of nothing in particular. The skipper, too old a hand to be impressed by the beauty of the evening, was probably quietly pleased that he had brought his ship out in eighty-seven days, a remarkably smart passage. We, for'ard, saw but one thing—a hard job of work done and a spree ashore ahead. It was a very satisfying evening.

Eight bells rang out mellowly. We drifted on.

My first watch contained no duties, so I put my donkey's breakfast on the forehatch in the hope of snatching a couple of hours' rest before we had to stow canvas, but at 10 P.M. three whistles summoned all hands to stations. We lit our riding lights in readiness and put them under the fo'c'sle head, thereby lighting up the foredeck. It was a weird, theatrical scene, with the maze of ropes silhouetted beside the masts, and now and then half-naked brown figures glistening with sweat casting long black shadows the whole length of the foredeck.

The end came half an hour later, when we got the order to clew everything up.

The scene was still dramatic—the cries of the crew singing out at the tackles, the squeal of the blocks, the rattle of the chain sheets.

"Starboard anchor, all clear!"

The Mate knocked out the catting pin with a maul.

The anchor went down with a shattering, terrifying roar. In the ensuing silence a little cloud of rust dust drifted away on the night air.

7
Australian Interlude

[*The crew of a sailing vessel worked as hard in port as at sea. It was not uncommon that a crew, after months at sea, might have only a single day of leave ashore even though in port for weeks or months. Some had none. One of the jobs was to get rid of a thousand tons or so of ballast after the run from Europe. Alex Hurst did not dodge hard work, but, according to his book* Ghosts on the Sea Line, *discharging ballast was not his idea of fun.*]

Most of the grain fleet sailed out to Australia in ballast. Very few of them ever carried water-ballast and when they did I imagine it was a very mixed blessing. Once they had arrived at their loading port the majority of the ships entered on the most arduous and soul-killing of all the jobs that fell to the lot of the square-rigged seaman—the discharging of her ballast. A cargo block was rigged between the masts over the ballast holds, a platform was built from one section of the hatch over to the side, and a trolley set upon it. One man worked the winch; two men in the hot sun, usually the mates, worked the trolley on which the baskets of ballast were deposited after being hauled up from the hold, and which were then run along the platform and tipped down a chute over the side. Everyone else was down in the hold filling the baskets. In one ship we had four baskets in circulation with three couples in each hold and, when possible, one man to work the hook to which the baskets were attached. It was usually exceedingly hot; it was continuous and heavy with the dust getting in our eyes, but it was probably better than the chalk ballast so often loaded in the Thames, which set solid and needed pick-axes to free the mass before it could be shovelled into the baskets. The whole essence of any sort of tolerability to the job was that each and every man should do his uttermost because, if one was sufficiently unlucky to work with a man who failed in this, the effort to fill the basket before its turn came again became unconscionable. The temperature was about 114 degrees in the shade, and there were occasions when a couple would find themselves working in a portion of the hold which was in full sunlight.

— · — · —

[Not all ships in the latter days of sail went out to Australia in ballast. James Bisset recorded the mix of goods in the cargo when he was apprentice in the County of Pembroke, *as well as the work the crew did in port. Bisset went to sea at age fifteen as an apprentice and served six years in sail, making four voyages around Cape Horn. He later became a master mariner.]*

On the day of our arrival at Hobson's Bay, we were towed into the Yarra River and berthed at a wharf in Victoria Dock, about four miles upstream, at the edge of the city of Melbourne. There our cargo was discharged by the labor of stevedores—and a strange assortment of merchandise it was! The list of items published in the Melbourne *Argus* of 12th January, 1899, showed that we had brought to the thirsty colonists, among many other things, 2,170 cases of stout, 50 cases of ale, 2,595 cases of whiskey, 20 cases of champagne cider, and 25 quarter-casks of brandy!

This hard liquor was only a small part of the merchandise that came out of our hold. There were 5,160 bags of Cheshire salt; 50 tons of rock salt; 60 bags and 100 kegs of borax; 400 kegs of sulphate of copper; 40

kegs of potash; 13 cases of magnesia; 100 drums of caustic soda; 15 kegs of soda ash; 17 drums of calcium; and 916 kegs of bicarbonate of soda.

Building and construction materials we brought to Melbourne included 61,800 slates; 12,000 firebricks; 1,550 cases of tin plate; 1,064 bundles of hoop iron; 262 cases of window glass; 275 fire tiles; 10 tons of pig iron; 259 reels of wire netting; 116 kegs of nails.

Sundry items included 10 bales of hemp cord; 94 bundles of sheets; 26 cases of mangles; 316 cases of paper; besides, as *The Argus* reported, "a large quantity of iron, steel, general soft goods, and unspecified merchandise." This was a typical mixed cargo of manufactured goods, not of a perishable or urgent nature, exported to Australia from Britain in those days of cargo-carrying under sail. As a sailing vessel has only one hold, the stowing of such a mixed cargo required forethought and skill, to avoid shifting or breaking of the packages. The return cargoes, which were usually of wheat or bales of wool, could be more easily stowed.

While the cargo was being discharged, the crew, including the apprentices, worked a ten-hour day—from 6 A.M. to 6 P.M., with an hour off for breakfast and lunch. We were kept busy chipping rust overside and scraping grass and barnacles from the hull as the lightened barque rose in the water; painting overside; overhauling the running gear and standing gear; serving and blacking down the rigging; sending down sails for the sailmaker to overhaul, and bending them again; greasing down the masts; painting the boats and deckhouses; polishing brass and woodwork; and doing everything else that the ingenuity of the Mates could find to keep the crew from idleness and to make the vessel shipshape and Bristol fashion and get her ready for the homeward voyage.

— — · — · —

[Sailing ships always carried live animals—cows, goats, sheep, ducks, geese, chickens, and pigs—except at the very end, in the 1950s, when the Germans

installed refrigeration in the Pamir *and* Passat. *By the 1930s, only pigs and perhaps sheep or chickens were taken along, to be slaughtered at intervals in a three- or four-month voyage. Alex Hurst notes in his* Ghosts on the Sea Line *that he was in charge of getting pigs on board in South Australia.]*

Fresh meat was occasionally provided by the slaughter of a pig. It was unusual for a ship to carry more than four or five and, on the homeward trip, the stringent economy of the ships led them to keep one almost until the moment of arrival in the United Kingdom, in order that they might comply as cheaply as possible with the regulation that the crews be fed on fresh meat in port.

One voyage we procured the pigs from an aboriginal farm in South Australia. They were brought down to the port in a cart which was backed into the water so that we could take the animals into the lifeboat and sail them aboard. By the time that the cart had been manoeuvered into position the pigs were in a highly suspicious frame of mind, and the position was not improved by the refusal of the driver to back his cart far enough, with the result that his tail-board was well above the gunwale of the lifeboat. As soon as the back was opened the first pig literally crash-dived into the boat, knocking one man over the side, and then went over the side himself. Both swam splendidly but, whilst the man struggled back into the boat, the pig, swimming in fine style— and let no one deny their abilities in this direction—made off down the Gulf as though to go round Cape Horn on his own. We found it quite impossible to get it into the boat from the water, for it was by this time in a very overwrought and unco-operative condition, and we had to drive it back to the shore and beach the boat. When we finally had all five in the boat, each squealing and protesting, it was no joke, for all were intent in getting over the side. I was holding the tiller with one hand and hugging a porker with the other, and the others were in similar case, so it was as well that we had a wind and did not have to row. Those pigs were the very devil to get aboard when we finally did arrive back at the ship, and there is little doubt but that it is easier to handle a full-grown elephant with the proper gear than a maddened set of pigs with no gear. They are very apt to eat charcoal at sea, which is normally the sign of a depraved appetite, and I recollect the misery with which we once beheld all our worm-infested pigs slaughtered and thrown over the side.

I was lucky to be promoted above my fellow first-trippers early in my first voyage, my superior size and knowledge of the workings of the ship more than outweighing my linguistic deficiencies (which were quickly rectified), and in consequence I escaped the worst feature of the pigs, which was cleaning out their styes. This was at its worst in bad weather in a loaded ship, when it was not advisable to let them out owing to the angle of the deck and the amount of water on board. The pigs were usually housed just abaft the fo'c'sle head, and it was necessary to swill and shovel until the stye was reasonably clean. There was always a big wooden trough as their one article of furniture, and this seemed to serve as dining-room in which they ate their wheat, slush and scraps (it was plain they were consistently unable to digest the wheat) and in between whiles it served as bed and lavatory. To clean the styes without letting the pigs out was never easy, and it sometimes happened that the inmates did succeed in escaping in bad weather. In that instant they would be swept into the scuppers in a welter of ice-cold Southern Ocean, and there they would struggle until the stye-cleaner, clad in oilskins and sea-boots, came to try to retrieve them. Neither man nor pig could stand well on the wet, slippery decks, and it was no light amusement to wrestle—for that is the only word to describe the action—with a wet, cold, squealing, shivering and terrified porker on the road to Cape Horn. It represented a scene which no landsman would ever imagine or conjure up, with the grey seas eternally thundering by, and the gaunt spars swinging dizzily aloft above the tragi-comedy on deck.

In one ship the five pigs were all housed in one big stye, and as soon as the weather was good enough they were given the run of the deck all day. Putting the pigs back in the evening was usually an easy enough task if a man were reasonably patient and took good care to prevent the wretched animals from getting too excited. This seldom happened in practice, at all events in that vessel. On one historic occasion when more difficulties than usual were being encountered (or manufactured), one porker, taking fright when already demented and crazed with panic, took some sort of dive at the sty which was slightly raised above the deck for the sake of dryness, and became firmly wedged underneath, being unable to move in any direction. His squealing organs were unfortunately unaffected, as it took all hands save only the helmsman and the master a good half-hour to release the creature, but by that time he was suffering from advanced hysteria and did not cease squealing for half the night.

When a pig was killed its blood was kept and mixed in with an ordinary pancake mixture to make blood pancakes, which were quite black and extremely appetizing. The majority of shore people turn up their noses at the very thought of this dish, but the hard facts remain that they were very good indeed and that those people who turn up their noses have never tried them nor, come to that, ever lived on a regular sailing ship diet for any length of time, if at all.

On the whole the cabin ate slightly better then the fo'c'sles, but the Finns seemed to show very little initiative at any form of helping themselves to food. When a pig-killing was bungled once and very little blood was saved, all of which was reserved for the cabin, I saw fit to divert some into my own pancakes, but found that my shipmates viewed the exploit with dumb amazement. This apathy was always incomprehensible to the English-speaking members of the crew.

Another ship had two small stye, one on each side of the break of the fo'c'sle head, and each housed two animals at the start of the voyage. It was not a particularly satisfactory arrangement as all four were much the same in appearance. If the couples were mixed up when they were returned at night they set up a terrible squealing and commotion until, for the sake of the common peace, they were re-housed, because if not they would keep it up all night until they were released again in the morning.

From their behaviour on deck, it was impossible to see that any two had more affection for each other than for the others, but there it was and it became necessary to mark them with red lead, each pig's back being numbered. After the first was killed there was only one pig left in one sty, and he always rent the heavens each night, even if the other two were correctly paired off, so we found that it was better to house all three together which, although it created a slum condition, seemed to satisfy the entire porcine population as well as the first voyagers, who had only one sty to clean instead of two.

The master of that ship was extremely parsimonious, particularly where the killing of pigs was concerned, and was always very loath to have them despatched until the ship was practically in port. The story is told of him that, when this sort of thing was going on during the long passage of a full-rigged ship which he had commanded in the past, the crew could finally bear it no longer, so a man went a little way up the rigging and dropped a heavy iron cast block on a pig, so that it was either killed or had to be despatched. The crew was delighted, for fresh meat appeared to be at hand, but they had not reckoned with the captain—the entire carcass was salted down! The only time that we could be really sure of a pig was on the Finnish midsummer holiday.

On one occasion the second mate was sick, and the third mate was taking his place. He was a nice enough fellow but rather ineffectual, and one evening told me to put the pigs away. Feeling in good fettle, I neglected all the rules of driving them gently with the merest coaxing and started them round the decks at full speed, shouting and yelling, so that, with the cheering from all the fellows who were watching, the pigs were soon charging about in a demented state and the situation became completely out of control. The porkers were making a terrific row, which was almost matched by the cheering and shouting on deck, and there is no doubt but that those animals showed a very fair turn of speed—it is surprising how many facets and qualities of swine one discovers in a sailing ship—and soon the pandemonium was complete. The third mate was evidently terrified of the Old Man appearing on deck so, having given everybody a good run for their money, and to put an end to the performance and save what was left of the third mate's face, I tackled a pig in rugger fashion and brought it down. I got up clasping it to my chest, finding it heavier than I expected, and took it back to its habitation in style (although to hear it one would suppose it being taken to the guillotine), and so I dealt with the other two. A couple of evenings later I was coming forward to replenish my red lead pot when I found the third mate quietly putting the pigs away himself, as he had evidently felt a fool on the previous occasion, and was now carrying out the operation with the utmost care and patience. I came up behind quietly and gave one pig a smart kick in its hams. It was in no wise hurt but startled beyond all measure, and it dashed back under the third mate's feet, throwing him on his back, which further startled the other two, and in a trice all three were dashing round and round the foredeck in squealing frenzy. It was never possible to put those pigs to bed easily again after that!

—·—··—·—

[Captain James Learmont was an outstanding master in sail. He went to sea at age twelve in his father's coasting schooner in Scotland. He went on to command three big square-riggers, including the Bengairn. When the Bengairn's coal cargo from Australia in 1907 shifted and threw the ship on her beam, Learmont righted the vessel and saved her, the only ship to sail back from that route after her cargo had shifted.]

The carriage of coal from New South Wales to Valparaiso and other West Coast [of South America] ports was responsible for the loss of more ships than any other trade that I have known ... day after day on reading the overdue list you would see the names of ships out of Newcastle, N.S.W., quoted for re-insurance, but they never arrived.

This trade in all did not last thirty years. In its infancy, the ships engaged were of the old semi-clipper type and differed very much from the large steel ships that were built in the 1890 period. They did not have much cubic capacity *[that is, cargo capacity]* and had to be trimmed "hard" *[loaded as full as possible]* to bring them down to their marks; indeed, with light gas coal you could not get them down. Also, they had considerable flare that prevented them from heeling badly when loaded. The modern steel ship had a great cubic capacity, and in design was just the reverse, for their "tumble home" offered no support once they began to heel.

In our case with ordinary *[heavy]* steam coal we had hundreds of tons of space empty when fully loaded. Trimmers were not very concerned; as long as they got your full weight under the hatches they were paid. Loading more fully in the midship section and leaving the ends free would have been safer, but they were a law unto themselves, resenting interference by anybody.

This continual loss of ships on passage from Newcastle to the West Coast had naturally given me concern for a long time as I knew it formed a large part of the work of a sailing ship. . . . I had talked to my father for years about these losses and he considered that they were due to fire, but I would not accept that and maintained that the cause was the cargo shifting. In cases of fire there was always the chance of being picked up, for as a rule you had time to abandon ship, whereas in these cases no one was ever saved. I always ended the discussion by saying that if ever my cargo shifted I would chop the masts out of her. . . .

With three lower topsails set and the foresail, the *Bengairn* was speeding away toward the southeast before a rapidly increasing wind. My barometer was low, the sea was one mass of phosphorescence and it somehow seemed uncanny. I cannot explain my change of attitude on this particular occasion in relation to the weather; it was most unusual for me to be under only lower topsails . . . somehow I had a premonition that I should be cautious. . . .

Next day it blew much harder and the seas were rising but she went along without doing much damage. On the following day the seas were very heavy and she with the wind on the quarter was lurching heavily. After one particularly heavy lurch I heard an ominous sound coming from the hold and she failed to right herself . . . I ordered the . . . helm up so we would get away before the wind and so bring wind and sea astern, but she was as if dead and failed to answer the helm. First I ordered them to let fly the lower mizzen topsail sheets in an endeavour to make her pay off, then the lower main topsail sheets, but the list increased. The sea was now making a clean breach *[waves swept over without restraint]* of the whole of her starboard side. To relieve her, I next ordered the fore sheet to be let go, and Frank literally dived under water to do this; how he managed to keep himself from being caught in the wire foresheet, that was torn out by the threshing of the foresail after he had slacked it off, I don't know.

On deck the scene was one of desolation; as the big combers came along they swept everything before them overboard. From the minute she heeled over it was really a terrifying sight, a fine ship on her beam ends with the seas battering the whole of her starboard side as she lay helpless, unable to escape from their fury as they stripped her of anything that was movable.

The ship was to all intents and purposes in her death throes, but we had to save her if possible in order to save ourselves. All the boats on the lee side had been swept away, and with the heavy list you could have walked outboard on her weather side, so it was useless to think of trying to lower the one remaining life boat. There was a movement by some of the crew while I was down in the hold to lower that boat, but Frank stopped it saying, "When the Capen says lower that boat, we'll lower it, but not before. Get away from here." As he was carrying an axe his words had weight.

The heel of the ship was such that one-half of No. 2 hatch between the main and mizzen masts was under water, and this hatch now became our principal concern as the tarpaulins started to wash off. Unknown to us, the bulwark stanchions under the strain of the ship lying on her side had been sheared off in the scuppers and water was pouring in there as well as through the No. 2 hatch. When the carpenter sounded the well *[checked for leaks]* he found four feet six inches of water. As the sounding-pipe was amidships, she must have had much more on the lee side.

Close the hatch we must if we wanted to see daylight again. Every conceivable plan was tried to get spare tarpaulins over it with lashings but they were washed back on us. I then decided on trying with a brand new lower topsail bent on a new rope as if it were the jack stay on a yard. After getting sufficient rope on each end we hove it tight by using the two capstans on the weather side which was free of water. When the sail was bent we furled it, using rope yarns as stops. Easing the capstans, on our hand and knees we pushed the furled sail over the combings, literally diving as the sea was breaking clean over us, but it soaked the sail and somehow helped by increasing its weight. At last with a final heave over it went, and we yelled, "Heave away!" The rope, a four-inch manila, took the strain; the sea couldn't budge him. Then by diving again we cut the stops and the sea helping us, covered the breach with the sail. With an additional coil of rope we were able to secure it firmly around the hatch combings.

We had secured the hatch but our position was still perilous. With so much water in the ship, her freeboard under ordinary conditions would be reduced by two feet; but now, on her beam ends, it was only a matter of time how long she would last.

With darkness coming on and the gale unabated I decided to cut the topmast backstays and let the top hamper go. As soon as the seizings were cut on the mizzen the topmasts doubled over above the cap and the whole lot went in a mighty crash. . . .

The loss of the top hamper on the mizzen relieved the ship considerably so I decided to cut the main away as well. This action eased the leverage for in all on each mast, topmast and topsail yards, topgallant yards and masts with royal yards would weigh about forty tons. Eighty tons was not much, you might say, but at an angle of nearly 60 degrees of heel, it was only when the ship was relieved of this weight that you realized how much it had affected her. Though the lee rail was submerged the force of the seas breaking on the hatch was not so heavy and I could see we had still a fighting chance. On soundings being taken we found that the securing of the hatch had been successful as the water had not increased. Those who understood the boiler were put on the job of making preparations for raising steam to pump the ship out. Mustering all hands on the poop I fed them with what food we could get, which, as the galley was washed out, was bottled stout and Australian biscuits. . . .

By way of the sail locker, all hands got into the after hold and started to move the coal over from the starboard to port by means of a basket and trolley. On account of the heavy list the incline was such that a tackle was necessary to pull the trolley up to windward. . . .

Meanwhile, the men working on the donkey boiler had filled the boiler with water, and started to raise steam. It was, in the circumstances, a very trying operation as everything had to be fitted under great difficulty. Even the shipping of the funnel *[smokestack of the donkey-engine]* was a problem. When we did get steam we were very scared about the effect of the list on the boiler . . . however, we got the pumps going by using the winch and the messenger chain.

Night and day trimming went on with only brief stops for food and drink. Once I felt that we were reasonably safe, with the improvement in the weather, I decided that the crew would do better if they had rest. . . .

After the men had a rest, by the aid of hand pumping we were able to reduce the soundings in the well while giving the donkey boiler a rest. Owing to the list we could only use the weather pump handle so to aid it a "bull rope" was used which any number of hands could tally on to.

With the ship gradually righting herself through pumping and trimming we were faced with a new danger; the broken spars that were hanging over were cutting the lower rigging at every movement and I was afraid that if they sagged further the jagged steel might pierce her under water, which would finish us, so I decided to get clear of them somehow. With the mate I went aloft, which was more a case of crawling than climbing on account of the list. On the lower cap we were over the sea.... With an axe I cut the wire brace runner that was holding the wreckage and as soon as I got it half way through the whole lot went....

Working day and night at trimming the cargo and at the pumps we were gaining ground. I was at both jobs along with the crew, hungry, dirty and sleepy. The passing of days had not meant anything to me but about now I realized that it was five days since the cargo shifted.

Although the wreckage was now clear of the ship, it was, on account of the lee backstays, still attached, but at least eighty feet under water. By means of life-lines we were now able to get down to slip the screws and let it go. By this time we had secured the yards on the foremast and set some sails. At last she was answering to her helm. As Sydney was our nearest port we set sail for there.

We made the land one evening at Jervis Bay about one hundred and twenty miles south of Sydney. The signal station on sighting us evidently reported our condition, for at 8 A.M. next day two salvage tugs were sighted steaming at full speed towards us....

We were indeed a sorry-looking mess as we entered Sydney Heads, but the ship and her crew were safe, not a man had a scratch. The starboard rail was still under water when we anchored off Garden Island.

— ‥ — ‥ —

[Captain Learmont was not content with getting his disabled ship safely back to port. He then undertook to rerig her with his own crew.]

Now there was much to do, surveys to be held, tenders prepared and the ship to be squared up generally. For one thing the half-deck where the apprentices lived was completely gutted, nothing left but the steel bulkheads; their chests and their clothes were all in the corner, a mass of pulp. . . .

These tenders were drawn up in five separate sections: (1) to repair the damage sustained on deck, bulwarks to be straightened, etc.; (2) to supply two topmasts, two topgallant masts, four topsail yards, four topgallant yards and two royal yards with all the fittings necessary to restore the main and mizzen masts to what they were prior to being cut away; (3) a complete suit of sails; (4) four new boats, two of them lifeboats, a jolly boat and captain's gig; (5) the rigging of the main and mizzen masts with new backstays and fore and aft stays, halyards, sheets and all the necessary blocks and ropes. . . .

When we came to the fifth and last section the trouble started. There were three firms tendering but they had been a little too smart, for their estimates were within five pounds of each other and anyone knowing what this tender embraced would see that they had put their heads together and decided how much it would be and who would get it. . . .

Now my attitude was distinctly hostile . . . I was warned that my attitude was going to delay the repairs but this did not alter my decision. Throughout this discussion I knew that we were not dependent on help from the shore to do this work providing we could get the material. I had in my mates and apprentices skilled seamen who could re-rig the ship, as most of the rigging we had cut away to save the ship had been previously fitted or renewed by them. . . .

As soon as the first delivery of five inch wire was made it was cut up in the required lengths. First in order were the main and mizzen stays. As they were "set up on their ends," or rove through iron blocks on the main deck and doubled back on themselves, this was a big job requiring immense purchase. This purchase was obtained by using three sheared blocks, "luff upon luff," which made a double tackle. Once the stays were sufficiently tight, by the aid of powerful rigging-screws they were brought together and seized off with wire. This was important for so much depended upon good seizing when the tackles were slacked. This work was performed by Mr. Brodie, the second mate, who could handle wire against any rigger. Now my policy of training my apprentices was bearing fruit.

I had a splendid officer in my mate, Mr. W. F. G. Martin; his measurements were most exact, for he was an expert in trigonometry, which was borne out later in his examination for extra master when he obtained the highest marks that had ever been awarded. He had his work admirably planned. The less experienced of the hands available to him he employed in preparing the wire, such as worming, parcelling and serving it ready for splicing or turning in as the case required.

[Because Captain Learmont had to cut away his upper masts in order to save his ship, his most difficult job now was to rig new topmasts. The account that follows is the most technical passage of the book. The reader who does not care to translate from the glossary may read it if only to sense the economy and precision of sea language. Learmont's spare narrative tells a sailor exactly how he set and secured the heavy and awkward upper masts in position high above the deck. Any sailor could accomplish this difficult and possibly dangerous job with just Learmont's brief description.

Upper masts had to be hoisted aloft and then joined to the lower masts by heavy steel rings or bands or "caps." The caps were usually fastened in place on the heads of the lower masts after the topmasts were hoisted aloft. Learmont believed that caps would be stronger if they were fastened before the masts were raised. But this meant, because of the limited reach in height of the sheerlegs, that the topmasts had to be raised upside down and then rotated 180 degrees and their lower ends dropped down, or "rove down," through the caps. His operation entailed determining the balance point of the topmast and rigging cables to its lower end and through the caps by which to rotate the mast 180 degrees and then to "rove" it down through the caps. He then secured the topmast in position by means of the "fid," the heavy steel bar used for that purpose.]

In ordering my spars I had specified that the topmast caps should be riveted on, as the sheerlegs would ship them, meaning that, instead of the topmasts being "sent up" they would be rove down. From experience I knew that fitting caps aloft was not satisfactory, for with heavy lower topgallant yards they worked loose in time.

The topmasts were fifty-eight feet long, like huge steel tubes, and the usual way would have been to get them on end, and then by means of a gantline each spar would be rove up through the trestletrees and lower cap. The next job would be to get the topmast cap aloft, heated, ready to shrink to the head of the topmast and rivetted. My idea was to reeve them down with the caps already fitted.

As I had so much to do I gave the contract of fitting the topmasts and sending up the topsail yards to Morts' [the shipyard], as we were under their sheerlegs. For two days they tried to ship the topmasts and failed. I made a suggestion to them as to how to do it, but as good Australians they wouldn't accept my plan. Then the manager sent for me and I went along to his office to find out what he wanted. Addressing me he said "Captain, we are going to cut those caps off and send the topmasts up in the usual way, for we cannot ship as you arranged." My reply seemed to surprise him; "No, you will not cut the caps off. Give me the use of your sheerlegs and your driver and I will ship those topmasts." His look was one of amazement, but he called his secretary and declared a contract which I signed without hesitation. The terms were that Morts' Dock would give me the use of their sheerlegs and I would be responsible for any damage.

Returning to the ship, I told the mate to take accurate measurements from the head of the sheers to the lower caps. The distance was twenty-three and a half feet, for the lower masts were about sixty-five feet above the water; the topmasts were fifty-eight feet long as already stated and weighed about five tons each.

I decided to sling the topmasts twenty-two feet from the heel, that was seven feet from the centre. I then rove two wires up through the trestletrees and lower cap and back down on deck, where they were rove through the length of the topmast from the heel and secured to the cap. Waiting for low water when we would get the maximum space between the head of the sheers and the lower cap, the topmast was hoisted aloft by a single wire with the cap hanging downwards and the heel uppermost. When it was high enough orders were given to heave away on both heel wires. Slowly and steadily the huge tube overended, just as you would set the lugsail of a small boat by bowsing down on the tack tackle. When the topmast was vertical and entered the cap the order was given to lower away. With the weight on the wires the balance was well maintained, and it went to its place on the trestletrees on the fid.

The mate and I were aloft, and we had a difficult job, first in guiding the topmast in, as there was no rigging to hold on to, and then to ship the fid, which weighed about two hundredweight.

The operation was watched by the master-rigger of Morts' and his gang with much interest. When I came down from aloft I had something for them to hear, saying "Fancy me having to do a little job like this when I have so many important jobs on hand."

The ship was moved along and next day at low water we shipped the other topmast. . . .

With the topmasts shipped I left the mate to carry on; he had much if not all the rigging for the topmasts ready and had even rattled down the topmast rigging itself. From Morts' I ordered a large quantity of different-sized internal strops for blocks. I purchased a big stock of hundreds of fine blocks. I purchased a big stock of tallowwood (an Australian tree) and from this the carpenter made hundreds of fine blocks. Hearing that a marine-store-dealer had bought salvaged gear from the wreck of a French ship at Newcastle, I obtained from his collection many useful blocks, especially in the large sizes.

Now the old ship was taking shape, and it was nice to see her when the topgallant masts were sent up and the topmast stays fitted. The latter was a big job, for the double stays were at least two hundred feet long, and the four hundred feet of five-inch wire weighed at least three tons. This was all part of the gear prepared and fitted under the direction of the mate. . . .

We had plenty of hard work in Sydney, but we had pleasant times when opportunity offered. For myself it had been a busy time but my way was clear; I set out to do a big job and it was accomplished without a hitch. Our returning with the cargo shifted, the only ship which had ever come back, had awakened the authorities in Newcastle. Later I heard that an inspector had been appointed to supervise trimming. When we were ready for sea, reporters from the Sydney papers visited the ship yet again, and a long account of the re-rigging and the financial result appeared in the papers. In London, Lloyd's Shipping Gazette printed the story and a leading article headed "An Enterprising Skipper."

The *Olivebank*, like many of her contemporaries built in the late 1880s and early 1890s, was decorated with "painted ports" that emphasized her fine sheer line. Note the wheelhouse at the stern protecting the helmsmen. A seaman on the mizzen royal yard is casting off gaskets prior to setting the mizzen royal as the *Olivebank* gets under way. *Courtesy of The Mariners' Museum, Newport News, Virginia*

The *Archibald Russell,* here almost under full sail, was the last Cape Horner built in Great Britain. The "twist of the sails" is evident, particularly on the foremast, and the spanker is unusual. Four-masted barks were found to be the most economical and easiest to handle of the last of the Cape Horners.
Courtesy of San Francisco Maritime National Historical Park

The wooden full-rigged ship *A. J. Fuller* was built in Bath, Maine. Americans built wooden Cape Horners long after Europeans had converted to iron and steel vessels. The *A. J. Fuller* had single topgallant sails, rather than double as was common on most of the last Cape Horners. *Courtesy of San Francisco Maritime National Historical Park, Plummer/Beaton Collection*

This young sailor, with a big smile, seems to be enjoying windy weather with seas coming aboard the *Castleton* in bright sunshine. In very heavy weather, even the boat on skids above his head was not immune from damage by seas coming aboard. The *Castleton*, a full-rigged ship, was dismasted and scrapped in 1926. *Courtesy San Francisco Maritime National Historical Park, George Dickinson Collection*

The helmsmen here on the *Hesperus*, later renamed *Grand Duchess Maria Nikolaevna*, were without a wheelhouse and exposed to seas breaking over the stern. Two helmsmen were often necessary in heavy weather. In the right foreground is the binnacle housing the compass. *Courtesy San Francisco Maritime National Historical Park*

The *Penang* was a typical three-masted bark, more economical to operate than a full-rigged ship in the late nineteenth and early twentieth centuries. *Courtesy San Francisco Maritime National Historical Park, New Zealand Herald Collection*

A view of the *Parma* from her bowsprit, taken in 1932. The safety netting in the foreground was designed to catch sailors swept from the bowsprit by breaking seas. This German innovation was rarely found on vessels from other countries. The photograph was taken by part owner Alan Villiers. *Courtesy of The Mariners' Museum, Newport News, Virginia*

Crewmen on the *Parma* take up the slack on a brace in typical conditions on the way to Cape Horn. A safety net is rigged to reduce the chance of being swept overboard. *Courtesy of The Mariners' Museum, Newport News, Virginia*

Seamen are securing the mainsail while seas sweep the deck of the *Garth-snaid,* a three-masted bark. The main uppertopsail is furled in response to the heavy weather. The *Garthsnaid* was dismasted in 1922. *Courtesy San Franscisco Maritime National Historical Park*

Under full sail, the *Herzogin Cecilie* waits out a flat calm, typical of the doldrums, but crewmen are kept busy over the side chipping rust and painting the hull. The *Herzogin Cecilie* had an extended poop deck, or raised main deck, that made for much drier and safer working conditions in bad weather.
Courtesy of The Mariners' Museum, Newport News, Virginia

The *Viking*, built in Denmark, carried its raised poop deck far forward, like the *Herzogin Cecilie*. Like many of the German-built Cape Horners, the *Viking* was steered from a wheel by the main mast. She carried an outer jib topsail. *Courtesy of The Mariners' Museum, Newport News, Virginia*

The graceful *John Ena* makes her number. Men are aloft on the fore and main upper topgallant yards and on the mizzen lower topgallant yard, no doubt making up buntlines after sails are set. Note the unusual triangular mizzen course and spanker. *Courtesy of San Francisco Maritime National Historical Park*

The *Lawhill* is about to pick up a tug off the coast of Washington State before the First World War, when the windjammers could still afford such assistance. There are men on the fore and main upper topsail yards securing the sails, and men on the forecastle head are ready to pass a towline. The *Lawhill* never carried royals and sailed well without them. It is just possible to see that her topgallant masts were rigged behind her topmasts, a very unusual arrangement. *Courtesy San Francisco Maritime National Historical Park, G. E. Plummer Collection*

Looking aloft from the steering wheel, up the after side of the main mast of the *Pamir*. Two triangular "tops," working platforms, support and spread rigging for the topmasts and topgallant masts. *Photo by Norman M. MacNeil, courtesy Mrs. Joan Gutensohn*

After discharging a cargo of grain at South Shields, England, about 1929, the *Winterhude*, in ballast and high out of the water, is towed to sea. The pilot is descending the Jacob's ladder and the upper topsails are being hoisted. A sailor on the main lower topgallant yard is casting off gaskets to loose the sail. The helmsman's job at the exposed wheel at the stern is to follow the tug. *Courtesy South Tyneside Borough Council*

Looking aft on the *Pommern* as she is tacking, or going about. The main and mizzen courses have been hauled up and the main staysail, in the upper left corner, is aback, probably as are all the sails on the foremast behind the viewer, forcing the ship's bow off the wind. *Courtesy of San Francisco Maritime National Historical Park*

Looking forward along the deck of the *Pamir.* The Liverpool House breaks up the open sweep of the deck. Compare with the deck view of the *Pommern.* The complexity of rigging explains the necessity for precision in seamens' language. *Photo by Norman M. MacNeil, courtesy of Mrs. Joan Gutensohn*

The *Grace Harwar,* old and tired, rusted and worn, is in ballast. The helmsman is just visible at the steering wheel on the stern. The fore and mizzen royal yards are missing. She was the last commercial full-rigged ship. This picture was probably taken shortly before she was scrapped in 1935. *Courtesy San Francisco Maritime National Historical Park*

The *Tusitala* was the last commercial American squarerigger, probably photographed here about 1928. She is typical of the full-riggers built in the 1880s that were superceded by the more economical three and four-masted barks of the 1890s and early 1900s. Like the *A. J. Fuller*, she had single topgallant sails, and here she is temporarily missing her fore royal yard. As is evident, and unlike the *Grace Harwar*, she was well cared for during her last years under the American flag, operated perhaps more from sentiment than as a business proposition. *Courtesy of The Mariners' Museum, Newport News, Virginia*

The *Moshulu* was the largest squarerigger in the world in the last Grain Race in 1939. She is preserved in Philadelphia. *Courtesy of The Mariners' Museum, Newport News, Virginia*

The *Passat* is "ghosting" along in catspaws of wind. She was one of the last two squareriggers to pass Cape Horn, in 1949, and is now preserved in Trave-munde, Germany. *Courtesy San Francisco Maritime National Historical Park, Adrian Small Collection*

The *Pamir*, under New Zealand ownership, gets under way from Wellington to San Francisco during the Second World War. Seamen on the fore and mizzen uppertopsail yards are loosing sail. When the sails are loose, the yards will be hoisted to stretch the sails. The Liverpool House shows clearly and the double spanker gaffs were typical of German-built Cape Horners. The *Pamir*, in 1949, was the last commercial squarerigger to pass Cape Horn. *Courtesy of Museum of Wellington, City and Sea*

8
Across the Southern Ocean

[The sailing route east from Australia was first south into the high lati-
tudes, where the windship would find the strong favoring westerly gales that
could send her eastward across the immense distances of the South Pacific
Ocean, to Cape Horn or to the west coast of North or South America. Ray
Wilmore found wonderful sailing in the swift John Ena *in those high*
southern latitudes.]

Br-r-r-r! Cold, windy and wet. There is no routine work on deck
now; just standing by and sailing. And how we are sailing! Every piece
of canvas is set. There's a strong wind on the starboard quarter, we're
heeling far over to port, lee rail almost under water at times, and the log
has shown twelve to fourteen knots per hour during the past twenty-
four hours. What a ship! What a thrill! Bad times ahead are forgotten
with this kind of sailing. Petty grievances are forgotten and all hands
are happy. The watch stands close-huddled under the break of the
poop or in the lee of a deck house and we brag about how she takes it.
We're proud of our ship, and well we might be. She's the prettiest,
grandest thing I have ever seen afloat.

The Old Man paces the deck, his now be-whiskered face wreathed in smiles, beady eyes sparkling. We're going places, and in the right direction. Only Mr. Carlson seems serious. He stands and watches, studying everything, squints frequently into the binnacle, scrutinizes the horizon closely, and talks occasionally in a low, quiet voice to the Old Man, presumably discussing the advisability of shortening sail. Not yet, apparently, as no orders come. The skipper resumes his pacing and the mate his watching, and on we surge, cutting a sharp gash through the high rolling seas or now and then riding over one and dipping into the next.

It's a great day. We're making knots. Who cares what's ahead?

———·—·—·—

[In the course of hundreds of days and nights far from land, the old windship sailors saw marvelous things. Rex Clements, in the Arethusa *in 1903, delighted in evoking the moods that strange and wonderful phenomena at sea could inspire.]*

That night while standing my two hours lookout on the fok'sle head my vigil was broken in upon by a startling apparition. It was a dark, starless night with a chill breeze moaning out of the east-south-east, and I paced back and forth across the break with my eyes searching the blackness ahead. As I walked briskly up and down I observed a pale light shape and collect itself out of the gloom, far distant but straight ahead of the vessel's track. I did not at once report it to the officer on watch, for it didn't look like a vessel's light, but seemed more to resemble an atmospheric disturbance.

As it drew closer it resolved itself into a huge ball of pale glimmering fire, seemingly dancing down on us on the crests of the waves. I didn't know what to make of it and sang out "Light right ahead, Sir!" to the mate on the poop. Mr. Thomas was evidently nonplussed too, for a moment afterwards our helm was put up and we fell off a couple of points. The strange gleaming globe neared rapidly and from it came a sound of whirring and rustling, with the noise of raucous cries. Several of the men were looking out over the rail and "big Mac" gave utterance to the general wonderment:

"What are ye?" said he, "devil or man or baste?"

The uncanny object swept down on us, grazed our shoulder, and went swirling and gleaming by. As it did so the mystery was explained. It was a dead whale. Stripped of every scrap of skin, with its blubber exposed to salt water, it glowed and sparkled all over with a shimmering phosphorescent light. The processes of decomposition had swelled it to a monstrous size, and its bulk lay on the water like a great bladder. Around it screamed and circled an uncounted multitude of birds, swooping, fighting, and tearing at it with their beaks. Every species of feathered inhabitant of the Southern Ocean, I should think, was represented; all squawking and uttering hoarse cries, as they hovered and picked greedily at the banquet provided. The grotesque apparition was gone in a few minutes, swallowed up in the gloom astern, with its luminous halo and noisy following. It made a very weird and not easily forgotten sight. What a ghost story it would have given rise to, I thought, if seen from a little distance by the daring but credulous mariners of old!

——·—·——

[But not all strange phenomena were so easily explained. Rex Clements could only record, not explain, another.]

Hard, stormy weather followed us till near the ninetieth meridian, when we hauled up and steered more to the nor'ard. One dark, moonless night just before we got clear of the "forties," with a fresh breeze blowing and the ship running quietly along under t'gallant'sls, there occurred a most uncanny experience.

It was about four bells in the middle watch, the "churchyard" watch, as the four hours after midnight is called, that it happened. We of the mate's watch were on deck—the men for'ard, Burton and I under the break, and Mr. Thomas pacing the poop above our heads. Suddenly, apparently close aboard on the port hand, there came howling out of the darkness a most frightful, wailing cry, ghastly in its agony and intensity. Not of overpowering volume—a score of men shouting together could have raised as loud a hail—it was the indescribable calibre and agony of the shriek that almost froze the blood in our veins.

We rushed to the rail, the mate and the men too, and stared searchingly into the blackness to wind'ard. The starbowlines, who a moment before had been sleeping the sleep of tired men in their bunks below, rushed out on deck. Shipwreck would hardly bring foremast Jack out before he was called, but that cry roused him like the last summons. If ever men were "horrorstruck" we were.

Even the old man was awakened by it and came upon deck. Everyone was listening intensely, straining their eyes into the blackness that enveloped us.

A moment or two passed and then as we listened, wondering and silent, again that appalling scream rang out, rising to the point of almost unbearable torture and dying crazily away in broken whimperings.

No one did anything, or even spoke. We stood like stones, simply staring into the mystery-laden gloom. How long we peered and listened, waiting for a repetition of the sound, I don't know. But minutes passed and still it did not come and slowly, like men coming out of a trance, we began to move about and speak to each other again.

We heard it no more and gradually, one at a time, trickled back to the fok'sle and half-deck. As far as the occupants of the latter were concerned, no one evinced any inclination to turn in and we sat around, smoking and discussing what the sound we had heard could possibly be. Nobody slept much more that night and thankful we were when the grey dawn broke over the tumbling, untenanted sea.

This was all. In bare words it doesn't sound very dreadful, but it made that night a night of terror. For long enough afterwards the echoes of that awful scream would ring in my ears and even now it sends a shiver through me to think of it.

Who and what it was that caused it we never learnt. We hazarded a variety of guesses, many of them farfetched enough. The cry of a whale was suggested, but I never heard a whale utter any sounds with its throat. Some other sea-monster, somebody else thought, that only rarely comes to the surface—but this was more unlikely still. The scream of seals or sea-lions on an island beach was another hypothesis—again, the nearest land was Easter Island, six hundred miles to the north'ard. Besides, the shriek we heard had certainly a human, if not a diabolic, origin. Whether it was, as some imagined, a shipwrecked boat's crew who saw our lights and in their extremity raised a sort of death-scream, or whether, as others asserted, it had a supernatural origin, remained a mystery insoluble.

Some time after, Nils, our taciturn Russian Finn, who was as superstitious as big Mac, told me we should have called out: "Jou wass come here, oldt man," and the thing, whatever it was, would have come and done us no harm. Nils evidently thought it was a sea-spirit. Who shall say? For my own part, I hold with Hamlet that "there are more things in heaven and earth than are dreamt of in our philosophy" and certainly more than one can put a name to.

———— · —— · ————

[In October 1908 the Denbigh Castle *sailed with a load of fuel from Cardiff for the west coast of South America. From mid-December until March 1909, she beat in vain against westerly gales to round Cape Horn. Six ships went missing off the Horn that year and others were seriously damaged. When her cargo shifted, the captain of the* Denbigh Castle *abandoned the attempt to thrash around Cape Horn and ran eastward across the South Atlantic, Indian, and (with a stop, after 253 days at sea, at Freemantle, Australia) South Pacific oceans to her destination, where she arrived late in November, 1909. It was the first voyage of apprentice Albert A. Bestic and a rough introduction to the profession in which he eventually became a master mariner. He describes the approach to their destination in South*

America and one of the reasons why that coast was difficult for sailing ships.]

It was fully three days after first sighting land that the Old Man decided to steer a northerly course. No little experience was required to take a sailing-ship up the west coast of South America. If a vessel got too close to the land there was danger of her losing the wind altogether. On the other hand, should she be too far off, she might pass her port, as lighthouses were inconspicuous, and the ports were rather alike in appearance. That a vessel should not pass her port was of the utmost importance since owing to a current moving north and light airs, she would be unable to retrace her path. The only alternative would be to stand out to sea where she would find enough wind to work her way to the southward again. This could easily add another fortnight or more to the passage.

As we were over four hundred days on our passage from Cardiff, our captain could hardly be blamed for ensuring that the *Denbigh Castle* did not pass her port. The result was, however, that we entered a belt of calm through getting too close to the shore. Our position was about fifteen miles south of Mollendo. All we needed was a breeze lasting two or three hours to bring our long passage to an end. Instead we lay rolling heavily to the long Pacific swell, our sails flapping so helplessly that the larger ones had to be hauled up to prevent them chafing.

Now a great anxiety began to assert itself. We were getting closer to the shore. Although we were drifting slowly northwards with the current, the big swell was also lifting us sideways. Restlessly the Old Man paced the poop hoping for a breeze. Apart from the oily swell, the surface was so devoid of ripples that the ship lay reflected in the water. And with the passing of each hour the shore was perceptibly nearer. Presently "Old Jowl" *[the chief mate: Jowl, taken from the Welsh word "Diawl" meaning "devil"]* blew his whistle. "Watch stand-by to take soundings!"

"What's the idea, George?" I queried as we took the end of the lead-line from its roller on the poop for'ard outside of the rigging to bring it to the fo'c'sle head. "Surely, there's plenty of water beneath us? I've always heard that the sea is very deep off this particular coast."

"There's probably too much underneath us," answered George, "I expect the Old Man wants to find out if it is shallow enough to drop anchor. It's the only way to stop her from drifting on to the beach, so far as I can see." Mr. Owen was waiting for us on the fo'c'sle head to secure the 14 lb. lead on to the end of the line. Although we had been to sea so long, this was the first time I had seen a deep-sea sounding taken. Already the men were standing on the ship's rail, about twenty feet apart, each with a small coil of lead-line in his hands. Mr. Owen "armed" with tallow the bottom of the lead, which was slightly hollowed, and when all was ready gave "Old Jowl" a wave. The mate waved back and, with a warning cry of "watch there, watch!", Mr. Owen flung the lead overboard. The sailor nearest him watched the coils slipping away from his hands in diminishing circles until, finally, as the last coil went without the lead touching bottom, he echoed Mr. Owen's cry to warn his neighbour that the responsibility now lay with him. "Watch there, watch!" The cry was echoed by each man in succession until at length the line was running out through the hands of "Old Jowl" on the poop.

Suddenly it stopped. The mate bent over the poop-rail and jerked the line up and down to ensure that the nature of the sea-bottom would adhere to the tallow. "Ninety-six fathoms, sir," he announced to the Old Man.

"Ninety-six, eh? Well, we're within the hundred fathom line, anyhow. We'll take a sounding every hour." We tramped in the 192 yards of lead-line along the deck until finally the lead itself rose up to the poop-rail and, at the yell of "hold it!" from Mr. Owen, we paused expectantly. "Old Jowl" lifted the lead inboard and, having examined the tallow, reported "rocky bottom" to the captain.

"Watch there, watch . . . Watch there, watch . . ." We carried out the evolution four times and, with each sounding, the depth became less, each time the shore was correspondingly nearer. We noticed too that, as the water shoaled, the big swell increased in height. Our last sounding had shown fifty fathoms, which was a questionable depth to hold a ship to anchor in such a swell, but the Old Man decided to risk it. The splash of the anchor, the rattle of the cable speeding through the hawse-pipe seemed like a death knell to my hopes. For months I had been longing to hear that self-same splash, but then I had anticipated that the ship would be in Mollendo Bay, not off this waste of forbidding mountains with not a house in sight.

"Well, now that we're here, where are we?" queried Gogan jocularly as we adjourned to the half deck after taking in all sail.

"The question is," answered Charlie, "are we going to remain here or are we to drag anchor? Did you notice that big swell breaking on the beach when we were up aloft?"

"I certainly did," I answered emphatically. "Seemed to break into big surf-curling rollers about a quarter of a mile out and then just race madly for the shore. I wouldn't give a ship much chance if she were caught in that lot."

"That's what I thought," George commented. "Still, we have the second anchor to let go if she doesn't hold with the first one. I didn't like 'Old Jowl' saying that the bottom was rocky. There would be a better chance of the anchor getting a grip in sand."

George and Charlie exasperated me. Why all this chatter about anchors? Why should we be anchored at all, with Mollendo and our letters but fifteen miles away and apparently forgotten? I had yet to learn the lessons taught by life in sail that to rail against fate only increases discontent. "Where is this all going to lead us?" and I flung my cap angrily into my bunk. "We might not get an offshore wind for months with these high mountains protecting us. And if the wind comes in from the sea, we'll be on a lee shore. All you chaps talk about is the ruddy anchors. You'd think that we wanted to stop here for good."

"It's no good getting worked up about it," George shrugged. "You have to take the knocks as they come, and the present problem for the Old Man is to keep the ship off the beach." Suddenly there was a dull rumble and the ship vibrated throughout her hull. George paused for the noise to cease. "There goes the second anchor. Looks as though the Old Man doesn't feel happy about things."

Apart from an hour's individual anchor watch which everybody had to keep in turn, we had all night in our bunks. We drew lots in the half-deck, and the midnight to one fell to me. We had to make a list out and give it to Mr. Owen so that he or the mate would know who was on duty at a certain time. Mr. Owen gave us instructions. "There aren't lights to take compass bearings of," he said, "so all you can do is keep your eye on the anchor cables and lead-line. Put your hand on the cable every quarter of an hour and, if it is vibrating, you'll know it's caused by the anchor dragging along the bottom. The lead-line is hanging from the poop-rail with the lead just clear of the bottom. Lower it down each time you come aft from the cables and see if the depth is getting any shallower. Another point, if the line moves forward instead of remaining up and down, that's another indication the ship is moving astern. Then there's the swell. If it gets bigger it may be because the ship is getting closer to the shore. Listen to the sound of the surf, too, in case it might be getting louder. If you have the least suspicion that there is any change, report to the mate or myself. We are working watches as usual tonight. Is that all clear?"

"Yes, sir," we chorused.

Sleepy-eyed, I turned out and relieved Gogan at midnight. "Glad to see you, old man," he greeted me with a grin. Anchor lights are burning brightly, Mr. Owen is in the chart-room and all is well. I'll go and report to him that you have relieved me, and then heigh-ho for that little cart that's waiting for me in the half-deck where I can get an even strain on all parts." With a final nod, he went to the chart-room and presently I saw him disappearing through the half-deck door. Suddenly I felt lonely. I stood on the poop and looked at the sky with its twinkling stars and a big golden moon lapsing majestically into the west. The peaceful outlook, however, was marred by the distant roar of the surf, and the memory of the racing broken water which I had viewed earlier in the day from up aloft.

I went forward to the fo'c'sle head which rose and fell rhythmically to the advancing swell. As her bow lifted, the ship would be carried astern and, taut and quavering, the anchor cables would emerge from the sea, to subside again as the vessel slid into the following valley. I placed my hand on each cable in turn but could not feel any violent vibration or the jumping which Mr. Owen had warned us about. I then went aft to look at the lead-line.

The chart-room clock showed only five minutes past twelve. I realized that my hour was going to be a long one. Supposing the ship dragged nearer to the shore while I was on watch? I kept wandering from the poop to the fo'c'sle head and back again carrying out my instructions. Tense and anxious, I stood listening to the distant roar. Did it sound louder? The swell, too. Surely this hill now approaching seemed much larger than its predecessor? Should I call Mr. Owen, probably having a little doze on the chart-room settee, to tell him that I felt unhappy about the safety of the ship? No, the cables were all right, and so was the lead-line. If I did call him without definite justification, would it not appear as though I were shirking responsibility?

I welcomed the arrival of George to relieve me at one o'clock. Gone was the anxiety of the cables, the lead-line, the roar of the breakers and the rising swell. If the ship rolled over and over to her doom in the surf, George would be blamed, not me. Responsibility! How many times have I envied the captain who, to my boyish mind, led a life of ease and tranquillity. How wonderful it must be just to give orders and watch one's crew carry them out! No going aloft to fight the kicking canvas, or down on deck to be buried under Cape Horn seas. How little did I realize that the captain was mentally with us in our battles, hoping that the sail would be secured without accident, concerned lest someone might be injured or washed overboard. Probably on this particular night he lay uneasily in his bunk tempted to break the etiquette of a captain and go and examine the cables and lead-line himself. By doing so, he would have shown distrust of his officers.

A good officer will brook no interference from a captain. He takes the orders but the captain must not show him how the job is to be done, or display any doubts, without justification, that it is not being done efficiently. In such a case I have heard an officer remark to his captain, "There is no necessity to have two good men on the job, sir, so I'll leave you to carry on."

At ten o'clock the following morning, which happened to be a Sunday, what we dreaded most happened. Mr. Owen who was on the poop at the time was the first to give the alarm. The ship took a big sheer bringing the swell broad on the bow, and the anchors failed to bring her head-on again. Obviously they had broken their hold. It seemed almost inconceivable that, after all our perils, we should finally be wrecked fifteen miles from our destination.

"All hands on deck!" How many times, I wonder, had we heard that familiar call since leaving Cardiff? All hands on deck when the ship was lying at anchor, and on a Sunday morning! The men came aft making choice and varied comments about the poor *Denbigh Castle.* "Never know what this ruddy ship will be up to next, s'help me . . . she's the most unlucky old basket I've sailed in yet . . . proper bitch she is, an' no mistake . . . reckon we'll be lucky to ever get home in her. . . ."

At the first warning cry from Mr. Owen, the Old Man came hastily out of the chart-room and summed up the situation at a glance. "We'll see if we can do anything *[that is, try to pull the ship ahead]* with the kedge, Mr. Mate." He turned to "Old Jowl". "Put one watch getting the lifeboat over the side, and the other can get the kedge ready."

"Old Jowl" stumped rapidly to the break of the poop, took a deep breath and bellowed the order. There was never any mistake about what the mate wanted done. In calm or storm, the roar came from the depths of his lungs with equal volume and intensity. "Port—watch—clear—port—lifeboat—starboard watch—get kedge ready! You see to the lifeboat, Mr. Owen; I'll look after the kedge."

It was a forlorn hope from the beginning. The kedge is a light anchor chiefly intended for use in the calm waters of harbours or rivers to shift a vessel from one berth to another when she is without power. It is small enough to be hung over the stern of a row-boat by which it can be taken to a required position and then dropped, thus enabling a vessel to haul herself over to it by means of a rope or wire. In the days, too, before schooners had engines, they could sometimes be seen bound for sea, going stern-first down a river on a tide dragging a kedge-anchor underneath the forefoot. By such means the vessel was kept under control and prevented from getting broadside on to the stream.

Captain Evans was faced with an extremely different proposition. In principle his idea was to drop the kedge-anchor ahead of the ship and heave her further out to sea. He must have realized that, as the two big bowers were refusing to hold the vessel in the heavy swell, such work with a kedge-anchor was bound to fail. He may have thought of the inquiry if the ship were lost. "Tell me, Captain Evans," some official at the inquiry might murmur, "did you not take any action to try and kedge your vessel clear of these existing dangers?" Possibly the Old Man, in anticipation, was taking no chances.

The preparations for kedging took up much time which, no doubt, seemed longer to us, in the increasing roar of the breakers. The wire strops holding the lifeboat in its chocks had to be released, and the canvas cover removed. The tackle-ropes for lowering away the boat had to be coiled down so that they would not become entangled. The boat had to be lifted, swung out, and the davits secured in position in an outboard position. She then had to be lowered and cork fenders held between her and the ship's side so that she would not bump in the heavy swell. Finally, when we did get her into the water we found that she leaked badly as she had not been afloat for months and her timbers had shrunk.

By the time we dragged her for'ard with the painter, leaping and swooping protestingly over the swell, "Old Jowl" had the kedge anchor ready and hanging over the side. Here indeed was a dangerous job. At one instant the boat would be in the hollow between two seas ten feet below the ship's rail, then she would come soaring upwards threatening to put the kedge through her bottom to say nothing of injuring some of the crew. After one such escape, the boat was pulled farther for'ard and a long sling placed over the body of the boat, the ends of which were secured to the kedge. The kedge was then lowered away until it finally hung from the sling underneath the boat.

When the Egyptians built the Pyramids, they at least had the consolation that there would be something to show for their labours. The crew of the lifeboat had to row against the high swell hindered by a kedge-anchor hanging beneath the boat, but they also had to tow out the kedge-rope. With two men straining at each oar, the sweat streaming off their bodies in the hot sun, they fought gallantly for every yard gained. Further, their craft was only kept afloat by two men constantly bailing.

With the other apprentices and the starboard watch, I stood on the swinging fo'c'sle head watching the boat creeping slowly away. When the crew were about a hundred yards distant, it was evident that, through sheer weariness and the ever-growing weight of the trailing rope, they could go no farther. "Jowl," said the mate, "that's as far as they'll ever get," and, making a funnel with his hand, he yelled to them to let go. We could see Big Charlie whipping out his sheath-knife and sawing away at the sling and, as the rope disappeared beneath the surface, we knew that the anchor had gone to the bottom.

"Right, men," said "Old Jowl", "take the rope to the capstan." Glad of action, we jumped to obey the order. Too long had we been standing idle listening to the sound of the surf growing louder, and watching the tell-tale vibrations of the anchor-cables. Clickity-click went the pawls of the capstan as we walked around. Alas, the rope was coming in too easily. It was obvious that instead of heaving the ship out to the kedge, we were heaving the kedge home to the ship. In less than half an hour it broke the surface and hung dangling from the fo'c'sle head, its flukes shining like polished silver due to the friction of being dragged along the sea-bed. "Old Jowl" shrugged his shoulders and turned towards the poop. "Kedge anchor hove home, sir," he called out to the captain.

I could see the Old Man shrug his shoulders resignedly. "Bring the hands aft, Mr. Evans," he called out, "and get them to clear the other lifeboat ready for lowering."

The other lifeboat? "Say," I said to George, who was beside me, "what's the idea?"

"Blessed if I know," he answered, "unless he's getting ready to abandon ship."

"Abandon ship?" I exclaimed, "but. . . ." I paused helplessly. "You're not leg-pulling, are you?"

George jerked his thumb significantly shorewards. "You can work it out for yourself. If the ship gets into that lot, nobody would survive. At the first couple of bumps the masts would come down, and I wouldn't like to be aboard trying to dodge 'em. The breakers in there must be over twenty feet high. They'd sweep the ship fore and aft, and then. . . ." he left the rest to my imagination. My whole being protested. Better almost to be overwhelmed by the furies of Cape Horn, or to be hurled ashore on the Crocodiles than undergo this cold-blooded, ignominious ending on a fine and sunny day, only fifteen miles from safety.

Suddenly Gogan came up to us. "Do you know," he exclaimed excitedly, "I believe we are going to abandon ship! I've just seen the steward bringing up a pile of stuff from the cabin on to the poop, provisions, and gear belonging to the Old Man. What a lark! We'll all go home as D.B.S. (Distressed British Seaman) in one of the P.S.N.C. *[Pacific Steam Navigation Company]* steamers. Plenty of grub and nothing to do. Why we'd be home in six weeks!"

"Oh, shut up," growled George. "Here, give us a hand to get this boat cover off." We worked at the boat in silence. I felt glad that George had shown his disapproval of Gogan's point of view. It proved that I was not the only sentimental fool, as Gogan might have described me.

"Mr. Evans," called the Old Man, "tell Mr. Owen that we're not going to hoist his boat up. Tell him to stand off an' we'll beckon him alongside when we want him. Mr. Owen waved his hand in acknowledgement of "Old Jowl's" bellow.

Even as the ship dragged, there had always been the hope that the anchors might catch up as the water shallowed, but that had not materialized. A heavy lurch from the ship made me look around and I saw that a hill of water, much higher than its fellows, had thrown the bows of the vessel skyward with her anchor-chains taut and vibrating ahead. It passed down on each side of us as though its crest might break at any moment. Barely a cable astern, it toppled over and, in a seething smother of roaring foam, raged shoreward with spray rising above it in a smoky spume.

The Old Man watched it, his knuckles showing white under their tan as he clutched the taff-rail, and then turned to the mate. "Tell the hands to get that gear the steward has brought up into the life-boat and then stand by to abandon ship."

Poor old *Denbigh Castle*! I glanced aloft at the towering masts and yards. How difficult to conceive that, within an hour or less when she struck, they would come hurtling downwards; that within seconds they would become a mass of tangled wreckage destroying the very hull which they had propelled right round the world. The words "abandon ship" were her death sentence, and to me it seemed as though some innocent person had been unjustly condemned. Surely, I thought, a reprieve must come from somewhere.

It came, and in the form of a reedy wail as though in protest against the Old Man's decision. It had a choking sound at times not unlike a man trying to clear his throat. Suddenly it stopped and, as though petrified, we stood gazing at one another in astonishment. Again it started and, with one accord, we rushed to the starboard rail and looked out to sea.

A small antiquated-looking tugboat had rounded a projecting point of land and was coming towards us.

She was the most ugly-looking craft imaginable, in outline not unlike a crude child's toy such as might be seen in any huckster's shop. Her cigarette-like funnel was higher than her stumpy mast, and the paintwork on the rickety bridge was neglected and peeling from the heat of the sun. Even as we watched open-mouthed, the steam showed from her water-choked whistle, and once again we heard the reedy wail—a pathetic sound that would have brought grins and caustic comments from listeners in any British port, yet to us it was heavenly music. Ugly? To our eyes she had all the beauties of a millionaire's yacht. She was superb, majestic.

Almost unbelievingly we watched her struggling over a swell to disappear into the deep hollow when only her grotesque funnel and mast could be seen above the water. Next instant she would clamber into sight pushing foaming water from her bluff bow, giving the impression of a speed she could never possess. A figure on the funny little bridge took off his cap and waved. An unintelligible hail in Spanish floated across the water through a megaphone, which seemed to break a spell. "Old Jowl" came clumping down the poop ladder towards us, his face portraying an excitement which I had never thought he possessed. "Get for'ard, all of you! Get that seven-inch hawser on to the fo'c'sle head and some heaving lines," he rapped out with the precision of gun bullets. "Two hands down the chain-locker ready to stow the cable; get that capstan connected up to the windlass, carpenter; come along, men, jump to it. There's no time to play around."

The little tugboat rounded up and maintained a position about twenty yards off our starboard bow. Her captain, a swarthy little man with a fierce-looking handle-bar moustache which put "Old Jowl's" completely to shame, yelled orders to us and to his crew alternately. Sometimes he would rush off the bridge and, with hands raised above his head and eyes rolling wildly, engage in an excited harangue with one of his officers. We interrupted by flinging a heaving-line across his quarter deck. A flood of orders came from his lips, and a substantial looking tow-rope was secured to our line which we hauled aboard and made fast.

"Hold on, everybody!" The yell came from "Old Jowl". We glanced seawards as a mighty swell traveled rapidly towards the ship. Its crest reared upwards into an ominous narrow ridge which looked as though it could tumble over at any moment into terrifying surf. The bow of the *Denbigh Castle* soared as though lifted by giant hands. I glanced at the tug. She had just topped the summit and I could see a good third of her keel. We all whipped round and looked aft to follow the course of the sea. The deck lay deep in a steep hill downwards towards the poop, and I saw the solitary figure of the Old Man gazing anxiously upwards. As the swell swept amidships leaving the hull unsupported at each end, it tumbled aboard on both sides and, as though demented, the water rushed around the decks. Next instant our bow was swooping into a steep valley.

We clung desperately to our respective holds, dreading that she would strike bottom and that the masts would come crashing down in our midst, but she lifted again, still waterborne. Never had such a strain been put on our anchor-cables in that initial assault, yet, although they groaned, they did not snap. We found out later, however, that some of the links had been badly twisted.

A stream of vitriolic Spanish from the tugboat turned our immediate anxieties into amusement. Her captain, with his moustache twisting about Harry Tate fashion, kept darting from one side of the bridge to the other with astonishing rapidity, and at times would drum on the canvas dodger with his closed fists as though to emphasize his commands. A comical tinkle came from her telegraphs; foam boiled under her stern and she started to move ahead. Her crew stood on the quarter-deck paying out the tow-rope. How slender that tow-rope seemed when we thought that not only did many thousands of pounds' worth of ship and cargo depend upon its strength, but quite possibly our own lives. Fascinated we watched. Suddenly, when the tugboat was about a hundred yards ahead of us, the tow-rope rose clear of the water. It quivered like a fiddle-string, and flung off spray not unlike a dog shaking its coat after a swim. The *Denbigh Castle* gave a lurch forward and the cables slackened.

"Capstan, men, capstan!" bellowed "Old Jowl". We grabbed the big capstan-bars and, fitting them into the sockets, started tramping around. The pawls, or ratchets, which prevent a capstan going backwards with a weight, clicked merrily. Inch by inch the anchor-cables crept through the hawse-pipes and down into the chain-lockers where they were stowed in such a manner that they would run out without becoming entangled next time the anchors were dropped. Although the captain of the tugboat appeared to be a lunatic, he knew his job. Skillfully he maneuvered his little vessel so that we had only slack anchor-cable to heave in. "Roundy come roundy," as sailors say, and round we went until presently there came a check. The anchors were directly underneath us ready to leave the bottom. By now the vessel had moved out over a hundred yards seawards and, in consequence, the swell was not so high. "Lift 'em up, lads, lift 'em up! Let's get out of here." "Old Jowl" made a few circles himself pushing on a capstan-bar to inspire our efforts. With straining backs and feet slipping, we forced the capstan round until at length we knew they must be clear of the bottom. "Old Jowl" made an "all clear" signal to the tugboat captain who acknowledged it with a toot from his whistle. Once again the tow-rope tautened and, in response to the strain, the *Denbigh Castle* started moving ahead. She was saved.

I looked at the tugboat, hidden at times by the black smoke issuing from her cigarette-like funnel, at the tow-rope which was pulling the *Denbigh Castle* seawards to safety and to Mollendo. Momentarily my thoughts reverted to fourteen months before when the tug was towing us down the Bristol Channel and I had longed for the moment when the tow-rope would be released. Now I would not have cared if we had a tow-rope tied to the ship all the way home.

—··—·—··—

[James Bisset described discharging coal from the County of Cardigan *on the west coast of South America in 1904. He was now second mate on this, his last voyage in sail.]*

The Captain went ashore in his gig, to make arrangements for discharging the cargo. On his return he informed the Mate and me that the consignees would provide bags, into which we would have to fill the coal, with the labor of the crew, no shore labor being available for this work. Assuming that each bag held one hundredweight of coal, we faced the task of filling 40,000 bags to clear our hold of coal—a dismaying prospect in that torrid climate.

On the morning after our arrival, a lighter came out from the shore, laden with empty bags. It was propelled by a crew of six Peruvians, with sweeps. We hauled the bundles of bags inboard with a hand-worked dolly winch and stacked them handy on deck. In the meantime the main hatch had been opened, and a gang of our seamen now began shoveling coal into the bags, which were roughly sewn up, and hove out of the hold, one bag at a time, with the dolly winch, and low-ered into the lighter. The capacity of the lighter was 400 bags of coal.

At our best working speed, handling one bag at a time, we could lift forty bags an hour. A little simple arithmetic indicated that it would take us a hundred working-days to discharge the cargo at that rate. With allowances for Saturday afternoons and Sundays off, and Saints' Days and "surf days" (when lightering was impossible) this rate made it evident that we would be . . . a very long time.

On the Captain's orders, we therefore opened the fore-hatch, rigged a second dolly winch there, and arranged for two lighters to come along side simultaneously, dividing the crew into two working gangs, in accordance with their watches at sea—one under the eye of the Mate and one under my eye.

Never before or since have I felt such a slave driver! The fo'c'sle hands we had engaged at Newcastle declared that discharging cargo in this way was not the proper work of seamen, and should be done by shore labor. There was a good deal to be said for their point of view, but apparently the consignees had stipulated this method of delivery when placing their order for the coal, and the Captain decided to save William Thomas & Co., Ltd., the expense of engaging shore labor to fill the bags—even if such shore labor had been obtainable in this benighted port.

Work went on from 6 A.M. to 5 P.M. daily, with half an hour for breakfast, and three quarters of an hour for midday dinner. With four men and a boy in the hold, filling and sewing the bags, and two men and a boy on deck in each gang working the dolly winches, and the Mates pushing bags over the side as the bags came up, all were soon black, and the decks were smothered in coal dust. The whack of fresh water remained at one quart per man per day. There were no facilities for taking in water . . . , and the Captain was obliged to hoard our reserves.

The only fresh provisions obtainable from on shore were pumpkins, sweet potatoes and scraggy and gristly meat, as cattle did not thrive in that tropical region. After a few days, when the crew began to grumble seriously, the Captain brought off a supply of the local grog, a fiery spirit named anisou, and served out a tot to each man at 11 A.M. and 4 P.M. daily, to keep them going.

Choked by coal dust down below; roasted by the blazing sun on deck; with no means of going ashore on Saturdays or Sundays, and nothing to do ashore even if a boat were available; thirsty, hungry and tired; the men quarreled and fought among themselves and resented every order that was given to them. On Saints' Days and surf days we kept them at work down below, filling and sewing bags and stowing them on deck ready for discharge.

— — · — · — · —

[Camaraderie was a strong tradition among the crews of sailing vessels in ports on the west coast of South America. A vessel might be assisted in getting under way from often difficult anchorages by the crews of other ships. The departure of any vessel was always celebrated by all the ships in port. Rex Clements recorded the ritual celebration on the eve of the Arethusa's *voyage on the long road for home.]*

The night before a laden vessel's departure, her company invariably went through the ceremony of cheering.

A pretty sight it was, particularly when several ships were going through it together.

After hoisting the youngest member of the ship's company aloft on the cargo-fall, with much waving of the Red Ensign, singing of shanties, and a subsequent drink apiece out of a bottle of "chain-lightning" provided, preparations were made for the main ceremony.

A stout wooden framework was constructed. To it were attached riding-lights in the form of the constellation of the Southern Cross. A smart ship, anxious to do the thing thoroughly, would bend on a long swinging outrigger to carry two more lights, representing the twin Centaurs.

As soon as it was dark and the ships in the harbour had knocked off work—sufficient time being given to their crews to have had tea—the homeward-bounder hoisted this structure to the foremast head, with all its lamps lit and shining brightly. It went up to the strains of "Lowlands low," "Old Storm-along," or some other favorite hauling shanty. When high enough, the song ceased, the gantline was belayed and everything was ready for the principal part of the performance.

The ship's bell was first rung violently; then, stepping to the rail, the loudest-voiced man on board would sing out: "Three cheers for the 'Fiery Cross'"—or whatever the name of the vessel next alongside might be.

Hard upon the words three cheers were given with all the united force of the crowd's lungs.

A moment later and the "Fiery Cross" would respond by ringing her bell, calling "Three cheers for the 'Arethusa'", and giving the same with as much noise and volume as possible.

Again ringing the bell, the "leather-lungs" of the homeward-bounder would bellow:

"Three cheers for the 'Atlantique'"—a Frenchman perhaps this time—and another three shouts would wake the echoes.

The "Atlantique" would answer with a tremendous roar, for those Frenchmen carried big crews—"'Eeep 'eep 'urray!'"—and a faint voice might be borne from across the Bay, "Good old Johnnie Franswor!"

Once more the homeward-bounder would rattle her bell, cheer the next ship, and receive her answering salute; while all the time the starry fabric aloft swayed and glittered in the mesh of the fore-rigging.

So it went on until all the ships in the harbour had been cheered. It was not permissible to overlook a single vessel; the humblest windjammer would regard the omission of her name as a deadly insult. In a port like Iquique where, in those days, there were never less than half a hundred vessels, the operation was no light matter.

It might happen when two vessels were going through the ceremony together, and their turn came to cheer each other, that such a ringing of bells and roaring of cheers would break out as fairly startled the bay, and might have disturbed the slumbers of dead-and-gone old mariners in the grave-yard on the far-away hill-side.

Usually it took two or three hours to announce with becoming courtesy her impending departure. Then all hands slowly lowered the Southern Cross and its companions to the deck, and with hoarse throats the "Farewell" shanty, sweetest and most wistful of all, heard only before a clipper spread her white wings for home, was sung as a finale:

> The billows roll, the breezes blow,
> Good-bye, fare ye well: goodbye, fare ye well;
> To us they're calling: Sheet home and go;
> Hurrah! my boys, we're homeward bound!

Another allowance of grog perhaps might be forthcoming; the lights would be put away, the framework unlashed, and all hands turned in, in readiness to weigh anchor first thing in the morning.

The Cape Horn Road

[James Bisset, apprentice on the County of Pembroke, *later served in forty-four ocean-going vessels. He became captain of the* Queen Mary *and* Queen Elizabeth, *was knighted Sir James Bisset, and ended his career as commodore of the Cunard White Star Line. He could speak with authority on the responsibilities of shipowners and shipmasters, and in retrospect commented on the conditions that were part of the passing of sail.]*

Standing to the southward in fresh southeasterly breezes, we made good progress and, in two weeks, picked up the roaring forties and ran into cold and dirty weather. It was usual in cold weather for the crew to be given "burgoo" (porridge) for breakfast. The cook had to be reminded of this. He grumbled and said that the weather was not cold; but next day we had our burgoo, and every morning thereafter for a week. In that time we had squared away for the Horn and the decks were awash, with high running seas astern, and gales of icy wind.

Then, the "burgoo" disappeared from the breakfast menu. "The oatmeal is finished," said the cook. This left us with only hard biscuits and coffee for breakfast. It was Christmas at sea—my fifth Christmas at sea—and if I wasn't a sailor by then I'd never be one. This voyage had now lasted a little more than thirteen months, since our departure from Liverpool in November, 1901. We were still living on provisions taken in at the beginning of the voyage. The Captain had not thought it necessary in June at Newcastle to replenish the salt provisions and groceries. There, these would have been readily procurable. He knew then that we were bound for the west coast of South America, with the prospect of delays there and a long homeward voyage.

He had neglected also to take in provisions at Callao in October, even though he knew that we were bound for the Chincha Islands and homeward on the long haul around Cape Horn. Finally, he had neglected his last chance to take in provisions which could have been sent out to him in November, from the port of Pisco, in the supply steamer running to the Chincha Islands. Such carelessness, or meanness, may have been due to a failure on his part to examine the stores as the voyage proceeded; but more likely it was due to instructions given to him by the owners to avoid expense in ports. Such instructions, which were handed to shipmasters and marked "Strictly Secret", were drawn up in legal terminology designed to exonerate the owners and put the blame on the Master of a vessel for almost any mishap that might occur. They cast the utmost responsibility on the Master and at the same time restricted his freedom of action in a hundred different ways, especially in incurring expenditure.

A shipmaster had to know much more than navigation and seamanship. He was required to have a working knowledge of accountancy and business methods and of mercantile and maritime law, applicable at sea and in many a foreign port. As all blame was put on the Captain when anything went wrong, even when the mishaps were due to the avarice or business acumen of the owners, he was viewed as the symbol of tyranny, meanness or ineptitude in all adverse contingencies, even though he was himself intimidated by the tyranny of his secret orders.

At the end of a voyage his accounts would be scrutinized by the owners and every item of expense questioned. It was impossible or very difficult to economize on port dues, towage, purchase of ballast, and various other working expenses on a long voyage; but the owners—who in most instances had never been to sea themselves—were intensely suspicious of any purchases made by shipmasters in foreign ports if these included provisions and stores. They had reason to believe that some shipmasters would make a profit on the side from such deals. For this reason the owners preferred to supply all necessary provisions and stores in the home port, under their own supervision, at the outset of the voyage.

The *County of Pembroke* had been provisioned at Liverpool for a twelve-months voyage. This would have been sufficient if we had succeeded in picking up a cargo in New Zealand, for a direct home run without undue delays; but when we were ordered to Newcastle, Callao, and the Chincha Islands, the voyage was extended by many months. In these circumstances the Captain could have used his own discretion or could have cabled to the owners for permission to take in extra provisions and stores.

If the accounts of the voyage showed a loss, the Captain would be blamed, whether it was his fault or not; but this voyage was a profitable one. We had carried three cargoes—general merchandise to New Zealand, coal to Callao, and guano for the run home—with no undue waste of time as time was reckoned in cargo voyages under sail. It was therefore an act of excessive meanness to economize on the food required by law to be supplied to the crew, especially in such a trifling expense as that required to lay in enough oatmeal to line the bellies of the crew with burgoo for the few weeks that we would be in cold latitudes while rounding Cape Horn.

— · — · —

[Fresh water was scarce and strictly rationed on ships that were routinely at sea for three or four months. Pumping out the daily ration was supervised by an officer, and in heavy weather it could be a major undertaking. Apprentice Jones wrote that the pumps were located on the British Isles *in the worst possible position for that job in bad weather.]*

Alas, for a fond parent's admonitions on the necessity for preserving bodily cleanliness at all times, there was now no fresh water available for washing one's face, on arising from slumber, or for washing one's underwear—apart from the problem of drying the washing if any could have been done.

But fresh water for tea-making and cooking is a necessity which cannot be dispensed with; and, although the ship was being deluged daily with thousands of gallons of pure fluid from the skies, in the shape of snow, sleet and hail, the practical problem of getting buckets of fresh water for the drinking-and-cooking rations of the officers and crew became, for a special reason, a worry of the first magnitude while the gale continued to rage.

The difficulty arose from the position of the ship's watertanks. There were two of these, built into the hold just abaft the mainmast. Around the base of the mast a strong teakwood rail was fitted, with rows of belaying-pins on which to make fast the braces from the mizzen-yards. At the center of the after-rail was a teakwood pillar, to which was fitted the hand-pump from the tanks—kept padlocked, and by a strict rule to be used only in the presence of an officer.

Under normal conditions of sailing this was a handy place for the pump, as the ordinary ration—a bucket of fresh water for every three men, for all purposes—could be conveniently drawn there, at a pre-arranged time, and carried in the buckets aft or forward along the decks to the officers' and men's quarters.

But in a Cape Horn Snorter, which continued for weeks, the position of this pump was, of all positions on deck, the most exposed to seas breaking on board, and no shelter whatever was possible there from the deluges that continuously swept across the decks, as sea after sea pounded the vessel's weather side.

To be thirsty in the midst of raging torrents of water was the plight of the Ancient Mariner of Coleridge's famous poem:

> Water, water, everywhere,
> Nor any drop to drink. . . .

But our plight, though not yet as serious as his, seemed serious enough to us, as we saw the only fresh-water pump on the ship submerged intermittently beneath the swirl of icy salt water.

To draw a few buckets of water from that pump, once a day, was a task requiring the strenuous efforts of all available hands in a watch—perhaps eight and an officer—exposing themselves to discomfort and danger.

Ten buckets of water per day constituted the full ration for the thirty persons on board, but, in the circumstances, we were lucky if we could draw five or six buckets without mishap.

The procedure was acrobatic. Lifelines were stretched taut along the deck, on both sides. By these the men and boys hauled themselves along to the pump, holding the empty buckets above their heads, to keep them free from salt water and spray. As the seas broke over the rail at irregular intervals, each man had to keep one hand free to clutch at ropes or anything else that might be handy, to prevent himself from being knocked down by the rush of water and swept into the scuppers, with risk of serious injury, or even of being swept overboard.

Arrived at the pump, two men or boys stood balanced on the teak-wood rail, about three feet above the deck, and two more, about three feet above them, on a platform of planks lashed to the tackles of the topsail and topgallant halyards.

The men on the upper platform had charge of the empty buckets, with two or three men ready to lend a hand passing the filled buckets forward to the forecastles or aft to the poop.

On the deck the officer of the watch and two men or boys stood by the pump, up to their waists in water, and lashed themselves to the rail. As opportunity occurred, between seas, when the pump was temporarily free of the flood, a bucket was passed down, and, with frantic pumping, was partly or nearly filled before the next sea broke on deck. It was then snatched by the top men and passed in relays to its destination, held as high as possible to avoid flying salt-spray.

This routine, which may seem simple when described in words, was one that required considerable agility in a howling gale or blizzard, with the ship rolling and lurching in mountainous seas. It often required an hour or more of concentrated effort to obtain six or seven buckets of water from the pump, before further efforts would have to be abandoned through the sheer exhaustion of the men and boys in the working-party.

Even then, only one bucket in three would reach its destination tasting like fresh water, as it was practically impossible to keep it free from salt splash and spray.

When I think of modern steamships and motor-ships, equipped with complicated plumbing, taps accessible in all parts of the vessel, wash-basins, baths, hot and cold water laid on, and suchlike luxuries, I sometimes wonder whether seafaring men of today could even begin to imagine the miseries of life on sailing-ships, in which water was rationed in buckets, under the conditions I have just described.

— · — · —

[*Elis Karlsson described in his* Pully-Haul *a typical night in the roaring forties along the way to Cape Horn when he was a seaman in 1926 on the* Herzogin Cecilie. *The mate here orders the crew to the "Port fore-braces."* *The crew knew that they were to pull on the line from the left-hand end of the yard for the lowest and largest sail on the foremast when the Mate slacked off on the right-hand, or starboard, end of the yard. The yard would thus be turned from its position to catch the northwest wind to a new position to catch the southwest wind as the wind suddenly shifted.]*

A dark, wet and windy night engulfed us when we took over the watch. Spray-mixed rainwater gurgled in the poopdeck scuppers and streaks of phosphorescence marked capstans and hatches, as the water sluiced and swirled over the foredeck. Within the distance of a cable-length round the ship, the backs of big, eastward-rolling seas were lit by a ghostly light caused by the gale-carried rain, while the troughs were abysmal shadows. The rain swept over the ship, beating on the straining sails with a noise that muffled the rumble of breaking seas; its icy coldness numbed our faces when we ventured out from the lee of the donkey-house, behind which we huddled. When we came on deck we had been told by the Mate to stay there and not to go either below or forrard for shelter under the fo'c'sle head.

The Mate's behaviour made us face the icy blast at frequent intervals. Against the background of the ghost-white sea we could see his back silhouette a few paces from the wheels and the struggling helmsmen. Facing aft he stood, swaying to the motion of the ship, his head lowered like a charging bull, staring into the stinging rain, sparing only a quick glance for the binnacle and the head of the ship. Apart from the few paces taken to and from the binnacle at intervals he did not budge, and when two bells drew near he whistled for the police and sent him aft to look at the chartroom clock. He obviously expected something to come at us from the murk astern.

Time dragged by in wet misery; waiting for we did not know what we huddled there, some of us leaning against the steel bulkhead of the donkeyboiler house; others had jammed themselves between the two cylindrical water tanks; some disregarded the deluge and sat on deck, their backs to the bulkhead—they had given up trying to keep reasonably dry. Nobody attempted to speak; the wind and the noise of the rain would have drowned any normal voice anyway.

Perhaps it was getting near four bells (2 A.M.) when the rain turned into an almost solid mass of water, which fell on us with a deafening roar and made us gasp for breath. Two whistle-blasts shrilled and the Mate bellowed as he ran to the starboard brace pinrail:

"Port fore-braces!"

With a couple of stumbling leaps over the heaving deck we were at the port fore-brace, ready to haul. One of us slid down the starboard poop-ladder and fought his way through the swirling water to the starboard capstan; he shouted to the look-out to haul in the slack on the tack as he paid out a few feet on the sheet.

I cast a glance aft as I hauled. The wheels were a flurry of oilskin-clad arms and wheel-spokes as the helmsmen put the rudder hard a-port. Aft, on our starboard quarter, a faint, pale glimmer of light could be seen through the opaque curtain of water.

Suddenly the wind was gone, completely gone! The sails hung slack in the rain, while the water gurgled in the scuppers and the rain hissed as it beat the seas. A few seconds of this and the downpour ceased as suddenly as the wind; its noise diminished as it left us in its wake. A clear night sky with brilliant stars from above the now visible horizon astern was revealed, and it grew bigger as the deluge swept eastward. With violent jerks the sails filled to a fierce blast from south-west. The starboard mainsail clew lifted ominously, but the ship responded to the helm in time, helped by the braced-in fore-rigging. We heaved home foresail sheet and tack, then braced in main- and mizzen-riggings, and the ship was brought back on her course. It was now a lovely, star-lit night with not a cloud to be seen and the ship heeled to a south-westerly wind of gale force. After clearing the deck, we gratefully stripped off oilskins and sou'westers.

—·—·—·—

[*Karlsson described a typical and important weather pattern of the southern ocean. Captain Roald Amundsen, crossing the southern ocean in his vessel* Fram *on his way to Antarctica and the first journey to the South Pole, explained the pattern this way:* "The wind is for the most part of cyclonic character, shifting suddenly from one quarter to another, and these shifts always involve a change of weather. When the barometer begins to fall, it is a sure warning of an approaching north-westerly wind, which is always accompanied by precipitation, and increases in force until the fall of the barometer ceases. When this occurs, there follows either a short pause, or else the wind suddenly shifts to the south-west, and blows from that quarter with increasing violence, while the barometer rises rapidly. The change of wind is almost always followed by a clearing of the weather."[10]

Captain Alan Villiers, on his way to Cape Horn in his little full-rigged ship, Joseph Conrad, *wrote:* "We were two weeks out before the first storm blew and then it was a mild one—hard from the nor'ard first with rain and the glass falling (about twelve hours of this), and then with a slight lift of the glass, the jump to south-southwest. One has to watch these jumps closely so that they do not catch the vessel by the lee: but in the South Pacific it is usually possible to see when they are coming, if only with a few minutes' warning. This is enough. There is a hesitant lull, or a heavier rain, or an instant's clearing of the southern sky: then stand from under! With a gust of violence that shakes the ship and scares at once all the tumult from the north wind's sea, the south gale comes! One becomes used to them after a while. After the wind has jumped to the south, it usually blows the sky clear, and settles into a comfortable steady gale from somewhere about the south- · west—fair wind, and most helpful to the vessel's progress."[11]

The officer on watch who failed to "watch these jumps closely" *would find his ship and himself in trouble. The mate of the* British Isles *in 1906 had*

10. Roald Amundsen, *The South Pole: An Account of the Norwegian Antarctic Expedition in the Fram, 1910–1912*, Vol. 1 (London: John Murray, 1913), 154.
11. Alan Villiers, *The Cruise of the Conrad* (New York: Charles Scribner's Sons, 1937), 339.

served mostly in steam and was ignorant of the weather patterns of the southern ocean, as W. H. S. Jones, who fought the fire on the British Isles, *recorded.]*

Coming on deck one morning at 4 A.M., I climbed the poop-ladder, and fought my way across the poop-deck, against the icy blast coming from the port quarter, to the shelter of the weather-cloth in the mizzen rigging. The ship was surging along in a north-westerly gale under a heavy press of sail, only the Crojik and royals being fast in the gaskets.

At daybreak, the sky to windward was packed with dense masses of snow clouds, piled up into the heavens, one upon the other, with evil-looking streaks of green, grey and yellow, radiating from a western quadrant, to tinge the upper edges of the cloud-masses with varie-gated colours.

The eastern sky was a blood-red, as the sun rose behind a high "dan", or wall, of dense cloud that reached up from the horizon.

With first streaks of daylight showing in the sky, I was sent below by the Mate to call the Captain, and found him asleep, fully dressed, on the cabin settee.

"Daylight coming in, sir," I said in a loud voice from the cabin door. Instantly the Old Man was awake.

"What is the weather like?" he asked, as he walked across the cabin to tap and read the aneroid barometer, on the bulkhead.

"North-westerly gale, with heavy sea. She's doing fourteen knots by the sand-glass," I answered in accordance with the Mate's instructions.

Going up the companion-way to the poop, the Old Man walked aft, and looked in the binnacle at the compass before taking in at one glance the evil-looking sky, the low clouds scudding over the mast heads, and the ship as she lay down in a smother of foam and flying spindrift from the breaking seas astern, which filled the decks from rail to rail as they hissed and seethed past in their expended fury.

Striding forward to the lee of the weather-cloth, the Captain shocked our steam-boat Mate into action, in language more forcible than polite:

"Hell's damnation, Mister, are you deaf, dumb and blind? Look astern, man, look astern! The wind will come out of the south-west any minute now. Get all hands on deck, get the mizzen and upper t'gans'ls in, get the braces clear for running!"

"All hands on deck!" bawled the Mate—but it was too late.

Like the rest of the watch huddled under the weather-cloth, the Mate had been standing with his back to the wind, as he tried to shield his face from the blasts of rain, sleet and hail.

With a roar the wind came away from the lee quarter. The Old Man and a sailor clawed the wheel over to get the ship away before the wind. On deck, the carpenter and Paul Nelson let fly the upper t'gall'nt halyards, while the Mate and Second Mate, with men and boys, hauled the yards around, floundering in the surging water which cascaded across the decks. The dismaying sound of rending aloft, and the sight of great pieces of canvas being swallowed up in the spume and murk to leeward, reminded us only too vividly of our ordeal off Cape Horn a year previously.

Luckily, we were not taken aback, or the three sticks and all they carried aloft would have been over the side, or the ship on her beam ends with the coal cargo shifted.

As it was, the lee yardarms had been pointing directly into the eye of the wind, before the ship answered her helm and began to pay off [*turn away from the wind*], but that brief interval was long enough for the fore and main upper t'gans'ls to be torn to ribbons as they were shaken violently by the hurricane squall, when the halyards were let go, and for the huge mainsail to be split from head to foot.

With the yards trimmed to a nicety again, the ship tore along in the high confused sea, which now leaped into pyramids as the wind from the south-westward gradually changed the direction of the great rollers. On deck we hauled the torn mainsail up, standing up to our waists in the ice-cold surge, soaked to the skin, our fingers numbed, our teeth chattering with the cold, and water running out over the tops of our seaboots, as our half-frozen feet squelched inside them at every move we made.

The discomforts of the waterlogged and weary crew in no way clouded the seamanlike reasoning of the Captain on the poop, who, with a fair wind blowing, fumed and chafed at the delay as he looked at the mess aloft, the bare yards, and the remnants of canvas from the torn sails standing out as stiff as boards from the sails' roping.

"Get some men aloft, Mr. Fraser," he ordered, as soon as he saw the torn mainsail up snug in the buntlines. "Send the fore and main upper t'gans'ls down and bend and set others. Keep all hands on deck in the meantime."

It had to be done, there was no use growling. Our crew were mostly real sailormen, who had learned the lessons of bitter experience. Yet all knew that our mishaps were due to the Mate's lack of intelligent anticipation of the change in the wind. . . .

At our usual post-mortem debate in the half deck that evening, in the second dog-watch, we heard . . . that a hell of a row had been going on in the mess-room after tea.

The Second Mate, when handing over the watch to the Mate at 4 A.M. the previous day, had told him that the barometer, which had been falling steadily with the wind from the north-westward, was now steady and inclined to rise, but the Mate had apparently forgotten, if he ever knew, the old and trusty barometer doggerel—"the first small rise, after low, may indicate a stronger blow"—and, to my personal knowledge, had not bothered to look at the instrument that morning.

— — ·— ·—

[*Ragged nerves, short tempers, and quarrels would inevitably come from heavy responsibilities, prolonged bad weather, lack of sleep, poor food, and other burdens on officers of the old ships. Basil Lubbock commented.*]

From what I can see of the matter, I think this petty rowing between the old man and mates is pretty general in wind-jammers, and is chiefly caused by the old men getting livers on them, caused by not getting enough exercise; this, added to anxiety, worry, and excitable dispositions, is quite enough to account for the extraordinary exhibitions of childish temper which sea-captains so often give way to. . . .

[The captain decided to heave the vessel to in bad weather, but] The mate and his watch got into trouble, as they let the fore-yards come round too soon; and there was the devil to pay.

The old man raved and stamped on the poop, and forward, everyone was yelling and cursing at once, we starboard gang looking on and waiting with a kind of condescending superiority upon the poor port watch.

But in the end we got through the operation much drier than we expected to be, and we are now hove to on the port tack.

Directly the decks were cleared up, we went to breakfast.

Meanwhile, directly the mate came aft, all the old man's bottled-up wrath overflowed, and he fairly let the mate have it, raking him fore and aft with his cutting tongue as he stamped up and down, stopping every turn to shake his fist at the mate as he stood without answering a word.

"An' ye call ye'self a sailor! I guess you ain't used to square-riggers; it ain't the same thing as a fore-and-aft yacht, you know," with biting, sneering sarcasm.

On and on he raved; we caught snatches of it high above the gale. It was the worst row they have had yet, and all hands turned out to watch it.

"Ain't ye got nothing to say? are you made of wood? Damn it! what good are you at all I'd like to know? Call yourself fit to be mate of a ship like this! you're only a steamboat sailor, that's what you are, a blasted bridge stanchion."

It was the greatest insult he could think of, calling the mate a steamboat sailor, and one the mate did not relish, for he was a fine seaman, almost as good as the old man, and, like him, had never been in a steamer in his life.

Meanwhile, the second mate, with his back turned to the old man, leant over the break of the poop and soliloquized in a loud undertone:

"Oh, you beauty! Captain Bailey; oh, but you're a beauty! Go it! why don't you call him a liar, and a thief, and a robber! Oh, you bad-tempered old man; hit him, won't ye! why don't you eat him! Curse you! you'll stamp in the poop if you're not careful! How's your liver this morning? pretty so-so, eh? Oh, you devil you! couldn't I kill you, couldn't I jump on you, couldn't I bust ye head in!—oh, but I will some day, if ye don't mind, curse you!"

At last the old man rushed below, snorting with fury, and the show was over, and we went to our regal repast.

—·—·—

[A curse of the sailor's life was the appearance of salt-water boils after several weeks at sea. They were caused by the combination of vitamin-deficient diet and constant friction of clothing on skin soaked with salt water. Claude Muncaster and Paul Stevenson described the horror. First, Muncaster.]

Food? Well, at home we should hurl it at the pigs. Persson was saying that he read in a newspaper the other day an advertisement: "Ship's food for sale. Very low price. Excellent fodder for pigs." For all that, we had to eat something, if only to fill our stomachs, but it is about time that those responsible should be refrained from taking advantage of men's misfortune. A sailor's life is hard and hungry, so food-stores are shipped such as only seafarers and pigs could swallow and digest. No ordinary human being employed ashore could continue to do his work on this kind of sustenance. Persson showed me his arm: the boils had already begun.

He laughed. But it was really no matter for joking: these boils can easily develop into blood-poisoning if not treated with reasonable care. My medicine chest was continually being of service to some of my companions, and I was always tearing up linen for bandages. I wished I had brought a bigger supply. Finally Persson's boil alarmed me, and there was a thin red line all the way up his arm. I advised him to go to the Skipper, and after some persuasion he went aft reluctantly. The "Old Man" gave him a poultice made of porridge! To me it seemed curious that such treatment should be prescribed for a boil, yet it had the desired effect. Next morning a good deal of the matter had come away, though the arm was badly swollen and very painful.

It would have amused or angered any medical man to have watched the primitive methods of rendering aid. Koskinnen in his rough manner pinched Persson's arm for him, and got most of the stuff away. Then we bathed the wound in "Condy's", but the poisoning still remained partially. With no more scientific instrument than a match, Persson therefore poked about to extract the last bit of matter. Finally, with the aid of his fingers and accompanied by a loud cheer, he pulled out of his arm a piece of string about half an inch long. Persson was a brave fellow. During the whole of this episode the pain must have been acute, yet he never made a murmur. Only once he said "Gee!" and mostly he was laughing or said nothing.

[And Paul Stevenson wrote of boils on an American vessel bound around Cape Horn.]

Many of the men are now afflicted with the most grievous perhaps of all the ills with which sailors are cursed in cold, bad weather,—the dreaded sea-boils. These harassing sores are due to the friction of oil-skins and other clothes upon the wrists and neck, continually drenched with salt-water, and though the bad condition of sailors' blood generally is doubtless responsible for the dreadful state of the wrists of the sufferers, it is singular that mere friction combined with cold sea-water should produce such results. Sea-boils or salt-water-boils, as they are sometimes called, are exquisitely painful and very sensitive to any rubbing, and they must be bandaged and poulticed until it is time for the lancing, upon which a sort of core, like a short thick piece of sinew, is laid bare, which must be seized and plucked out. Two of these boils as large as plums will lay a man up; and any attempt to work him hard generally results in a high fever and his bunk for several days. Imagine what the suffering must be off Cape Horn when these boils are added to fatigue, cold, loss of sleep from frequent calls of all hands, and to the lethargy that comes from exposure . . . Coleman this morning showed me two dreadful-looking wrists; the left one was particularly bad, with a deep rent or cavity in the flesh itself that a silver dollar would not cover; not bleeding, but mortifying and sloughing terribly, presenting a sickening spectacle. Coleman says that some of the others are a good deal worse than he is.

— — · — · — —

[Maintenance of the ships went on in all but the worst of weather. A home-ward voyage of three or four months was just long enough to get a ship ready for inspection by the owners. A mate hoped for his own command if the owners were pleased. The captain could lose his job if they were not. Alan Villiers, in his Falmouth for Orders, *noted that this ancient routine went on even on ships that were on their last voyage and condemned to the break-up yard.]*

Why must sailing ships have such rotten, soul-searing, miserable jobs always associated with the voyages that they make? Nobody takes any notice of them in port; the only people who see them at sea, mostly, are their crews. They never know the voyage, now, that will be their last, when the knackers of the break-up yards will claim them and they may go to sea no more. Yet voyage after voyage has its scraping at teak-wood with the extremely primitive and sadly inefficient tools of sand and canvas, in the foolish endeavour to remove all the oil and varnish in order that more may be put on, to be scrapped off by the same inef-ficient means on the following voyage: voyage after voyage has its end-less chipping of rust, and scraping of paint, and daubing of red lead, and washing of white paint, and scraping of decks. We had our share of all these in *Herzogin Cecilie*. The hands must be employed!

We scrubbed the teakwood and washed all the paint on the road to Cape Horn. Neither, in any conditions, is enjoyable work; the only kind of work that is ever enjoyable is that which is congenial, into which one may throw the energy of mind as well as body. What could anyone find congenial in washing paint? In a great Cape Horner, flying along in 55° S. for the bleak headland from which it takes its name, it might easily qualify as the World's Worst Work.

Scrubbing teak, you first put some strong caustic soda solution on the varnish, then you smother that with sand and scrub the lot with canvas as long and as hard as you can go. Then you wash off with salt water, and if all the varnish is not gone—mostly it isn't—and the mate is about, you begin again. If the mate isn't about, you go somewhere else. Every blessed deck-fitting in the ship seems made of teak, or bound with it—the big charthouse aft, the skylights, the compass stands, the pin-rails, the fife-rails, the companions, the very deck-buckets, the sides of the flying bridge, the wheels (four of these, all huge), even the older of the belaying pins—and nothing can be neglected. And it is all so insufferably cold, and insufferably irksome, and damnably useless, and hellishly painful.

But scrubbing teak, bad as it is, is a much better job than washing paint. You put the caustic solution on with a wad on the end of a stick—the longer the stick the better—with the teak; with the paint you put it on with a wad in your hand. You can manage to escape some of the caustic with the teak; with the paint you have to put your hand into the bucket, and you escape nothing. And that caustic solution is strong. It is strong enough to remove the paint, if you rub too hard—which we didn't do very often—as well as the surface dirt that is upon it. And what could remove paint could scarcely be recommended as a manicure preparation for the ladies.

Nothing would keep out the caustic. We tied sacking closely round our wrists, and bound it tightly with strands of rope; but the only thing this achieved was to keep the caustic always wet around us. Soon everybody's hands were in a fearful state. With so much hauling on wet ropes, clawing at wet canvas, gripping of strong wheelspokes, fooling about with heavy wires, one's hands were in a bad enough state without having to put them continuously for hours in caustic soda. In those high latitudes cuts and minor skin wounds refuse to heal, eating into the flesh right to the bone instead, remaining deep and open, though they do not bleed unless they are knocked. Then how they do sting, ye gods! Queer, obstinate breaks come in the flesh of the fingers, that never close, and never bleed, and never cease paining. The possession of two or three of these was surely pain enough; but the accursed caustic burnt every scratch and minor skin break—of these we had many—into a deep, pulsating cut, right to the bone. It burnt the skin from the hands, first turning it leathery, with small sores; then brittle, with larger sores; and then the old skin went, leaving very soft, new skin in its place.

Then the caustic played havoc! The soft, new skin came on the tips of the fingers first and it could not stand up to the ordeal. It had not a chance, really; and soon it broke, bringing right on the fingertips sores more malignant than ever. These hurt abominably; then it was difficult to carry on. Dropping the soda-wads every now and then to haul on wet braces or sheets did not improve things. I counted thirty-eight sores upon my right hand one day; and my right hand was merely typical of the right hands of the watch. It was impossible to open it right out, and equally impossible to close it right up. It pained continuously, even to the extent of interrupting one's sleep—and at sea that is an accomplishment which takes doing. To haul on the hard, wet ropes brought the blood from a score-odd open burns; on the backs of the two first fingers, malignant sores had gathered at the nails; farther down all the fingers lesser sores clustered as thickly as freckles on a sunburnt child. In places, particularly at the wrists and on the back of the hands, the skin had gone altogether. Here the soda had dripped from the wads all day; nothing would prevent it. The left hand was little better than the right, though it was not used so much. Both palms were so leathery that they were not much affected, but the backs of the hands and the fingers were enough.

Let it not be imagined that the mates of the *Herzogin Cecilie* were hard taskmasters, for they were nothing of the kind. Each took a kindly interest in all the boys, and each was respected by all the boys in return; and all of them flung themselves into that soda-washing with an energy and determination that, though it took a good deal of willpower to sustain, was an encouragement and an object lesson to us all. Everybody knew that the soda-washing meant burnt hands and more misery when we already had enough on the decks of our great four-masted barque, with nineteen boys to do what ninety did, racing for Cape Horn; and everybody also knew that it had to be done. It was only a sailor's job, that was all. And if some of the younger boys felt a bit dejected about it at times, wet through, cold and chilled to the bone, they always carried on.

So we got it done; but we had reached the South-east Trades on the other side of the Horn before all our sores had gone.

— · — · —

[Rare is the ship that now voyages in the high southern latitudes, across the three oceans of the world. Powered vessels don't need the strong winds found there to drive them on their way, and so the high latitudes now are far from the main ocean commerce shipping lanes. Gone perhaps forever is the terrifying and exhilarating sensation of sailing a great ship in the roaring forties. The climax of that experience came as a vessel was well along on its way to Cape Horn, as Ray Wilmore described it on the John Ena.*]*

We're into the thick of it now. I see, hear and feel things that I just can't believe. They beggar all description. Had I known that weather like this could be, I would have said no ship could live through it. I don't see how we do. In my wildest imaginings, bolstered by stories I've read and heard, I've never conceived of conditions such as we are now in—the Roaring Forties in all their winter fury. I'm beginning to know the reason for that involuntary shiver and that ashen look I've seen creep over the faces of some of the old-timers when this region has been under discussion. We are, of course, just in the outer fringe of the area now, but already I can understand why the very name is enough to strike fear into the hearts of anyone, no matter how hardy, who knows its meaning.

The wind shrieks and roars incessantly, like all the steam whistles and sirens in the world turned loose in one gigantic and continuing salute. When the waves reach a certain height the wind clips off the tops and sends them smoking across the surface, smoking like a prairie fire driven before a high wind. It drives in on us in constant sheets.

We are under shortened sail: down to upper t'gans'ls.[12] The deck is constantly awash. Every sea we encounter comes aboard. Sometimes they pass clear over the tops of the deck houses. We stand all our watches on the poop; that is, we try to stand, but with now and then a cross sea breaking in. The following rollers and the cross seas keep us wallowing at unbelievable angles, twenty-five degrees to port then to starboard. All day the pendulum has been swinging that way. Then, too, there is the rise and the dip as the mountain-high following rollers overtake us in rapid succession. They travel at a speed that makes it seem as if we are going full speed astern, in spite of the indication from the log that we are clipping off fourteen knots an hour.

It's terrifying to watch one of these high, greenish-black, white-topped waves bearing down on us, rising high above our stern then, seemingly, lifting us by the buttocks and pointing the bow downward at an angle from which I'm sure, momentarily, we shall never recover. The wave moves on, lifts the whole ship, lifts the bow and drops the

12. Wilmore may have meant upper *topsails*, not t'gallant sails. From the diagram, it is clear that carrying the latter is not much reduction of sails.

stern kerplunk; the ship quivers and shakes as if trying to recover from a near-knockout blow. There is a terrific roar as the churning, wind-clipped crest of the wave overtakes and passes full length over the ship. We hang on to whatever we can grab, close our eyes and hold our breath. It's over quickly and we find ourselves settled down in the trough with the mountain moving on, but just astern is another one, and we hang on and wait and wonder and hope. And so it will be all day and all night; probably many days and nights, maybe weeks, and always the wind shrieks and howls. We will be wet and cold, nothing will be dry or warm. One long night-and-day struggle, man against the elements.

When we previously had mountainous seas some days ago, we were heading almost directly into them. I thought they were bad when they broke over the bow, sending spray and foam up into the rigging, but these following seas are worse and they make steering a nightmare. I spent the hardest and most terrifying two hours of the trip during my trick at the wheel this afternoon. I was in a lather of perspiration the entire time, notwithstanding the near freezing temperature. It was work, work, work, every second. The ship would yaw and run off before the wind with every following sea. She seemed to slip and slide, first at the stern, then at the bow, then sidewise with the wind. Before I could do anything about it, the ship would be off course a couple of points. There she would hold and hold and wouldn't come back. Then all of a sudden, with the orneriness of an unbroken bronco, she'd over-reach the mark by a couple of points. So it went all afternoon, two points north then two points south of the course, wallowing in the trough, climbing the side of a mountainous sea, sliding down the other side, completely awash most of the time. . . .

Inside the bunkhouse things are in a mess. We have about six inches of water in the room. We bail and bail, but every sea higher than the door board lets in more gallons of water. It rushes back and forth across the room and slaps up under the lower bunks, the bottoms of which are boarded with tongue and groove to keep out the water, but that doesn't mean much. The water splashes and slops about so much that everything in the room is wet. Blankets, donkey's breakfasts, clothes—all are soggy wet, with no chance to dry them. It would do little good to dry them anyway; they would quickly get wet again. We are wet all the time. We don't even bother to take off our wet clothes when we turn in for a few winks of sleep. All we take off are our boots and oilskins.

We have to wedge ourselves in our bunks, building up the outer edge of the mattress by stuffing bundles of old canvas, old clothes or rope under it so when we turn in we fit down into a V between the mattress and the sidewalls and can't be rolled out. Even at that, we frequently have to brace ourselves against the upright stanchions to stay in. Frankly, the bunks are about the least inviting spots on the ship. If we could stand up in a corner, and could learn to sleep standing up, that would be more comfortable than lying on our soggy donkey's breakfasts covered with wet, smelly blankets. What a mess!

— ·· — ·· —

[Weather on the road to Cape Horn would normally be expected to be bad. Superimposed on bad weather could be "Cape Horn Snorters," which were worse. Elis Karlsson described a snorter in 1936 when he was chief mate of the Herzogin Cecilie.*]*

The Second turned aft to go below and then he stopped, a look of awe on his usually placid features as he stared aft.

"That's a nasty one," he said at last.

A blue-black curtain covered the sky astern of us, and a thin, luminous, silver-white band extended from one quarter to the other, where the approaching squall touched the sea. It was a monster, both in size and appearance. In its dark heart formless shadows swirled and writhed: the demons of the west winds at their revels. And in a few moments we would be in the midst of it.

I blew two blasts on my whistle, and the watch gathered. I shouted: "Jansson, Koski! Slack fore-upper topsail sheets till the preventers take some of the strain! Hirvilahti, Saari! Do the same in the main rigging. Mattson, Gronlund, mizzen rigging. Move! Bjork, give a hand at the wheel! The rest of you, stand by!"

The hands jumped to it, and I hurried aft to get my oilskin coat out of the chart-room. On my way I passed the Captain, standing facing aft on the small standard-compass bridge; apart from a quick glance to see what the hands were doing, his eyes were fixed on the swiftly approaching squall, trying to read its hidden secrets. Was it all wind, or wind and hail, or hail only? Would the wind be steady?

The hands had barely finished their tasks when it hit us. The deep tone in the rigging rose suddenly to a brutal howl and the deck under my feet gave a jerk as if the ship had stumbled; then she leapt ahead. The day was swept away and twilight descended with the hail-filled wind, and the surface of the sea was beaten into smoky spume. The smaller, irregular wave formations were flattened or torn to shreds; the big west-wind rollers, too mighty to be flattened even by such a wind, rose steeper at their crests and hurried their pace. For some moments the ship kept up with the seas. On the wind-flattened ridge, with surging white water up to her rails as if in a huge foam-bath, she stormed along with a rumbling avalanche of breaking crest under her, her jib-boom pointing into the valley below and ahead. Slowly she lost the race as the undertow made itself felt, and her bows were lifted by the shoulder of the sea; for a while she lingered on the windward slope, her jib-boom thrusting at the screaming murk; slowly she sank down into the comparative quiet of the valley, which echoed with the turmoil above, where the hail-mixed spindrift beat a frenzied tattoo on the straining canvas. Astern another towering ridge approached, its crest spilling over and drenching the ship up to her topsails. Higher and nearer the wall of rumbling water reared, until it seemed inevitable that it would engulf us; steeper and higher it rose until the foam-flecked mass leaned over the ship. But her stern lifted, slowly at first, then more swiftly, and in the next fantastic moment she was carried down the slope in the welter of the collapsing ridge, miraculously unhurt and intact.

I had stayed where I was when it struck, leaning back against the wind and steadying myself against the port cru'jack sheet capstan, clamping my whistle between my teeth and tensely watching the sails, bellying up there in the hail-filled twilight. Something must carry away, nothing can withstand this, I thought. In my mind I was feverishly busy checking up on the gear, although I knew full well that nothing could be done. When had I renewed that wire, when had I turned that sheet-chain? Would that sheet-block sheave be strong enough?

Every now and then I glanced at the helmsmen, and eventually it dawned on me that they hardly moved the wheels. And yet the ship was definitely on course, dead before the wind. She had no time to roll in her headlong rush to eastward, and she was sailing herself!

And how she sailed! Up and up went her bows, with the jib-boom barely visible in the swirling murk, as she stormed up the slope of a sea. Slowly, slowly, she would lose the race with the breaking crest in front and sail between the two towering ridges for a while. Then gradually her stern would lift higher and higher by the overtaking sea, the jib-boom almost dipping in the dark waters of the trough and the deck sloping forward at an impossible angle. At the moment when she seemed intent on sailing herself into the deep, the crest of the sea astern would collapse with a hiss and a rumble, the white waters of the crest carrying her along in a swift, spectacular surge.

I was watching spellbound the most awe-inspiring, and at the same time the most magnificent, sight I shall ever see. I knew then that nothing would carry away; nothing would stop this marvellous ship in this her hour; she was part of the elements; as she was carried eastward in the heart of the gale, ship and elements were one. The spectacle was so overwhelming in its display of power that ordinary awareness, stark fear, or even apprehension vanished and were replaced by an exultant feeling of one-ness with the elements and the ship. I knew then that all was well and stood there revelling in it all, a spectator yet a part of it.

I awoke with a vague feeling of regret that it was all over; the gloom around us had gone and the wind had lowered its voice. The ship had commenced her roll and the swirling mass of the squall had left up in its wake. I recovered my sanity and walked aft.

The chart-room clock read 8 hours 45 minutes. Reading the log I found that the ship had sailed a little over 14 nautical miles since 8 o'clock: an average of 19 knots! Loaded to the marks and in an extremely heavy sea, this fine ship had in that three-quarters of an hour maintained a speed perhaps never equalled by another loaded sailing-ship in the twentieth century.

But the miracle of that three-quarter hour was not the ship's speed; by rights she ought to have been unmanageable in that wind and with that sea running. I thought I knew the Duchess well; I had reason for that belief, for had I not sailed in her as able seaman, learning all her tricks—as I had thought—from a helmsman's angle? And for three years as Chief Mate I had spent many a long watch controlling—or trying to control—her wild antics when running easting down. And yet this day she has steered herself!

—·—·—

[But most ships, of course, would not steer themselves; indeed, in very heavy weather it could be that ships could hardly be steered at all. Dewar Brown described the difficulties of steering the Winterhude *in such conditions encountered in 1934.]*

It is a terrifying experience to see the rudder take charge of the wheel, and exceedingly dangerous both to the safety of the ship and for the helmsman trying to regain control. The terrific pressure exerted on the rudder by the long seas as they surge up astern and sweep for'ard in a welter of broken water, caused the wheel, if released for a single moment, to spin with the force and momentum of a fly-wheel. It was a demoniacal menace that had to be checked before the whole steering gear jammed and the ship was rendered helpless at the mercy of the seas. When conditions were tough, we were secured to the taffrail by a length of rope fixed around our shoulders to avoid being thrown and thereby losing control, and when conditions were particularly bad, the wheel was doubled by a hand to the lee wheel, and we were both roped to the rail. The relieving tackle was never unshipped, yet despite this fact the back kick on the steering gear, due probably to worn pintles, was really severe, so much so that after six weeks of incessant wrestling, doing my trick with a kicking wheel, my arms were completely numb and dead from the jolts and jars endured. Fortunately, however, I lost no power in them, but it was some little while before normal feeling returned.

— · — · —

[*The great danger in the southern ocean was that overtaking waves could break over the stern if a vessel did not run fast enough or rise fast enough to the seas. A sea breaking over the stern could and did sweep helmsmen from the wheel, smash the wheel, and cause the ship to stumble and lurch out of control. The damage could be fatal to men and ships. Claude Woollard, an apprentice here and later a master mariner, described an accident on the* Penrhyn Castle *in 1903 that could have been disastrous. The* Penrhyn Castle *went missing in the southern ocean in the winter of 1915, perhaps from just this kind of accident.*]

We had by this time sailed more than half-way across the South Indian Ocean and had passed well to the northward of St. Paul's Rocks, when the barometer steadily fell to below twenty-seven inches, and shortly afterwards the wind and sea rose rapidly. I imagine that the captain had not anticipated such a change in the weather conditions, and instead of "heaving to" as he should have done, he now found that the seas were too dangerous for us to attempt such an undertaking, so the alternative was for us to continue to run before it and trust to providence.

In a short time the fury of the wind and sea had been whipped up, and the "greybeards" which attempted to overtake us astern, with crests seemingly over a mile long, commenced to rear up, and at times we would see a tremendous green sea with a boiling whirlpool of foam on its crest approach as if to overwhelm us—the next moment the ship's stern would be lifted to it, as it roared past on each side, part of it breaking with tremendous force over the main deck with a heavy crash. In spite of this, most of our work lay there and often enough, struggling and staggering waist deep in the water-logged deck, the watch hauled away on halyards and braces, sometimes being washed into the scuppers and nearly overboard but still clinging to the rope they were hauling on.

There was nothing like a good chanty for putting new life into the work, and the hands roared and bellowed out the chorus until they were nearly hoarse. It all helped to keep us from being too crestfallen and miserable. Crash—and a sea breaks over them; one gasp and a splutter and they were under water again, swept off their feet and knocked helter-skelter until they lay all tangled up in a heap, battered and bruised, but still very much alive. Scrambling to their feet, they went at it again, working like demons until the task was accomplished, and still singing chanties amid the howling of the wind.

In spite of our reduced canvas, we tore through the water for hours, the seas becoming more dangerous each hour, and when darkness came we wondered if we should ever see daylight again, for the danger now was the risk of "broaching to" and possibly foundering.

Towards one bell in the middle watch, a huge wave hit the rudder with appalling force and swept over the poop, crashing on to the main deck in a roaring torrent, filling it level to the top of the bulwarks. Both the captain and I had seen this wave approaching high above us like a monster and a sight to strike terror into the stoutest heart, and we both sprang into the mizzen rigging. The ship staggered under the blow and then gave a sickening roll to starboard under the terrific weight of water, and all life seemed to be knocked out of her. It was a horrid sensation to feel the old ship gradually sinking under our feet and we wondered if she would ever right herself again. Slowly, however, she shook off the weight of the water from her decks and became a thing of life again, but not for long.

The shock of the sea hitting the rudder had caused the wheel to spin with such momentum that the helmsman on the weather side had been flung clean over the top and he landed on deck on the other side, stunned and to all appearances dead. The helmsman on the other side was, however, thrown clear and being only slightly hurt, scrambled to his feet again, and made a wild grab at the rapidly revolving wheel and hung on to it like grim death, exerting every muscle in his body in a desperate effort to get it over and get the ship back on her course again. The compass light had unfortunately been extinguished by the flood of water, and the ship was now rapidly swinging into the wind.

I jumped to the wheel and together we got the wheel up, but to no avail, for there was no response. Horrified, we realised then that the ship was "broaching-to" and that we were in a very serious position, with little chance of saving the ship from foundering. Round she swung, sea after sea sweeping her decks and carrying away all our boats and almost smashing through the decks. All hands were by now alerted and were standing by ready to face the worst.

At last, and it seemed an eternity, she came up into the wind, and a frightful pandemonium now ensued as the sails we carried were taken aback and with a fearful report blew to pieces.

The feeling that the ship was sinking under one's feet with the weight of water on her decks and the slashing about of those three sails as they were literally blown to threads, will forever remain as a very frightful and vivid recollection, for few have survived such an ordeal to tell the story and for a mercy we lost no lives and had no serious casualties. It certainly ranks as the most terrible experience of my life at sea.

We lay "hove-to" for two days after this dreadful experience and it was a heavy and dangerous task going aloft later on to clear away the shreds that were left and to bend on three other storm sails, and this we did without an accident, in spite of the heavy swell running.

—·—·—

[Rex Clements also experienced the terrible effects of being "pooped" on the Arethusa.]

It was just after four bells in the afternoon watch, following a shrieking squall that exceeded all that had gone before, and while the barque was still wallowing like a half tide rock, that we saw a monstrous, foam-crested breaker rolling up astern.

We had seen many before; this was but a giant among giants, coming on with unopposable stride. It was the behaviour of the hardly-pressed barque that troubled us. She lay like a gladiator, sore-stricken and fainting, careless of the clamour around and the uplifted sword of the exultant foe. Buried deep under a weight of water, there was no life in her.

Higher and higher the comber rose, with a toppling, concave crest, swiftly overtaking the ship.

We doubted the staggering hull would ever rise to it and there was little need for the old man's hoarse shout:

"Hang on all!" We sprang for stanchion and backstay and clung desperately to them. The towering grey-beard swept down on the ship, came up with her, and was met by no answering rise.

High above the taffrail—forty or fifty feet—it loomed, and the next minute it fell.

The fall of the firmament from above could not have been more terrible. Six feet above the poop deck we were buried under a black weight of water. For the space of a few seconds we knew not if the barque still floated or was being forced down to the depths inexorably. Through instinct more than exercise of will I hung on, with the strangle-hold of a nightmare upon me and the deadly thunder of water in my ears.

I felt my shoulders were being wrenched out as demon-fingers plucked at me; then the weight of the avalanche lifted and I knew the blessed feel of light and freedom again. It cannot have lasted more than the space of a few seconds, but it sufficed me to learn the meaning of that word that in eternity a thousand years are but a moment.

The bosun and I had jumped for the port mizzen rigging and had been climbing to the topmast backstay. As the water passed we looked up. The great roller that had pooped us had swept for'ard and buried the ship deep under a green swirl of water. Even as we looked, two walls of water rushed in over the submerged bulwarks and collided down the length of the ship. The hull settled and felt dead beneath our feet.

"My God, she's gone!" said the bosun.

I glanced at the fore t'gallant yard, motionless against the sky. It was the last thing I ever expected to see. Nothing of the ship was visible, save the deck of the fok'sle head, like a lonely rock. Another bucket of water would have done for us.

For a few seconds we lay, as it were, stricken and a-swoon. Another white-lipped monster was rolling up astern, but before it reached us the gallant old barque seemed to make a mighty effort. She quivered and laboured heavily up, throwing the water from her main deck and lifting her streaming bows. As the roller swung down on us, her stern rose slowly to it, and it surged on and under, lifting the barque on its shoulders, spouting cataracts from every port.

The worst was over; we had come through that and were ready to face fresh onslaughts with confidence.

But what havoc it had played with us! As I looked aft I saw big Mac at the wheel and the old man, bareheaded, at his elbow. The wheel box was utterly gone and the well-oiled steel couplings stood bare to the spray. The binnacle still stood, but the cabin skylight had gone to matchwood. Tons and tons of water had fallen below, flooding the cabins and filling them with a litter of wood and splintered glass. The top of the lazarette was smashed in and the fragments of the scuttle held only a broken hinge. All the poop gratings, the covering board and the weather cloth had disappeared utterly. The poop was swept bare. What had happened on the main deck we couldn't see, but the flying bridge was smashed and the boat lashed on top of the house— a full seven feet above the deck—was stove [*smashed*] in and lay, a dejected raffle of boards and broken edges, held together only by the lashings in which it was swathed.

Nor had the men escaped. All hands were there, but more or less battered. Several of them were bleeding; the second mate was propping John Nielsen, white-faced and barely-conscious, up in the companion. The old mate lay under the mizzen rigging with his foot doubled up in a tangle of ropes, unable to rise. The steward, who was below in the cabin, was nearly drowned. There was no escape for the water up to the height of the pantry flap and it lay three feet deep in the saloon and cabin, swishing about with a wreckage of wood on top and a reef of broken glass underneath. He was all night bailing it out.

All through that shrieking afternoon, with never a jot of abatement in wind or sea, we ran blindly on our way, two men at the helm and the old man, broad-shouldered and bare-headed, standing before them, conning the ship. The binnacle was useless, broken for all we knew, for the Flinders-bars had gone with the skylight. Eye alone had to guide the ship now. Night came, and still the old man stood there, and next day broke and he hadn't once moved away. He rarely spoke, but with eyes ranging to port, to starboard, and aloft, directed the steering with motions of hand and arm. The navigators among us were fond of criticizing the old man, but that night he silenced criticism, as far as bad weather was concerned, once and for all. We should have been in bad plight but for his skill and endurance.

Fortunately our good main tops'l stood. We carried nothing away aloft, though several times we had to lay out on the yards and secure a sail that was in danger of being blown adrift. For the rest, all hands could only shelter on the poop—cold, hungry, and heavy-eyed, waiting for a break to lighten to windward.

The fury of the gale moderated a little on the following afternoon and we were able to repair the broken skylight and restore the water-logged cabins to some semblance of order. The old mate was put into his bunk, badly wrenched and strained, but Nielsen hung on to his duty, though his neck and shoulders went black through the violence of the blow he had received.

The wind still lessened and at nightfall we shook out both lower tops'ls and were able to bring the ship to her course. On the following morning it had dropped to a fresh gale and we set the upper tops'ls. The old mate gamely struggled on to the poop and directed the work from there. Tommy coaxed a fire into the galley-stove and we had a welcome cup of coffee. Chips was kept hard at work boarding up the skylight and the captain spent a long time adjusting the compass as best he could.

This gale blew itself out, but hard, stormy weather followed us for some time longer. Nothing so bad as our experience of pooping occurred again though, and under double tops'ls we ran wallowing to the north-east. . . .

It is impossible to describe the might and majesty of a Cape Horn sea. Words are not capable of such a thing. One is tempted to pile adjective on adjective and revel in terms that from the mouth of roaring typhoon dropped would seem hyperboles. It's all useless. Those who have not seen it cannot imagine it, and those who have need no shake of memory's wing. Seen from the deck of a little barque of a thousand tons or so, such a sea is the high-watermark of elemental majesty.

—·—·—

[Rarely did iron or steel ships leak much, particularly the last ones built. That was a blessing for their sailors; they did not normally have to spend hours a day at the pumps, as did the hands on even new wooden ships. But as they grew old—thirty or forty years old—even steel ships could leak under the stress of weather and slow deterioration. The Grace Harwar *was forty years old in 1929. Alan Villiers described a very hard voyage on which the tired old ship began to leak on a long passage to Cape Horn.]*

We found that the pumps were jammed. They wouldn't work. There was sixteen inches of water in the hold, and more coming in.

Still, sixteen inches wasn't so much. She wouldn't sink, if she developed no further leaks. We were not pessimistic.

Sailing ships' pumps are the most primitive and appalling appliances imaginable. They are situated in the wettest part of the decks, worked by all hands swinging on the handle bars of two huge fly wheels and heaving them around. Work! You heave on those bars for hours, before the pumps begin to suck; it is ghastly work even when the pumps are drawing. And now they would not work at all. There was no need to be unduly worried, although this succession of calamities was getting rather on one's nerves, on top of the sleepless night and the worrying weeks. The seas were sweeping across the decks so heavily that it was dangerous to remain there, but we had to open the top of a ventilator warily, and then the carpenter, with a hurricane lamp, climbed down into the bowels of the ship to get at the rose boxes of the pumps, in the bilges, and clear them if he could. The top of the ventilator was clamped down on him as he disappeared. He went down entirely unconcerned. It would have been a filthy and rotten job even in port, but he managed it. He cleared the rose boxes by scooping out from them with his hands the conglomeration of wet wheat which had fouled them, and climbed up into the air again.

We began to pump. It was difficult, with the ship's heavy rolling. When she rolled one way the lee pumps did not draw; when she fell back the other way, the axle of the flywheels slipped a little in its bed, with a jerk, and the bars all but came off. It was an all-hands job, of course. The starboard watch was on the starboard side, the port watch on the port. In the beginning there was some attempt at chanteying, which soon failed. We needed all our spirit—all our breath, indeed— to pump. Hour after hour went by with no alteration. It was freezingly cold; there was ice in the scuppers. Yet our bodies were streaming wet with perspiration and our faces steamed. The palms of our hands began to wear away, with the constant friction of the steel handle-bars. The seas washed about us to the waist, sometimes right over us. We did not think of trying to get out of their way. What was the use? We were wet through and through, as wet and cold and frozen as we could possibly be. We couldn't be washed away, because we were lashed there. The ship rolled and the washports clanged; the wind screamed and the seas roared and thundered; the spume flew right over the t'gal-lant yards, and the ship seemed to be racing on in a cloud of shrieking foam. We were glad of the short respite of our wheel tricks, away from the accursed pumps. After six hours the water was down to thirteen inches, which wasn't so bad. We had the leak under control, anyway. It was nothing serious.

And the west wind blew on. . . . We were on our course! It was splendid; it looked at last as if we were really on the way to round Cape Horn.

— — · — —

[After several weeks of such conditions at sea, the strains on the crew could produce a very grim view of the world, as Ken Attiwill found in 1929 on the Archibald Russell.*]*

I am fed up with the dirt that is everywhere, although we have been cleaning the ship ever since we left Victoria. It seems to me we make more damned mess cleaning things than we would if we left them alone. Personally I stink, and I am not used to stinking. Dirty clothes, dirty body, dirty bunk—(one of the pigs left his effects on my head-cushion one day when I had it on deck to dry in a snatch of sunshine: it has been impossible to remove all traces of the outrage)—dirty food, dirty dishes to eat it in, dirty work to be done, dirty faces to greet me, a dirty mirror to reflect my own dirty dial, dirty officers, and a dirty ship—everywhere dirt. It is nauseating and my senses rebel.

—·—·—

[Life has a way of adding injury to insult. Again, Ken Attiwill.]

Another big wave is out there. We can see it coming. Banked high up like a tremendous crumbling wall. It will sweep over in a minute. We are nearly at Andrastyrman's *[second mate's]* side. He sees the wave outside, grabs Gosta by the arm, and rushes with him up the poop deck steps. At the top he drops Gosta and turns to me.

"Look out, down dere," he screams. "Come up here."

There isn't time. I thud across the quarterdeck, clutch one of the iron poop supports, and swing on to the salt meat barrel. The wave curls up over the side, hangs there for a horrible second, and dumps itself with a sickening roar on the deck. The water rushes up to my knees, lashes my face, seeps through my scarf down my neck. That horrible sensation of icy water on my stomach. It swells up under the leg of my oilskin trousers, and pours into my rubber sea-boots. A minute later comes another wave, bigger than the last, and then a third, sweeping right over the poop and filling the quarterdeck as though it were a tank. I am swept away by the swirling powerful force of it. My hands are too numb to hold me to the iron support which I was clutching. My legs go out from under me. I am carried along— where? Where am I? Floating somewhere in the water. Good Jesus

Christ! Not overboard! Am I overboard? Out in that hissing mess where nothing can live or be saved? Am I out there, to feel my soul sloughing the dross of my cold flesh and bones? Am I out there to give a last despairing gurgle and sink and die? Where am I? To drown like a f'c'sle rat?—My mother stands before me in a vision ... everybody that I know ... all speechless, watching silently.... What in hell is this dirty damned business? I am living. I ... do not even think, beyond that burning question—where am I?

My behind suddenly lands on something hard. It is the deck. Even at that I haven't time to laugh. The wave is running out and has deposited me against the poop steps on the lee side. I am no sooner there than there is a sudden jolt at my knee and something very solid hits me. Pain, sharp stinging pain, and then a sort of numbness. What the—? The iron head of a capstan-bar, broken loose with the force of that wave, has come racing down the deck, to hit me in the pit of the stomach.

This is too much altogether. I am absolutely fed up. I scramble up. Ooch! I can't put the left leg on the deck. Feels as though it is in a place where men get ruptured, but I am not quite sure of the symptoms. Oh, to hell with the whole lot of it! I am fed up, and furthermore, I am through. Definitely. Let's get this thing taped off. I am through! I crawl to the *skans [forecastle]* door, wrench it open, fling myself inside and pull the door after me just in time to avoid another huge wave which hauls itself aboard. Finished with that tommy-rot. I'm *sjuk [sick]* now. Enter me up in the log book—*sjuk* and bloody fed-up. Damn and blast these wet clothes! I rip them from me, leaving only my singlet, and chuck them on the floor in a soppy heap. I scramble into bed and pull the blankets close around. Now blow your bloody whistle! Blow, go on—blow, like silly hell. I shall not be there.

—·—·—

[The danger of being swept overboard was very real. Many books tell of men lost or very nearly so, saved only by the smallest chance. It was a constant risk in the low-sided ships running heavily through stormy waves that regularly and frequently flooded green over the rails and filled the decks. Most older sailors could not swim. Probably most of the young sailors in the last days of commercial sail could swim, and in the calms of the tropics they often did, watching always for sharks. But whether a sailor could swim for safety or not was almost irrelevant, for the chances of being rescued from the wild seas of the southern ocean were small. In very heavy weather, when the danger of being swept overboard was greatest, a ship often could not even attempt a rescue without serious danger to itself. Alan Villiers wrote of the unusual rescue in 1929 of one soul who went over the side of the ill-starred Grace Harwar, *on which voyage one man had already been killed in the rigging.]*

It was not until nearly four o'clock in the afternoon that one of us went overboard.

It was so simple! It was a wonder it hadn't happened long before. It was the easiest thing on earth, to be swept overboard from the decks of a heavily running sailing ship, deep-laden, hard pressed by the sea and the wind. The ship scoops up a hundred tons of water over her lee rail. Then she lifts that rail, and rolls the water murderously down to the other side, dipping that under the water also. You are on the weather side, caught crossing the deck; you might be hanging to the life-line, but it doesn't matter much. If the sea is very heavy that won't save you. You are knocked down. And then you go slipping and sliding helplessly about the decks, and the sea emptys you out, before you can help yourself, over the ship's immersed rail. What is there to save you? Lots of things you might think, if you have only to think about it. But you would find that there is nothing, were you there.

That was what happened. The boy went so easily that at first we had not realised he was gone. The sea came—a great brute, green and grey, glittering and glinting right through—he was clinging to the life-line on the weather side, just abaft the main rigging, in the narrow open space on the fore part of the skids. We thought he was safe, hanging to the life-line. We were thunderstruck when we looked afterwards, and he was not there. The others of us were about the fife-rail, and we leapt high into the stays and on the whips of the crojack braces there, out of the way of the weight of the water. We clung there like monkeys, waiting for it to clear. It was in a moment of spell from the pumps, when we had cast adrift the lashings. The wind had gone down a great deal by then, and there was talk of setting the main tops'l. But the sea was still running savagely high.

It looked, on the face of it, as if this second life was gone as well. The Captain was on the poop and saw what happened; so did the helmsmen, shivering there. So did the mate, with his watchful eye never leaving the deck. The Captain flung a lifebelt overboard from the poop. He saw the oilskinned figure rise, a little astern of the ship, and grasp the logline trailing there. The ship was running on heavily, making about six knots, maybe, and the drag of the logline pulled the poor fellow's head under the water. He would have drowned if he had clung there. He kept his nerve, despite the apparent nearness of his end, and seeing the life-belt floating by, let go the logline and struck out a few strokes for the belt. We saw that he caught it, and put his head through. . . . It was so cold that he would die of exposure if he were left there long. What could we do?

It was dangerous to try to bring the ship to, in a sea like that. The seas would sweep her from end to end; the wind would catch the sails aback. Would her rigging stand it? Could the poor old ship, noble and splendidly game as she was, stand up to the added strain? Captain Svensson never hesitated a moment about anything: "Down helm!" he roared, the instant that the figure, tossed high by the heaving waves, swept by the poop. And down helm it was; the ship came slowly into the wind. The seas swept her decks, but they did no damage. She was carrying little sail; the rigging creaked frighteningly, and the masts groaned. But they stood. . . . Looking back, it was a big chance to bring the ship into the wind then. It was almost looking for disaster. Some shipmasters would not have tried it. But ours tried; and he won.

That was only the beginning. There were no falls rove in the davits,[13] and the boats could not be swung out. The two boats aft were lashed down on their skids, and lashed again. Huge manila lines had been passed around them fore and aft, and tightened down with spare capstan bars, and frapped about and lashed again, so that the boats would not shift with the ship's heavy working nor be washed away with the seas. There were no falls rove [rigged ready for use] because it was not thought they would be needed. In the ordinary course of events, they are not; and the new rope that would be required for them was very much needed for other purposes. There was not so very much new rope in the ship. . . .

Was anyone ever in a more hopeless predicament? Washed away from a heavy running ship, below 50 South, in a big sea and bad weather, with boats that could not be used? It looked as if it was absolutely hopeless even to think of saving that boy's life. Maybe it was too; but we had to try.

We smashed in the caulked-up door of the sail locker, in the poop, and slashed away the Cape Horn lashings of the port boat with an axe. While some of the boys saw to the rowlocks and oars and flung out of the boat all superfluous gear—water barrel, air tanks, biscuit cask, mast, sails—others dragged out new coils of rope from the sail locker and hastily rove off falls. No one was excited. Nobody lost his head. I never thought such coolness was possible; but if anything were to be of use now, coolness must prevail. The mate, strong-featured and with little to say, took charge of the actual preparations of the boat. One would have thought it was a little boat drill we were embarking on, in pleas-

13. The lines and blocks ("falls") used to raise and lower boats were normally removed when ships were at sea. The boats were brought in and securely lashed down so that they could not be swept away by waves breaking over the rails.

ant weather, to look at him. Efficiency and speed; he was perfect—not a command too many, not a raised shout once, not a word when it was not necessary; he said what it was necessary to say, at the right time, quietly. He gave such a splendid example that no one could be flustered. On the poop near by the Captain looked on, watchful; now and again he swept a glance back into the murk astern, and at the weather. The lee helmsman was gone to the mizzen top, whence he could still see the floating boy, not far away.

The weather, which was temporarily a little better, looked as if it might become much worse again at any moment. This was no part of the ocean to fool about in boats! There was a rain squall coming down, to blot out everything. Night was approaching.

Inside seven minutes the boat was swung out. The cover had been ripped off; everything was ready. The boat was over the side, ready to be lowered into the water when a chance came. The seas washed so high that they lifted it, at times; but there was not the same driving force in them now. The ship lay sluggish in the water, rolling heavily. There came an ominous creaking and groaning from the rigging.

The mate stepped into the after end of the boat. The Captain said the names of those who were to go, in a quiet voice. There was no need to call for volunteers; everyone was ready—every boy, with no exception, although they knew what it meant and they were all pretty tired. They went to their places, six of them. The others stood by to lower the boat, when the Captain gave the word. We had to be careful about that, lest she be stove in by crashing against the ship's rolling sides, and everybody spilled into the sea and helplessly drowned. We waited until she rolled that side down into the water and the sea skimmed almost to the bottom of the boat. "Now!" shouted the Captain. The falls gave way rapidly; the boat rode in the sea; the tackle-blocks were flung hurriedly from the hooks fore and aft in the boat; we pushed off and were away before that side rolled into view again. It was quick work. Almost instantly the ship had gone. She lay there, high above us now as the boat sank in the trough of the sea, looking curiously strange when one was accustomed for so long to know her only from the view-point of her own decks. *Grace Harwar, Mariehamn,* we read on the counter; that name meant something by then. The green moss came into view on her undersides, as she rolled.

It began to rain. There was a nasty low howling in the wind, though it was not then very strong. The sea was tremendous, seen from that tiny boat; yet she rode it splendidly and there was no fear attached to the management of her. We were too much concerned with the chances of saving the one who had gone to worry about ourselves. We knew that they were faint; faint, faint indeed. . . . We were almost without hope. And yet we had to try; he was not so far away, if he still floated. And if he clung to the life-belt, he would float.

The mate stood there aft, with a huge steering oar; I don't know how he kept his balance. Now the boat fell deep into a trough, and there was nothing save walls of foam-soaked green around. Now she was flung high on a crest, up and up until we thought she was going to take to the air; even upon the crests of the highest waves, the horizon was bounded by the third sea. We could not see far; never further than three seas away. In the troughs we could not see at all—not even the ship. The boys strained to their oars; the sailmaker, grim countenanced; the boyish Hagert and Sjoberg; French Peter and Filimon, coats flung off, soaked to the skin, worried, not saying anything. The mate said nothing but looked to the life of the boat. He glanced hard into the wind, when we rose on a sea. It looked ugly. It was already dusk, and the night was coming rapidly down. The Captain shouted to us a direction to steer when we left the ship, but we did not know where the boy was. We had no idea, in that heaving waste. We did not know where to begin to look for him. . . .

We remembered that the ship had been running before the wind, and steered back into it. We saw nothing. We tried to follow the oiliness of the ship's wake, where her disturbing foam still left a trace upon the waters. But the trace was faint, and was soon gone. There was no hope in that direction. We tried to watch some albatrosses, circling round, in the hope that they would circle over the figure in the life-belt—if it still was there!—but they came, screaming, and circled over us. Moments passed, and we saw nothing. It came on to rain much more heavily; the light was nearly gone from the sky now. It looked as if a heavy squall were coming down. We dare not go too far from the ship. We were a little too far already. What could we do, if a squall came down and shut her out? Would we find her again? It was not so very likely. It had happened before, at sea, that boats had put out after people washed overboard, and all had gone. . . . We gave no thought to things like that. The boys grunted at the oars; the mate scanned the seas eagerly. I never saw such a picture of splendid efficiency and glorious coolness in my life, nor heard of one. He knew the chances, well enough. He saw the squall coming down, and the darkness. He knew that not only the half-drowned wretch in the life-belt—if he was still there—was in danger. And yet he did not give in. He never at any moment even betrayed anxiety. He smiled! He swung the steering oar, this way and that, and now and then quietly exhorted the boys. There was no air of hopelessness about him, no faintest sign of despair. He struck no note of worry; we might have been upon a fishing trip, in quiet and sheltered waters.

I admit quite candidly that I had long since given up hope of rescuing that boy. What hope was there? I waited for the mate to signify that he, too, was throwing it in. We had not by then the foggiest notion of which direction to steer. The ship was over a mile away.

He did not give in. We kept on. . . . And then in the last moment of diffused light, we saw him! Not four boat's lengths away! It was a miracle, if there ever was one. We had been bound towards him all the time, and had no faintest idea.

We raced down to the life-belt and took him aboard, carefully, over the stern sheets for fear the boat would capsize. He was quite unconscious, and frozen almost stiff. We flung all the coats we had over him; French Peter tried to bring back some circulation as we pulled back to the ship, which had swung round a little to the wind now and was coming down to us.

Everybody was amazed when we brought him back aboard. He was given up for dead—gone hopelessly. As it was, he was pretty far gone; but he lived. There is iron in the bodies of these sailing ships' boys, and in their spirits, treasure without worldly synonym. He would have died if he had not been hardened by the previous hell. He could do no work for a fortnight. It might have been longer than that.

We were glad beyond words that we had saved this life. One was enough to lose—too much. We felt again that somebody was interested in us, that the hatred and fury of the sea did not wholly comprise our world. After fifty days of the Cape Horn road, in winter time, one might understandably be depressed enough, even if there has not been also something of tragedy.

The westerly wind held, thank God, and we sailed on.

— ∙ — ∙ —

[The public interest in the Australian grain races led many people, men and women, to sail as passengers, which provided additional income to the owners. W. M. Hutton was a somewhat elderly Scottish engineer who for years had traveled throughout the world. Apparently, he had been a passenger on the last British Cape Horner, Garthpool, *when she was stranded and lost on the Cape Verde Islands in 1929. Hutton wrote about his voyage in* Viking *in 1934 from Australia to Wales.]*

We are now in our fourth week out, and about midway across, when I come on the captain poring over a strange-looking chart, in German. It is the kind of chart that the landsman knows nothing of and that a nervous passenger should never see. It is being compared with an American chart of the same nature. On both of them there begins somewhere about where we are now, but away south, a red wavy line with a decided rise as it travels eastward, then a dip southward again to finish close up to the Horn. It is marked, "Northern limit of the regions in which icebergs have been encountered in months of March, April, and May."

When the import of this comes home, a great northerly bulge on the red line between 120° and 130° west takes on a rather sinister meaning. The peak of the bulge touches the latitude of 45°, and we are now down on 50° while the Horn itself has to be turned on 57°. We cross this red line on our twenty-fifth day out, and from then onward remain below it. . . .

The most phlegmatic ocean traveller would be jerked out of himself by the announcement that his ship was now heading into a region of uncharted reefs and shoals, even if it were clear weather and daylight. But in dirty weather and night time it would appear little short of madness. Yet that is, to all intents and purposes, what sailing through berg infested waters amounts to. If it is thus to a steamer which can stop, go astern, and steer at will, how much worse is it for a sailing ship which can do neither of the first two and the last but slowly in certain directions only?

Travelling a mile in five minutes, with visibility perhaps no more than the ship's length, it is a terrible thought to take to bed with you; after reading, in a supposedly dry-as-dust *Mariner's Directory to South Pacific Navigation,* such paragraphs as these: "There are few things in navigation more dangerous than these low ice islands in a dark night, when blowing hard, and with a high sea; all circumstances which unfortunately are likely enough to come together at this particular time when ice is most frequently encountered off Cape Horn. . . . In bad weather it will be prudent to lie-to." . . .

To a landsman's eye and nerves the apparent futility of the look-out comes home when he looks along that pitch black deck and cannot see even the nearest mast. Looks seaward and can see nothing but a pallid gleam of a breaking sea probably not more than a dozen yards off. And, simply by hearing alone, how can any look-out distinguish breakers on a berg from that confusion of breakers round the ship? It is even worse when one turns in. The ear becomes attuned to every sound. Was that a hail from the fo'castle head? What is that hurried patter of feet on the deck, which has become like a sounding board since you lay down? Only ten o'clock yet, and there won't be a gleam of light till six tomorrow morning—for eight hours in which we will have gone through numberless of these six minutes in which we travel a mile....

We are soon two hundred miles deep in that bulge I spoke of, when the wind falls away and leaves us helpless right in the middle of it. The far looking captain had it figured out two weeks ago that we would have the moon for that stretch, but here is the moon being wasted. In any case, the weather is too overcast to give more than fitful sights of her, although even at that she gives a certain luminosity helpful to the look-out.

There is some compensation in the thought that if we are making little or no headway, at least we are not driving along on to the unseen. But we must drive along sometime, and we are now too deep in the red to have any hope of getting out of it this side of the Horn.

Here I may say that although the bulge only measured a matter of two hundred miles east and west we were eight days in passing across it—one day's run being logged as ten miles....

It was on one of these ghostly dark nights that I was told I must either put my light out or cover up my deck light. This is a tiny strip of thick glass let into the deck and not much bigger than a pillar-box slot. Even the loom from this was interfering with the mate's vision. This darkness on deck is a feature of sailing-ship life hard to get accustomed to with us to whom artificial light has become a second nature. Dark spells gloom and depression to our modern ideas, but to sailor-men as distinct from steamer-men, darkness is the natural thing once the sun has gone down. To them it has become instinctive to take hold of the correct rope out of a dozen hanging close as herring along the belaying-pin rail. An artificial light would but confuse them.

Well muffled up and with my rabbit-skin balaclava strapped down over the ears, I stand with the mate the next night on the tiny bridge carrying the standard compass. Gradually my eyes acquire in some small measure this cat's gift of seeing in the dark. Yes, I begin to see the horizon, and away down in the south it actually shows as a whitish line here and there as if the faint after-glow of a long departed sun. But of course no sun ever set down towards the pole. "A whitish something," I say to the mate, but he is silent.

Having seen for myself that human vision—trained to it—is of some good after all, I turn in, more assured in my mind, to be awakened up by the Old Man himself, saying:

"No, don't light up—have a look through your porthole—you will see two bergs about seven miles to windward."

I think I can make them out, but no clearer than I had unconsciously done a couple of hours before from the bridge.

— - — - —

[*The southern ocean in the last days of sail was the loneliest place in the world. There is no land there, and very few ships, hardly anything to run into for thousands of miles. Nevertheless, night and day the crew stood look-out watch on the forecastle head, a miserable duty in the most exposed part of the ship. The great danger, of course, was ice. Ken Attiwill described the duty on the* Archibald Russell.]

The watch had changed. I am now on the f'c'sle, alone, keeping lookout. It is wretchedly cold, with an occasional shower of hail and a biting wind. The foresail swells its paunch with vulgar plops above my head. Waves crash over the side, even high up as this, and each time one comes across I have to turn my back and crouch my head deep into my shoulders to prevent the water from getting down my neck and running right down into my sea-boots. A trickle of this icy water down a man's stomach almost drives him insane. I know, because I have experienced it. I am now getting wise to many of the tricks of the trade. My clothing at present consists of three wet pairs of socks, two suits of underclothing, two pairs of trousers (one wet), a thick working shirt, a tight-fitting pullover, a thick high-collared astrakhan waist-length jacket . . . and a long woolly scarf. Over all this I have heavily-oiled trousers, jacket, and sou'wester, and rubber sea-boots which reach up to my knees. Still I am cold. This is a clumsy outfit. It gets in the way when you have to climb up the crazy rigging to the royals, and makes you sweat like a pig—although cold—when hauling ropes or struggling with the wheel. There are no pockets in the oilskin trousers or jackets. They would get torn in the rig, and moreover, would not be watertight. Also, the use of gloves in the rigging is disallowed: it hand-icaps the worker and lessens the speed of the work. Altogether it is extremely uncomfortable.

Up and down the f'c'sle deck to try and keep warm. Up and down—to and fro—a short ten paces from side to side to see that the lamps are bright and to watch for possible danger ahead or on either side. Up and down—to and fro—the deck is deep worn here. How many hun-dreds of poor cold wretches have walked it before me?

—·—·—

[Navigation, dependent on visibility of the sun or stars, was often rudi-mentary, and bad weather could preclude a determination of a ship's posi-tion for days or even weeks. Shipmasters therefore tended to avoid any land as much as possible and particularly Cape Horn and its outlying rocks. Some authors asserted that rarely was the Horn sighted, but, in fact, it was occa-sionally in view as the ships passed around bound east or west. Alan Villiers recorded a sighting in the Parma *in 1932, and his record shows that not always was the passage around the notorious cape stormy.]*

We have come round the Horn at last and are headed towards England.

We came round on the evening of Saturday, April 23rd, thirty-seven days from Port Broughton—two days longer than we had hoped for, but still not so bad. From Port Broughton to Cape Horn is over 7,000 miles, and to be driven by the wind over that distance in thirty-seven days is passable. A clipper ship might have done it in seven days less or even ten (perhaps); but we carry 5,200 tons of grain, we lost two of our best and most important sails, and we have a crew of boys. . . . Everybody is mightily pleased to be round and the Old Man walks the poop quietly humming a Swedish folk-song in the cold.

At daybreak I saw three shags fly past the poop; the rocks of Diego Ramirez bore three points on the starboard bow. We were slipping on slowly, passing between the rocks and Tierra del Fuego to the north, taking a short cut in the usual de Cloux *[the captain's]* manner. The weather was the same gentle westerly breeze which we held over from the previous day; we went quietly on under all sail—even the royals, flying jib, gaff tops'l, and jigger topmast stays'l—with a dry main deck for the first time in a month and sunshine in the afternoon. Sunshine! In Drake Straits! We might be sailing down Long Island Sound in summer, or in the Baltic: all day there was little sea (until a head swell came, indicating north-east wind ahead) and *Parma* went on quietly as if she were sailing down Spencer Gulf. There were cumulus clouds, fleecy—and, well, not too white or summery, if the truth must be told. But in the afternoon I walked the focs'l head looking at the blue sea— a heavy, severe kind of blue—the sky and the clouds, the Cape pigeons and the land; and with two leather coats on, two jerseys and a shirt, it was positively warm. There was actually some warmth—though white and meagre—in the rays of the sun. . . .

All day we had land in sight: in the morning Diego Ramirez, then Hermite Islands, Wollaston Island and the dreaded Horn itself. The seas broke sullenly on Diego Ramirez; we passed so close we could see the russac upon the central rock which seemed to be the largest of the three. The picturesque name of Diego Ramirez seems wasted on these bleak rocks over which the sea breaks fretfully, driving white spray half-way to the summits even upon such a day of calm as saw us pass by. Senor Ramirez was head pilot of the *Nodales* expedition in 1619 when the rocks were first seen by Europeans; hence the name which seems so much more appropriate to a South Sea atoll. But the Spaniards have given picturesque and mellow-sounding names even to guano islands. . . .

Tierra del Fuego and its islands raise their saw-like hills from the sea white and cold, grim and desolate in their snow-covered solitude. They suffer our passing in virginal disdain; yet there is a sense of threat about the whole area which is not pleasant to experience. Under its heavy snow the misnamed Land of Fire looks like South Victoria Land, at the Ross Sea; a high conical iceberg away in near the land adds to the threat and the similarity. (We do not like to see the ice.) Captain de Cloux says the land is unusually snow-covered, looking already like the depth of winter. But we have had a lot of snow on our way and the season has been bitterly cold.

All the afternoon we sailed along this inhospitable shore, slipping quietly by its cold loneliness. The high peaks of the Hermite Islands clustered thickly along the port beam. These are the southernmost group of the vast number of islands which form the so-called land of Tierra del Fuego; Horn Island is the southernmost of the Hermite group, and Cape Horn is its southernmost point. The Hermite Islands take their name from the Hollander admiral who commanded the fleet that sailed this way in 1624; Cape Horn itself was named by LeMaire and Schouten in 1616 after the town of Horne, or Hoorn, in West Friesland not far from Amsterdam. The summit of the Horn, which is a black promontory rising 500 feet above the sea, lies in 55.58° South and 67.16° West.

"A clear day here," says the South Pacific Ocean Directory, "is a very rare occurrence."

It is. We were very fortunate.

We came past the Horn itself at eventide with the moon out almost full, silvering the black waters: gently we sailed by still with our royals. Black under the moon, rising bluntly like the head of a sperm whale to its snow-surmounted summit, the dreaded bulk of the massive Cape stood solemn in a quiet sea. . . .

It hailed a lot in the first night watch and came down thick, just to show us that we *were* at Cape Horn; mains'l and crojack came in between two and four bells with better wind and a falling glass. We kept the royals on her as she increased her speed to nine knots, with the Horn and its surrounding islands in clear view now just abaft the beam. It was strange that while all the rest of the land was a bleak white, Cape Horn itself rose bare and black from sea to crest. Its head seemed sprinkled with snow but it was far from being snow-covered.

The Hazards of Ice

[The dangers of the southern ocean were not left behind once a ship was around Cape Horn. Antarctic icebergs tend to drift to the waters east and northeast of the Horn, and shipmasters were particularly anxious about them in summer months when they could be found there in greatest numbers. W. H. S. Jones noted that the British Isles *found ice there when he was second mate in 1909.]*

All was well indeed. We had passed the pitch of the Horn.

All day we stood away to the south-eastward, in the light breeze, with the sun shining in a clear sky, as we enjoyed the rare phenomenon of a Cape Horn summer. Next morning I had the Graveyard Watch, in bright moonlight, and noticed by the thermometer that the temperature was falling fast, but paid little heed to it, as we were now well to the southward.

At 4 A.M., at the change of the watch, we wore ship, as the breeze was backing around slowly to the south-eastward, and we stood away to the N.E., close-hauled on the starboard tack.

I had been asleep about two hours when I was awakened by loud shouts of "All hands on deck!" and the stamping of heavy boots on the main deck nearby. As I rushed out through the main deck door, I saw some of the watch on deck frantically hauling up the clew of the main-sail, while others were hauling the main yards around as the lee-braces were let fly. The Mate, half-way down the poop-ladder, yelled out to me, "Haul the foreyards aback, Mister, lively now!"

Without knowing what was amiss, I ran forward in time to get my watch, as they tumbled out of the forecastle door, tailed on to the weather fore-braces, and let fly those to leeward as the clews of the foresail were hauled up and the yards swung free, hauling them aback.

Puzzled at the reason for this commotion, I hastened aft. Dawn was coming in, and cold misty rain was falling. The Old Man was now on the poop, and the Mate was running forward.

I met him and asked, "What's wrong, Mister?"

For reply he pointed over the port bow. There, half hidden by the mist, was a huge iceberg, literally a floating mountain of ice, perhaps a mile long and at least 100 feet above the water.

"We were sailing slap into it when it was sighted," said the Mate hurriedly.

The fo'c'sle hands were now standing by on deck, staring at the berg, which was not half a mile ahead of us.

"Don't stand there gaping," bellowed the Mate. "Stand by the fore-braces!"

With the Old Man by the helmsman, the Mate and I made the air resound with orders, quickly obeyed. We wore ship and brought her around on to the other tack, after almost ramming the berg, as its pin-nacles and cliffs loomed dangerously near before the sails filled, and we bore away into clear water.

At that proximity to such a vast mass of ice, the air was freezing cold. This was the season when bergs, detached from the icefields of Antarctica by the summer thaw, drift northwards, a terrible menace to shipping rounding Cape Horn and the Falkland Islands. The immense size of the ice-mass astounded me, the more so as I realized that only a portion of its bulk projected above the water.

"A narrow shave!" the Mate commented to me. "The lookout sighted it only a mile ahead. He did well to see it in the mist in the dawn light."

As we headed away from the icy menace the Mate posted an extra lookout on the foreyard, and one on the forecastle-head. My watch then went below again, and I retired to my cabin to resume my interrupted sleep.

When I came on deck to take the 8 A.M. to noon watch the sun was shining brightly. I stood and stared in amazement. The ship was now close-hauled on the starboard tack again, and sailing slowly to the north-eastward in a light S.E. breeze.

To the eastward of us, the nearest about a mile away, were a number of icebergs, between fifteen and twenty of them, resembling a magical floating archipelago, of a wondrous but sinister beauty, extending from far ahead to the horizon astern. They were not white, as might be expected from looking at a small lump of ice, but of a scintillating greenish colour, sparkling like gigantic jewels refracting the sun's rays.

Colours varied in every part of each berg, as the morning sun cast shadows from the jagged pinnacles, and light played in the hollows and on the cliffs of ice, deepening the green to blue and purple where the shadows fell.

During the forenoon we sailed past berg after berg, many of them up to a mile long and over 100 feet high, and all changing in shape, colour and general appearance under the varying play of the sunlight, and as different facets of these great jewels were presented to our view while we sailed past them.

It was appalling to think what a hazard these beautiful but horrible things could be to mariners on a dark night, or in squalls of rain. How many fine ships, I wonder, have been caught in their cold clutches, stove in and sent to their doom in these icy waters? They continue to drift to a northern limit, nowadays well marked on charts, where they gradually disintegrate in the warmer water, and in the sunlight; but their melting must be a slow process, of many weeks, because of their huge size.

As we skirted the bergs the wind backed around to the south. Checking the yards in, we stood away to the north-eastward under full sail, to get clear of the ice before nightfall. In the afternoon the wind freshened, and we tore along on a course set to pass to the eastward of the Falkland Islands. Before dark we had lost sight of the last berg, which dropped below the horizon on our quarter.

The sky clouded over, the wind increased to a gale, but we didn't care a damn, as we were now well and truly clear of Cape Horn, and running to the norrard with a certainty of fine weather ahead.

We were in the Atlantic and headed for home. The usual holystoning of decks and cleaning of bright work, and painting ship, was the daily routine. Instead of being down on my hunkers with a holystone in my hand, I was now able to adopt a comfortable stance by the poop rail, from where I could detect any malingering and spur the culprit into greater activity. So we passed steadily through the Roaring Forties and bowled along in the S.E. trades, free of care.

— · — · —

[Not all ships were fortunate enough to avoid the ice. Contact with even a small piece—a "growler"—could sink a ship with a big hold and no partitions. P. A. Eaddy was lucky indeed to complete his voyage when his ship hit an iceberg in 1908.]

Of all the most depressing conditions to put up with at sea, especially in the cold weather latitudes, fog takes a lot of beating.

For several days now, we had rolled along, with the wind moderating at times almost to a calm, and our ship enveloped for the greater part of the time in heavy fog banks.

The wind still continued to keep abaft the beam but had hauled from the sou'-west into the nor'-west; the weather was bitterly cold, and the ghostly-looking driving fog banks sent a shudder down one's spine as one came on deck each watch.

Save for the slapping of gear aloft, and the gurglings and splashings as the deck ports clanged open and drained the main deck every now and again, the silence was remarkable.

Even the dreary dirge of the foghorn, sending three prolonged blasts every few minutes from the look-out's post on the fo'c'sle head, sounded muffled and strange. His cry every half-hour of "All's well" came eerily through the murk of fog, reminding one of a seagull's call on an outlying rock that was being passed by, close to, at night.

The Old Man stumped up and down the poop, stopping at frequent intervals to listen, and peer out ahead, the picture of a man very ill at ease.

"Let two men keep the look-out for'ard there, Mr. Craddock, one on each side of the fo'c'sle head, and keep two boys handy aft here on the poop, and let them keep a look-out on each quarter. By the feel of the air at times I fancy ice is not far distant. Let the fog horn be kept going frequently and listen for any echo which may come. Call me at once should any change come, or if you sight anything."

"Aye, aye, sir," replied the Mate as the Old Man stepped inside the chart-house door on his way below for a rest, as he had been on deck most of the night.

It was our watch on deck in the early morning from four o'clock till eight; the fog still persisted, but the Mate was anxious to get on with the "sand and canvassing" of the bright work.

At six o'clock, when the Old Man went below, the Mate, after posting extra look-outs, got the remainder of the watch on to the sand and canvassing. We were employed thus when seven bells was struck, and the other watch called.

Just as they had tumbled out, and were getting their breakfast in from the galley, old Tom Kidd, who was on the look-out, on the port bow for'ard on the fo'c'sle head, startled the whole ship's company with the cry of "Ice! Ice right ahead! Port your helm, port your helm! Hard up with it, sir; we are right on top of it!"

Surprise and consternation were on every face as we rushed to the weather rail to look for the ice.

"Why, it's only drift ice," said Thompson, who was standing next to me looking over the rail on the main deck near the break of the poop.

"No, it's not, look higher," I replied, gazing at a great whitey-grey wall that was taking a more definite shape all along our port side, the nearer we approached it.

It appeared like a monstrous white sheet hanging down through the fog, which even at this near distance almost obliterated it.

The ship was swinging off to starboard, the Mate having rushed to the wheel at old Tom's first cry, and helped the helmsman to swing her hard over.

We were on the port tack with the yards off the backstays, and were carrying all plain sail but the cro'jack, which was furled, and the mainsail, which was hauled up in its gear under the yard.

The minutes seemed like hours, and we were beginning to wonder if we should escape hitting it when "Crash!" The weather fore-yard arm and the end of our big spike jib-boom, took the impact simultaneously.

Down came the hundred-foot steel yard, with a crashing and tearing of gear and sails, and fell with a giant thud across the fore-deck and over the lee rail, the fore lower topsail hanging in festoons from its yard above it.

The great steel jib-boom was buckled upwards, parting bobstay and backstays from under it, and as the ship still moved ahead the port anchor was driven through the fo'c'sle head decking.

The figurehead, which had been our pride, was smashed into small splinters, and the pretty curve of our clipper bow was dented inwards considerably.

As we eventually came to standstill under the lee of the berg, the sails hung limp from our yards, the wind being all taken out of them by the height of the berg, which towered above our t'gall'nt yards.

Great lumps of ice, some weighing half a ton or more, fell from the top of the iceberg down on to our decks, which soon presented a sorry sight.

One of our boats on the for'ard deck house had her sides stove in with falling ice, while one of the large lifeboats on the after-skid was badly holed.

The donkey-boiler and winch on the fore deck also suffered a lot of damage, while the carpenter's shop on the port side, under the fo'c'sle head, was knocked all out of shape, when her bow struck the ice.

In several places on the main deck, great lumps had fallen right through the decking, and had landed on top of the wheat below.

Luckily no one was injured, for as soon as she struck, the Old Man had roared out, "All hands lay aft on the starboard side of the poop," and here we all stopped until the ship came to a standstill.

"Sound the well, carpenter," said the Old Man to Chips when we had sidled up alongside the berg and lay quietly with no more ice falling down.

"She is not making any water [not leaking], sir," called Chips to the Old Man after taking his first sounding.

"All right, try again in a few minutes," said the Old Man.

But after several tries with sounding-rod it was proved that the only damage we had was all above the water-line.

After a day of strenuous toil by all hands, we succeeded in getting things a bit ship-shape once more. The fore-yard was cut clear from its gear, where it hung balanced on the starboard rail, and was given a watery grave, taking with it the remains of our new hard-weather foresail. The decks were clear of ice, and temporary patches of canvas and timber nailed over where the ice had broken right through.

Towards evening we had drifted a little way away from the berg we had collided with and, as the day wore on, the fog lifted and let us see more of our surroundings. All round us were icebergs of all shapes and sizes. There was no opening at all visible, right ahead, when viewed even from the height of our upper t'gall'nt yards.

The berg we had hit was over one hundred and fifty feet in height, and approximately three miles long, while further ahead was a long low berg which the Mate calculated was about twelve miles long.

There were small icebergs all round us. Some rose like great buildings and church spires, while others were squat and low in the water.

During the day, one of the tall church-like ones, about a mile distant from us, out on the starboard side, capsized with a roar and a great splashing and upheaval of the water in its vicinity.

We seemed to have run right into the centre of a large ice-field, and the only way out now open to us was to double back on our tracks, and get out the way we had come in.

Late that afternoon a large four-masted German barque, painted black, passed close to us and made his number, afterwards asking us whether he could give us any assistance.

As our reply was being made the fog descended once more and blotted him out, leaving us to put in another night in company with the icebergs which we could not see, though we could plainly hear some of them grinding all night long.

For the next couple of days, the weather, luckily for us, was beautiful, and gave us a great chance to get the ship into sea-going order once more.

We had to repair the whole of our port fore-lower rigging as it had all been badly damaged in the collision.

Where the shrouds had been parted, we had to turn the broken ends in, and shackle on mooring chains to make them long enough to reach the screws.

We also had to pass a mooring chain right round the ship, with a large shackle at its center under the keel forward, on to which we shackled a temporary bobstay to heave the bowsprit down again.

Having no spar that would serve for a fore-yard, we had to dispense with two of our most useful sails, the fore-lower topsail, and the fore-sail.

There was some talk of sending the cro'jack yard down, and sending it up on the fore, in place of the fore-yard, but owing to the badly damaged state of our rigging on the fore, this was not done. In any case it would not have been nearly long enough.

The day after the collision the Old Man called all hands aft, and put it to the whole ship's company as to whether we should, in our damaged condition, take the ship in to the Falkland Islands, which were about two hundred miles distant, or carry her right home as she was.

The verdict, by a large majority, was to take the ship right home as she was; so we worked both watches all day from daylight to dark, to make her ready for the long passage that still lay ahead of us. Even though the weather was fine, working with heavy chains and wire seizing all day was cold work, and none of us was sorry when at last the job was completed, and we were standing well to the northward, and away from the ice-fields.

11

The Road Home

[The L'Avenir *was built in 1908 as a training ship for Belgium and was later owned in Finland. In 1937 she was sold to Germany to be used as a training ship. She disappeared at sea in 1938, perhaps from a collision with ice, returning from Australia with a crew of sixty, including forty cadets.*

Commander C. M. Butlin of the Royal Navy and his wife sailed as passengers on L'Avenir *in 1934 from Port Germein, South Australia, via Cape Horn, to Falmouth, England. There was at that time some interest in England in acquiring a large square-rigger as a training ship, England's last windjammer, the* Garthpool, *having been lost in 1929. Several Royal Navy officers sailed in the grain fleet to assess the practicality of such a venture, but nothing came of it. Whether Butlin sailed for that reason is not clear, but he apparently was the only one of the officers to record the experience. Butlin wrote of* L'Avenir's *wildlife, which was not unknown in other vessels.]*

As the voyage progressed, the presence of rats on board became more and more evident. When she arrived in Australia, *L'Avenir* had been fumigated in accordance with the regulations, but the efficacy of this is doubtful, considering the small number of dead rats found afterwards.

It was during the cold weather in the southern ocean that the rats began to be a nuisance, for they used to raid the galley every night. Not for food, for with over three thousand tons of wheat on board, they had no difficulty about that, but they had to get material for their nests. Any clothes left there overnight to dry were liable to have pieces eaten out of them; one almost new leather coat was ruined this way.

In the warm weather, for some reason unknown, unless it was an urge for pure seamanship, a rat would sometimes go aloft, not by the ordinary shrouds, but up the braces. It was easy enough to shake him off into the sea, unless Josephina the cat happened to appear. She was wonderful with rats and was not afraid of even the largest and fiercest of a family. Even before her kitten came off milk diet, Josephina would often be seen looking for it during the evening, emitting muffled mews, due to having a struggling rat in her mouth. She reminded one of a parent returning home from the City with a rather unwieldy toy for the young hopeful.

Towards the end of the voyage, the rats began to get above themselves. One evening, the steward's boy, the smallest person on board, was sitting reading when a rat ran up inside his trouser leg. Charlie (all steward boys answer to this) grabbed the wriggling bulge when it was above his knee, managed to crush the rat to death without getting bitten and then slipped out of his trousers as if they had caught fire.

Whenever the holds were opened for ventilation, one could see at a glance the kinds of damage that rats do to a cargo. Although there was no lack of wheat lying about, they had seemed to take pleasure in ripping open fresh bags.

We were unable to discover whether the rats obtained any fresh water, or whether they could get on without. Another problem remained unsolved; if eight rabbits consume as much pasture as one sheep, how many rats would it take to eat a human's ration?

—·—·—

[*When shipmasters were within a few hundred miles of the coast of Patagonia, they were always apprehensive of remarkable and dangerous weather that could dismast a vessel without warning. It is a phenomenon apparently unique to that region. Rex Clements described an example that assailed the* Arethusa.]

The estuary of the Plate . . . can produce its fair share of dirty weather, though compared to the terrors of the Horn it's an exhibition of mere childish petulance.

When we were somewhere off the mouth of that river we ran into a "pampero". These are hot violent winds blowing directly off the vast pampas of South America—hence their name. They are not of long duration, but of terrific intensity and almost unheralded.

This one caught us without a moment's warning. It was about one bell in the second dog watch; the ship was under t'gans'ls, and the bosun and I were yarning under the side of the house, when a black funnel-shaped cloud raced up out of the nor'west with tremendous speed.

The mate saw it coming. "Let go your t'gallant halyards," he shouted, hobbling aft to help the helmsman. The words were not out of his mouth before the squall hit us. There was a roar like a million bricks falling, and a sensation as though we were in the middle of them. I let fly the fore t'gallant halyards and Stedman scrambled over to the main on the opposite side of the deck. The barque was lying over at such an angle that he had to dig his fingers in the seams between the planks to claw his way to wind'ard. Even when the halyards were let go the masts lay over so much that the yards would not budge but stuck at the mast head.

All hands tumbled out on deck and, manning the clew-lines, hauled the yards down by main force. Stays'l halyards were let fly and hauled down and the barque righted to a more normal angle—for a few minutes her sides had been nearer the horizontal than her decks.

The wind rushed at us like a witch on a broomstick, the air grew black as pitch, and suddenly a rattling volley of thunder cracked and banged above our heads. Without hint or warning it exploded in an almighty crash. In an instant the lightning blazed out everywhere, zigzagging across the solid vault on every side and seemingly stabbing through and through the ship. For some minutes it was hell with the lid off. Then, with a hiss and a roar, down came the rain!

We worked blindly and frantically at the ropes in our efforts to quickly snug her down. The devil's tattoo of the wind, the pitchy darkness and the deafening thunder-roll overhead made concerted effort impossible and we worked as best we could individually, obeying orders when we heard them.

"Here," would come an urgent voice, blown whistling past one's ears, "bear a hand . . . this blasted clew-line!" A shape or two surged forward and a rope was shaken violently.

"You've . . . got the buntline. This . . . here!" A drenched figure bumped violently against you, a wet rope flicked your face and you grabbed and hauled madly at it.

Stumbling, cursing, half our efforts aimlessly spent, the t'gans'ls were clewed up, the stays'ls hauled down, while the fury of the squall lessened, the thunder dulled and the cataracts of rain settled down into a steady downpour.

It was still blowing great guns as we lay aloft to furl the bellowing canvas and restore the stampeding ship to some sort of peace and order. We snugged her down to tops'ls before the order was given to relieve the wheel and the watch sent below.

All that night it blew hard, and a busy time the watch had till daylight broke and the pampero sullenly blew itself out. Then we made sail and resumed the tenour of our day's work. In the brief log I always kept on my wanderings I find this encounter with a pampero summarized in the entry, "Incessant thunder and lightning; black as soot, and rain like water-spouts. Damn bad night!"

—··—·—··—

[But pamperos were not always without warning, nor were they always, as Clements noted, hot winds. Ray Wilmore on the John Ena *in 1911 found them definitely not hot.]*

SATURDAY, JULY 8 / 56TH DAY: Wind steady and strong and we're still sailing! . . . The barometer has been climbing, climbing. It is much too high to last in these latitudes and probably is but a warning. Look out for a sudden drop. We are in bad waters.

SUNDAY, JULY 9 / 57TH DAY: This day has been a real "breeder." Much too good; a glorious day for sailing; a strong, steady wind driving us along at a twelve knot clip by the taffrail log. The air is fresh and the sun almost bright enough to shed a little warmth. The barometer is still up: 31 it read at noon. That's all right if it stays up, but it is unnaturally high. Nevertheless, no matter what is in store for us, we have certainly enjoyed and are still enjoying the respite from high seas, wet decks, blustering gales, snow and ice. It has been a restful and delightful Sunday with not one disagreeable incident to mar it and no work except wheel and lookout duty.

The Old Man is a bit restless. He pops out on deck frequently, scans the horizon, sniffs the weather and disappears again into the chart room muttering "Goddam."

MONDAY, JULY 10 / 58TH DAY: The wind, the seas and the barometer are higher today. There is an ominous feeling in the air. In anticipation of things about to happen the skipper ordered sail shortened, stripping the yards down to t'gans'ls, and still we are riding fast. It looked silly to be taking in sail with wind and weather as good as it has been today. But it won't last. The Old Man knows a thing or two. His muttered "Goddams" in my opinion are more in the nature of prayers than curses.

This has been a day of tough, hard work, the first one for a long time. I have an hour left in this dog watch before going on deck again. Then it will be my trick at the wheel. It will be heavy duty tonight; I may have to ask for a lee helmsman. Time for a short rest now.

TUESDAY, JULY 11 / 59TH DAY: We're in for it! The wind, which has been steadily from the southeast, shifted suddenly to the northwest. No doubt about it, we're heading right into a pampero. The wind is terrific and the seas the highest and the most vicious of any we've had. Every sea breaks clear over the fo'c'sle head on the port side, pours down over the tops of the houses, smashes up against the break of the poop with a roar and a crash and washes out to sea over the starboard bulwarks. The bottom has all but dropped out of the barometer. The seas come over so fast that the decks don't clear at all; the waist is full to the rail all the time. The poop and fo'c'sle head are the only parts of the hull above water. Occasionally we rise and shed some of the water through the flapping seaports, only to dive in and fill again a moment later. Looking out from inside our bunkhouse, I can't figure how we are going to get our door open and keep it open long enough to crawl out over the splash board and make the bridge. It will be one man at a time: open the door, let the cabin fill, then jump. One jump to the top of the hatch, hoping for time to make a second jump; grab a bridge stanchion and swing up topside before another big wash comes aboard.

We'll pay tonight for the light weather around the Horn and the past day or two of pleasant weather.

It looks like a big night. I'm all set. In fact, the only thing I shed on coming off deck for our dog watch below was my sou'wester. I didn't even loosen the rope yarns around my neck, waist, wrist and legs. I expected we'd be called on deck before our time. We probably will be. I can hear sounds of much activity on deck, many orders shouted, much cursing, many feet pounding over the top of our bunk house. Well, I guess we can take it, and by "we" I mean men and ship.

WEDNESDAY, JULY 12 / 60TH DAY: Evening. The ship rides *[floats]*, thank God, and all hands are still aboard and able to be about, but ship and men alike are a sorry looking mess. The pampero that overtook us last evening beggars all description. Words, pen or brush could convey but a slight idea of the force and fury of the wind, the height and viciousness of the seas that swooped down upon us, seeming to fairly climb the masts and then drop to the deck, causing the ship to shudder and quake until it seemed she'd wrack herself to pieces. Today we have mostly rested, but we're still a worn and haggard crew, all but exhausted.

The wind had reached approximately full gale proportions when our watch was relieved at four bells (6 P.M.) yesterday for our dog watch below. The clouds were black and heavy and every sea we encountered came aboard.

It had turned bitterly cold and the rain that had been falling heavily all day was then driving in on us horizontally in alternating spasms of sleet, hail and snow. Every element was in its worst mood and steadily growing worse.

Royals and upper t'gans'ls were already made fast and, up to the time we turned in for our two hour rest and dinner the mate was determined to ride out the storm without further shortening of sail. Things were getting worse by the minute, however, and we had not been long below when we heard the Old Man order the starboard watch to the t'gallant halyards.

With more good luck than cleverness, I had managed to get our evening whack of bully beef and coffee, arriving safely with it by only the narrowest of margins. We ate hurriedly and in ominous silence, expectantly. Not one word passed between any of us. Now and then we glanced furtively at one another when a particularly heavy sea would crash down on top of our housing, but for the most part our eyes were glued to our mess-tins. We were waiting for what we knew must come—that bellowing voice of Mr. Carlsen—"All hands on deck." . . .

There was no waiting for the water on deck to subside and give us an even chance to get out. We literally dove out through the small opening above the door bulkhead. It was a dive to the hatch and a leap to the bridge, seemingly all in one motion, a desperate chance for each of us, but fortunately no one went awash.

If we hadn't sensed from inside the bunk house what we were into, the first instant on deck gave us a pretty full realization that we were well into the thick of what we had been talking about and expecting for days, but it was worse than the wildest imagination had conjured.

We couldn't stand upright; couldn't move except by lying down over the stout chain railing along the sides of the fore and aft bridge and dragging ourselves forward to the foremast where the starboard watch had been struggling with the lower t'gallant halyards[14] and clewlines for an hour or more without making any headway. They had been working atop the house, where the lines have been made fast ever since we entered the Roaring Forties. . . .

Little by little the fore lower t'gallant was clewed up. The starboard men had gone aloft when we took over the lines, so they were ready to get the gaskets around the bellied-out bunts of the sail and make fast as we tightened up on the clews. But it was almost like throwing a rope around a steel tank and trying to pinch it together. It took ten men to each side of the yard, but they finally made it and we moved on to the main and then to the mizzen t'gallants, our watch taking the dirty end of the job on deck in the water, starboard watch aloft. I don't know, at that, whether there was any choice of jobs. It was bad everywhere— aloft, on the bridge, at the wheel on the open poop, on deck in the icy water—cold, wet and tough all around. . . .

The wind and weather grew steadily worse.

From the t'gallants we went to the upper tops'ls. . . . It took the combined efforts of both watches on deck to clew up the sails, then all

14. Wilmore must mean here "bunt lines"; lower topgallant yards were fixed to a cap and had no halyards.

hands aloft to get the gaskets around and take in sail. At that, there were times when we all but despaired of accomplishing our purpose.

On each side of the masts the topsails belly out in three great bunts or balloons. There were twenty-two of us on the tops'l yards at one time, eighteen crew, sailmaker, two bosuns and the second mate, and we were close to an hour clewing up and snugging down each of those three sails. . . .

After a long and useless struggle, the combined efforts of all of us making not the slightest impression on the ice-coated bellies, nor getting the gaskets in an inch, Wilson went up to the yard above . . . , secured a line and lowered his two hundred and fifty pounds down to the face of the largest bunt. Holding onto the line and jumping up and down, he was able to force enough wind out of the belly to enable us, inch by inch, to draw in on the gaskets, finally getting the sail in tight to the yard. This reckless but most effective feat he performed time and again, until the upper tops'ls were made fast. . . .

It was about four o'clock yesterday afternoon when the starboard watch started taking in sail; five-thirty when our watch was called on deck. We had had our supper; the starboard watch had not. It was dawn this morning when our task was finished, every piece of canvas safely snugged down except the fore, main and mizzen lower tops'ls. They were left to give us steerage way, to hold the ship steady and, particularly, to keep the masts from wracking out of their steps. . . .

Tough as had been our struggle on deck and aloft, I doubt if the fourteen to sixteen hours of active battling put in by any of the crew had been as downright killing and bitter as those hours were to Big Martin and Kanaka Pete. They had stood the entire night through at the wheel on the open poop without relief. We on deck were moving about, working hard enough to sweat even when outwardly covered with a coating of ice. Martin and Peter could only stand and hold on, stamping their feet to keep from freezing stiff. One of them might take one hand at a time and beat it against his body to help circulation, but for the most part it required the full strength and handling of both men, (as Sails and I soon found out) to hold the ship on course.

Neither Martin nor Peter could talk when we relieved them. Their bodies, arms and legs were so benumbed and stiff that they could scarcely stand or walk. . . .

After a time a faint gray streak began to show on the northeast horizon. It showed a breaking cloud formation. The fury of the gale began to diminish. Sleet and hail no longer cut in at us. At eight bells it was almost daylight, the wind had quieted down; not even rain was falling. After the booming and zooming, howling and shrieking of the night, it seemed almost deathly still. . . . Belfast and Swede relieved Sails and me at the wheel, but by that time there was hardly need for a helmsman. The wind was practically gone; the sea had flattened out; the waist was empty of water; sails were beginning to sag and flap. It seemed incredible. The storm was gone. We had apparently blown right through it and out beyond the radius of the sphere wherein it had spent its vengeance.

—·—·—

[Once past the region of pamperos, the homeward-bound ship could expect weeks of moderate weather. The mates excelled in making sure that the good times were fully used in preparing the ship for port. American mates were particularly diligent in maintaining a smart ship. Ray Wilmore learned what that meant.]

All heads bowed and shoulders drooped this morning. Sailors' prayer books! Soon shoulders will droop more; backs and arms will ache. Holy-stoning of decks is under way—one of the most disliked tasks in a sailor's life.

A sailor's prayer book consists of two blocks of sandstone, each 12" long by 8" wide and 4" thick. Clamped together in a frame, they make a solid block 12" x 8" x 8" and weigh about thirty pounds per "book". A handle, like a mop handle, is attached to the frame. Each man is supplied with one of these instruments of torture. The deck is wet down, heavily sanded and wet again. Then, with backs bared to the tropic sun which fairly blisters the steel sides of the ship, and with the wet deck steaming in the heat, "devotions" begin. Back and forth, back and forth, the all but naked men push and pull the sandstone blocks, over and over the same swath until the grimy, weather-stained, paint and tar spotted deck is worn down to white new wood. Push and pull, push and pull, long swinging strokes in unison.

Four hours of this pushing and pulling and swaying under the sweltering sun sweats plenty of "grease" out of a man. We're all hard and tough after seventy-five days of the most demanding and grueling kind of work, but this new task seems to grind us down as well as the deck. It will take about two weeks of steady grinding to put the proper polish on the poop, main deck, fo'c'sle head and cabin floors. In a few days we will become accustomed to the new exercise and will strike a rhythmic swing. The aches and pains will ease up and it won't seem so bad.

Swinging the prayer books is not as bad, however, as the knee-blistering hand work that has to be done all around the edges of the decks and in the corners, against the houses and around the masts and all other standing parts. That work is reserved especially for those to whom the mates or bosuns want to administer punishment or discipline, or work out a personal grudge. Syd and Boston on the starboard watch and Green and Oscar on port watch will probably get most of the hand work.

I'm too tired for more scribbling tonight. Time for a couple of hours' rest.

FRIDAY, JULY 28 / 76TH DAY: Prayer books have been in full swing all day on each watch, but the going didn't seem so tough. It has rained heavily, so we have not had the sun on our backs, and the rain eliminated the necessity for frequent hauling up of buckets of water to wet down the sanded deck.

We finished the poop deck, and what a pretty job it is! The smooth, white hardwood decking fairly shines.

I got myself in the wrong with some of the old timers by putting too much enthusiasm and vigor into my work. All hands are expected to keep pace with the one who swings the longest and fastest stroke, which unconsciously and unintentionally I had been doing, so I was told in no polite words to slow down. I obliged, falling in with the slow and easy pace set by Steve Joy. Well, I guess there is no hurry. When we finish this job there will be something else. If, for example, we finish holy-stoning too long before making port, we will be aloft again with paint and tar pots. Then the decks will again get spotted and smeared and will have to be gone over again with the stones. So we might as well grind along slowly and stretch the job out at a comfortable pace....

Holy-stoning is gradually getting easier, not only because we are becoming accustomed to the labor, but the stones are wearing down and getting lighter each day.

—··—··—

[Even in the last days of sail, when only a dozen or so ships were at sea, the old vessels might sail together for a bit. Since they often left the same port in Australia at about the same time and followed the same route home, they had hopes of meeting along the way. Alex Hurst was in the Pommern *in 1939 when she came up with the* Olivebank *in the southeast trade winds. He described the meeting in* Ghosts on the Sea Line.*]*

After a comparatively short time we picked up a pillar ahead, almost like the distant view of a lighthouse, but we could make little on her. When the wind was aft she, with her bigger area of mizzen canvas, had the better of it, but when it hauled a little to the quarter we gained a bit and, by dint of judicious tacking to leeward, we came right up with her again under all plain sail in quite a fresh wind with a little water slopping aboard; the wind just free enough to fill the fore-and-afters, white caps on the seas and the tips of their swells running along the tops of the bulwarks. From our decks her three tall tiers of bellying canvas towered above us until they seemed to scrape the sky and then, although we passed close enough in all conscience, she suddenly swung in on us in a great picture of action so breathtaking in its beauty that we scarcely realized the danger of the daring manoeuver, faultlessly executed. As she came, rolling a little and magnificent in her great majesty of motion, it seemed that her raking bowsprit must tear into our spanker, but as we dipped so she scended, and our helmsman still swears that the shark's tail at the end of that great steel spike passed over his head before she dropped astern, throwing glittering sprays all the length of her and her bow wave running towards us with a steady roar from the teeth of her cutwater which impinged on all our ears as we stood spellbound, beholding a sight of such symmetry given to few men in our generation. Only belatedly did we wonder if it was not instead some unavoidable fate bearing down on us, because we were too drunk with the scene to appreciate its enormity. In swinging down the wind that ship had quickly increased her speed and thus carried her way until she had all but rammed us in a piece of seamanship which, if it left no margin for error, was certainly as consummate as it was spectacular.

The wind increased as the day wore on, and the clouds rolled away while the two four-posters went snoring through the seas at some thirteen knots in ideal deep sea sailing conditions, for the wind was as strong as it could be without knocking up too much sea. They sped on like two souls possessed, with bow waves running out ahead and wide stretches of foam down each side which merged with the wake to extend as far astern as the eye could reach. White water spurted from the scuppers and sprays flew over their weather rails; while their diving bows immersed the fair ladies who were their figureheads in baths of sparkling foam, as they danced on over the wrath of the sea, under the urgent and steady curves of the headsails.

As I observed this perfect scene from the end of our bowsprit, the headsails straining at their hanks above me and the crash of the bow wave drowning all other sound, so I beheld on the quarter that other ship which still kept company, heeling well over, her black sides wet with the spray that sparkled and glistened in the sun until its golden ball dipped into the western sea to tinge those curving sails with pink before they were hidden in the night. After an hour or so, a full moon picked her up as a bright square in the darkness, ever dropping further astern.

—·—·—

[Rarely would a sailor see his own ship under sail, but the calms of the mid Atlantic on a quiet Sunday afternoon might offer a chance to launch a small boat and row off a bit to admire a ship. Alan Villiers, as part owner of the Parma, would take particular pride in that great bark.]

In the calm we put out a boat and pull around old Parma. How big she is! Used for so long to her decks and her rigging, she seems like a strange ship from outside. She is big, and black, and rusty; as she lifts in the swells she shows the red boot-topping gone from her underside and the white anti-fouling of the nitrate carrier showing through. There are few barnacles as yet; the Good Hope way would have brought more.

She backs and fills; the sails slat and fill again; the sea gurgles round cutwater and stern with that sickening, bath-draining sound that tells of stayed progress. She has no headway—perhaps ten yards in ten minutes. Yet she does not look out of place; she does not look like a dead thing upon a dead ocean. She is having a little rest which she has very well earned. Good old Parma! She has done well for us to bring us here—how deeply she is laden!—and she is stout and strong, or she would never have stood up again from that battering in the trough of the Cape Horn sea. . . . It is difficult to believe that this is the ship that went through those violent gales of April, that rolled her sides beneath the seas on so many occasions, that pooped, and threw her focs'l head into the water. We put a little dinghy out, about twelve feet long, with room in it for four persons. In such a craft, passing by the *Parma*'s she looks like the *Majestic*.

We pull all round her, with one at the oars. The Old Man wants to look at his vessel. . . . Christiansen . . . bails for his life; the dinghy leaks badly and is by no means the ideal vessel for pulling round the North Atlantic. We are safe enough; the calm will last. If it does not they can easily pick us up from the ship.

The sea, so small from the big vessel, is huge to us now; we fall in the troughs and see nothing of our *Parma* but her rigging, only a ship's length away.

We are stirred by the beauty of the ship, just lying there in the calm, and we lie there on the oars and look at her while she drifts slowly on. She is very big and her masts are not high. She is not a clipper. She is a big hard-working economic windjammer, sails' last effort against steam—big in the hull, to carry much; small in the rig to carry it economically; fine-lined to sail reasonably; rigged with chain and wire for strength. But she has loveliness and grace; she follows nobly in the traditions of the best of sail, and blends perfectly into the peace of her surroundings. From for'ard and aft she is especially beautiful, where one does not notice the comparative shortness of the masts; she looks strong and powerful, as she is. Her bow is good and she looks an honest vessel, as indeed she is—a steady worker, an honest old deliverer of heavy cargoes, a staunch toiler of the sea world.

We watch the mastheads rolling quietly against the clouds, the bows lifting gently on the swells that send our dinghy tossing about, the long low sides of her—high to us now—gently rising and falling in the sea's slow breathing. We delight in the symmetry of her sails, the power of her upstanding masts, the ordered maze of her rigging. We see the browned figures of boys hanging over her rails, and take in such details as the red lead on the midship house, the blankets hanging to air on the railing of the flying bridge along the length of her. . . . Why is a sailing ship so beautiful? She is only masts and yards, and sails and hull—a steel hull and steel masts, and sails sewn from canvas. A bolt of canvas is not beautiful, nor is a gaunt steel yard lying in a dock; steel plates to rivet on to a ship's side are bare and ugly. Yet this creation from them all has a queer beauty which appeals to all men who see it— the *Baronessa*'s firemen no less than the *Hermonides*' master, the passengers of steamships and the dwellers of the shore.

"I like beautiful things—lovely women and tall sailing ships, sunsets and the wisps of smoke rising from the farmer's home upon some quiet countryside," writes a man in a magazine who probably never saw a vessel under canvas. The pictures of them appeal to him. I look up at the masts and yards from the boat; the man is right. There is such a grace and quiet loveliness about this ship as we like to think there is about beautiful women. Everything about her matches perfectly; her curves, her angles, her posture upon the water, the set of masts and yards, until the whole is a creation of symmetrical loveliness that the mind is better for the eye's beholding. She looks restful (not always!), faithful, true—demanding only understanding.

—··—··—

[The Tusitala *was a handsome full-rigged ship and the last commercial square-rigger under the American flag. In the late 1920s, she sailed between New York and Hawaii in the trade much like that of* John Ena, *carrying fertilizers to the islands and raw sugar home again. In her last years, she was commanded by Captain James P. Barker, who had earlier been master of the* British Isles *of which W. H. S. Jones wrote in these extracts. Captain Barker's son, Roland, sailed before the mast in the U.S. Merchant Marine and was third mate on* Tusitala *in 1928. He recorded an extraordinary natural occurrence at sea on her way home to New York.]*

The wind fell away again, and the afternoon found us floating on an unrippled sea. Mr. Hughes followed Jansen and me at eight bells—

4 o'clock—but instead of going below, we lingered on the poop, our attention arrested by a slow expanding discoloration in the sky away in the direction of Yucatan. I remember Mr. Hughes knocking his pipe out against the poop rail and hearing the brief hiss of the ashes meeting the still water. The mate frowned as he put the pipe in his pocket and strode across the poop toward the open cabin skylight.

"Captain," he called, "looks like a squall making up in the nor'west, sir."

My father hastened on deck and cast a sweeping glance all around the horizon.

"That's odd," he muttered. "The aneroid's steady." Then "all hands on deck," he roared. "Haul the fores'l up!"

The mains'l and cro'jik had long since been clewed up and left hanging in the bunts, for since noon not a catspaw had rippled the oily surface of the deep.

Jansen repeated the order as I followed him forward. With all hands on the job, we let go the fore tack and sheet and had the fores'l snugged up the yard in less than five minutes. No sooner had Jansen ordered, "Aloft and furl!" when Mr. Hughes called from the poop, "Get the t'gans'ls and royals off her. Look alive for'ard, there!"

Half an hour later, when the furled canvas had been marled to the yards and the men were back on deck, I returned aft. On the poop, the man at the wheel stood tense, expectant, his hands tight on the spokes. Mr. Hughes, I noticed, alternated his glances between the captain and the phenomenon that now blotched a portion of the western sky. He was clearly apprehensive, seeking some reassurance. My own sensations were curious, indefinable; it was as though something weird and strange, something that befalls men once in a thousand years, was about to happen.

My father raised his binoculars and stared through them across the sea. Suddenly his voice startled us:

"Damned queer! I don't know what to make of it!"

The cloud, writhing and twisting at the edges, had cast a shadow on the sea, yet the water remained serene, with not a single telltale white-cap visible. A sound, faint yet vast, and ever growing in volume, seemed to fill our world like a fluttering of millions of leaves. The air tremored with a soft vibration—movement, not of wind, which had been thrown up and outward from somewhere in the quivering jungles of distant Yucatan. Even *Tusitala* seemed to sense it. She rolled slightly, her rudder creaking harshly on its gudgeons and the yards aloft jerked uneasily at goosenecks and parrels.

I moved to the rail where my father stood, a glow of excitement in his eyes. Then, as the cloud swept across the sun, he wheeled suddenly and called out: "Watch your faces, men—your eyes!" There was passion in his voice, abrupt awareness of this manifestation of the earth's vibrating life.

"Swallows, by God! Millions of them!"

With a roar of countless fluttering wings the birds were upon us.

Throughout the confusion of the next few seconds, when men shouted with excitement as they sought to ward off the incredible multitude, the captain's movements, I remember clearly, were deliberate, steady, as though impelled by a benevolence, an apparent desire to destroy not a single one of the invaders of our hitherto peaceful domain. It was like a dream but the whirling force, hesitating briefly before speeding onward, evidenced the reality of frantic things—a vast migration bent on self-preservation, perhaps escape from some un-known terror beyond the western horizon.

Fast as the wind they came and as suddenly sped onward; but with the lifting of their shadow, it could be seen that thousands of them, doubtless too exhausted to carry on, had stayed behind. Aloft, the yards and rigging were black with them. Their dead by the hundreds littered the decks. Others, merely stunned by having flown against our tophamper, sought refuge in the scuppers and behind our running gear coiled on the fiferails at the foot of the masts. They entered the port and starboard foc's'ls, the carpenter's shop, the donkey room and, ignoring the astonished Augustine, perched on the shelves in the galley.

My father said that in all his years at sea he had never seen anything like it. He gave an order to Mr. Hughes and presently members of the watch were plying deck brooms, sweeping the dead into feathery piles, shoveling them overboard, where they floated pathetically on the still water—food for sharks that might be lurking astern.

The resting swallows remained with us, gathering strength for a renewed flight into the unknown. Then, with the tropical darkness, wind came, faintly at first. The ship stirred, and from high aloft came the sound of fluttering wings. Occasionally little bodies plummeted down to strike the hard pine decks, or to fall almost noiselessly into the sea. Attracted by the glow of the binnacle light which illuminated the bronzed, set face of the helmsman, a swallow fluttered out of the darkness, hovered for a moment over the wheel, then settled on the man's shoulder.

"There's a breeze at last, mister," my father said, as the mate loomed beside him. "Loose the courses! Set everything, sir!" He had spoken quietly, as though regretting the necessity of noise and commotion aloft; but as the servant of a commercial world, he was obliged to grasp every opportunity afforded by the wind gods. . . .

Dawn found *Tusitala* slipping through the Caribbean at six knots with a fresh breeze abeam. During the dark night watches many of the swallows had resumed their journey; hundreds of them, fatigued and helpless, had fallen to their death on the decks to be swept overboard through the scuppers when the crew washed down. Scores of others, obviously fully recovered, had elected to bear us company.

At breakfast that morning an inquisitive band of them startled and delighted the afterguard by flying through the open portholes into the messroom, where they fluttered and twittered excitedly about us, came to rest on our heads and shoulders and, gaining confidence, finally explored our victuals on the table.

Completely devoid of fear, they perched on the edges of our plates, pecking away with obvious satisfaction and boundless joy at bread and cereal and corned beef hash. One, less cautious, landed feet first in the butter dish, another tugged at a piece of toast, trying desperately to share it with the captain. . . .

As the days went by, the swallows departed in small groups, until at last only a few dozen remained. The lingerers continued to share our meals with boisterous enthusiasm, swooping down from aloft and through the portholes in answer to the pealing of the hand bell wielded by Lenahan. They became very tame, an intimate part of our little world. Apparently, however, they were still afflicted by some strange malady, for each dawn revealed more of their dead about the decks.

Finally only six remained—pathetic little things constantly seeking solace and refuge in human kindness. A low, enticing whistle from any man aboard would bring them swooping down from high amid the shadowy sails to take fly or cockroach from between thumb and forefinger.

Still green is my memory of the day—November 19—when I discovered that all but one had left us forever. Responding to my whistled summons, the last of the swallows flew toward me, not from somewhere high on the mainmast, but from the mizzen hatch a few feet away. As it perched on my wrist, head dropping, eyes half closed, its talons cool and tight on my flesh, I heard the captain's voice:

"You'd better take it below, out of the rain."

That afternoon a gale came out of the nor'west, smiting us hard. . . .

In my cabin, when I came down from aloft, the dim glow of my desk lamp revealed something dark against the whiteness of my pillow—the lifeless body of the last swallow.

—·—·—

[The Herzogin Cecilie *met the* C. B. Pedersen, *a Swedish four-masted bark, near the equator in 1928. The crews exchanged visits in the calm of the doldrums, and Alan Villiers described what happened when a squall came up while seamen of the* C. B. Pedersen *were on board the Duchess.]*

One of those heavy rain-squalls that had been hovering around the horizon earlier suddenly whipped down upon us, and for an hour or two it looked as if it were quite on the cards that we would have to take the captain, the chief mate, and the seven boys of *C. B. Pedersen* on with us to Falmouth. The wind howled, the sea rose, and the black rain shut out the other ship from our view. Seas came over the fore-deck; the ship lay over heavily and snored through the water; and the wind hauled around the compass with surprising rapidity.

The whole thing happened with startling suddenness. We had been slipping along very slowly before a gentle southerly air that would have taken a year to blow us to Falmouth, with no suggestion that the wind was going to get fierce all of a sudden, or do anything at all. There were those rain-squalls knocking about, of course, and we were very near the Line, where anything might happen. But the rain-squalls had been there two days and seemed to have no intention of making our closer acquaintance; and those of them that had reached us before had never had a kick in them. The one that jumped on us from nowhere that bright Sunday morning, however, had kick enough for six.

It began by catching us flat aback, which wasn't a pleasant beginning, by any means. Still, it wasn't so strong then and the rain was not so heavy. We rushed to haul up the cro'jack and mains'l and to get the yards around, but while we worked the squall worked too, and quickly reached a velocity that was dangerous. Every sail in the ship was flat aback; driving rain continually blocked the horizon; and we sailed backwards towards Cape Horn.

It was all hands on deck then, with a rush, and the boys from *C. B. Pedersen* came, too. We were glad of them! It would have been a job for us, even with all hands on deck, to get the eighteen heavy yards around with the wind howling against them the wrong way, and all the fore-and-afters shifted over, and the mains'l and cro'jack hauled up, and everything else done that had to be done to get the ship in order. The wind increased steadily. We thought it was just a squall, that would go as fast as it had come. But it wasn't, and it didn't go. The wind swung eight points in as many seconds after we had got the yards around and caught us all aback again. What could we do, with a wind like that? We wore ship then faster than we had ever done before. It was a wild scene, that, with the tropic rain falling solidly on the boys' faces as they ran about the deck, bawling their sailors' shouts as they tramped the braces, hauled on the clewlines and on downhauls, and the ship lying over until her lee rail smoked though the water and it was hard to stand on deck, and *C. B. Pedersen*—where?

That was the question. Aft our captain stood in the lee of the big charthouse with the captain and the first mate of the Swede, peering into the murk for a glimpse of the other ship. She had been upon our lee side when last we saw her; when the wind came we were too busy to look. With a wind like that, that must have caught her aback exactly as it did us, it would be fatally easy for the ships to drift miles apart in half an hour; indeed, it was quite within the bounds of possibility that by the time the horizon cleared neither ship would be visible to the other. We were doing fourteen knots, though we had the mains'l and cro'jack off her and many of the fore-and-afters in. It was a strange position in which we found ourselves, with the captain, the mate and half the focs'l of another ship on board; not knowing where the other ship was! It would be stranger still if we had to take them on.

When the ship was around, all hands, as thoroughly wet as they possibly could be, stationed themselves around the rail and searched through wind and rain for *C. B. Pedersen*. The captain and the mate from her were the coolest men aboard. Captain Dahlstrom had left his second mate in charge—he had no cause to suspect a sudden wind like that—and from the quiet way in which he took things he must have had perfect confidence in the ability of his junior officer. He peered steadily through the murk in the direction in which he thought his ship would appear, keeping his eyes fixed upon that place with quiet confidence, serenely unperturbed by the rain that smashed into his face and ruined his pith helmet, heedless of the wind that howled around him.

His confidence and his trust were rewarded, for he was the first to see, dimly through the driving rain, the blurred outline of his ship hurtling along not half a mile from us. Only for an instant he saw her; then the rain shut her out again.

The wind, still up to its mad tricks, had hauled around again then, though this time it didn't catch us aback. Braced hard by the wind, we were flying through the water back for Cape Horn. The compass showed that our course was south by east. We couldn't have that!

And yet we couldn't put about either, and bear away from *C. B. Pedersen* with half her crew aboard. We couldn't put about if she didn't know. We couldn't just go away and leave her there. What was to be done? The wind was stronger than ever; we were losing ground with amazing rapidity in a place where we least wanted to lose it and where, in all probability, it would be most difficult to get it back; we were sailing for Cape Horn when we should have been going across the Equator. The instant that we had seen *C. B. Pedersen* had shown us the second mate was about his business, with the small crew that was left aboard. The mains'l and cro'jack were hauled up, and he was clewing up the royals.

A bunch of signal flags ascended to our peak, and blew out in the rain. "I shall wear ship," they said. The second mate would know that he must wear ship, too. But could he see those signals? Seeing that we couldn't even see his ship, it was hardly likely. The only thing that we could do was to hang on until we saw him again sufficiently clearly to be sure that he could read the signals.

Anxiously we gazed into the rain again. All this time *C. B. Peder-*

sen's life boat had been towing alongside, going at a great bat with the spray flying over it. In the instant that the squall had come, seeing the danger of the boat being smashed to pieces if it remained untended there, one of the boys from *C. B. Pedersen* and an apprentice of ours slipped over the side and down into it. Then they let go the stern line and allowed the boat, fast now only ahead, to swing out wide. Then *C. B. Pedersen*'s boy sat at the tiller to guide her off and our apprentice stood ever ready to fend her off with a boathook. They must have had a great view of us driving through the water; they said it was magnificent, afterwards.

At length we saw *C. B. Pedersen*, more clearly this time, driving along on the strong wind in the same relative position as she was before, and the instant that we saw her the answering pennant flew to her peak. A smart officer, that second mate.

We wasted no more time then. So long as *C. B. Pedersen* was with us we must trust to a chance coming later for her people to get back aboard, though the wind then showed no signs of diminishing. It was blowing too hard to tack, so we wore her around. We raced those braces along the deck as we never had before, and everything went with a great swing. We had her around in less than a quarter of an hour, and when she was going course again—towards the Equator instead of Cape Horn—the wind dropped considerably though the rain was still with us. Not long afterwards the rain had cleared sufficiently for us to keep the other ship constantly in sight, and the wind dropped back to little more than nothing. Our anxiety was over.

It was dinner time then, and before they returned to their own vessel our visitors joined us at our fare of sweet soup and cooked preserved meat. There was plenty for all, and it was a memorable Sunday dinner. It had been a memorable morning, too.

A little after 1 o'clock both wind and rain had gone completely, and to the accompaniment of our music and our cheers the life boat set out again. It had been only a doldrum squall, after all, though it had been long enough and hard enough, in the circumstances, to cause us all some anxious moments.

—·—·—·—

[There were times and circumstances when it was not possible to change direction by "tacking" a square-rigger. The alternative was to "wear ship," turning away from the wind rather than into the wind, which was a more certain and often safer method of going about, but took more sea room. The Herzogin Cecilie *and* C. B. Pedersen *each "wore" ship twice during that squall to change their directions. Holger Thesleff described the process of wearing the* Passat.*]*

First she is made "ready to go about": the topgallant braces are belayed with a "by the wind" hitch to prevent their running out when they are cast loose. The lazy *[slack]* staysail sheets are made clear to be hauled in. The spankers and jigger-topsail are taken in, and the spanker boom sheeted amidships. Mainsail and crojack are clewed up, and you see that the sheets and clew lines are running clear. Some men from either watch are stationed on the fo'c'sle head to see to the head sails and the fore tack. Then the remainder of the starboard watch go to the mizzen-braces and of the port watch to the main-braces.

At an order from the Skipper the helmsman puts the wheel hard up *[turns the wheel so that the bow turns away from the wind]*, and as the ship falls away from the wind, you haul the mizzen- and main-braces until the yards are square across the ship. Meanwhile the men on the fo'c'sle head shift the jibs over the stays. When the mizzen- and main-yards are more or less at right angles to the mast you belay the braces provisionally, the starboard watch runs to the fore-sheet on the fore-deck and the port watch to the fore-braces on the midships deck. Then, the foreyards have to be swung round as quickly as possible, and the Skipper at the wheel sees that the ship does not luff too quickly.

You then sheet the foresail and take down the tack for the new tack. Before the wind is on the bow, the watches must dash back to the mizzen- and main-braces on the poop and the after deck to haul them close up as well. Usually there is not time for the staysails and they have to be left until after the bracing.

All that done, the free watch goes below and the watch on deck is left to see to the rest. The staysail sheets, which in the hurry were left provisionally belayed, are hauled close and the fore-sheet and tack likewise. The yards are trimmed better for the new tack. The mainsail and crojack are set again. The spanker boom is hauled out to leeward and the two spankers and the gaff-topsail set again. Then, while the loose ends are being cleared up, the helmsman stabilizes the ship on her new tack.

—·—·—

[The tedious and frustrating doldrums at the equator had to be crossed twice in every circumnavigation. Ken Attiwill captured the effects of the doldrums on the mood and temper of the crew of the Archibald Russell, *unrelieved by the novelty of ship visiting.]*

After another glaring day of doldrums we are rewarded with a dish of blah, in which porridge and rice and mouldy carrots play important parts. It puts us in the mood we want. The deputation follows immediately on the changing of the watch. The captain is on the poop. Nils is spokesman. He addresses the poop in Swedish.

"We would speak with the captain."

The skipper comes to the railing and waits, smoking a cigarette. Nils wastes no words.

"Do you think this is enough for a man's stomach after a hard day's work?" he shouts, brandishing a bilious-looking exhibit.

"Yes," replies the Old Man promptly.

"Well, we don't," retorts Nils.

The Skipper shows some interest.

"What are you going to do about it, then?"

"We go hungry. No man can eat this," Nils snorts.

"Well?"

"And the salt meat stinks from here to hell," pursues Nils, warming to his subject, although rather baffled by the skipper's attitude.

"That's a goddam lie!" shouts the captain.

"Is it a goddam lie?" Nils turns to the crew.

"Nej!" roars Erik, none the less enthusiastically for his not having been invited to do so. We had rehearsed this part differently.

"We cannot work all day with this," Nils exclaims.

"You bloody well will work with it. Anybody who wants to argue about that can come up here." The skipper adopts a bellicose attitude. "I am taking full responsibility for the food you get. Gå ur min åsyn!" *[get out of my sight]*.

We do as bidden, and go out of his sight. There is nothing else to do. The skipper is a big, powerful man, with forearms that bulge and ripple with brawny muscle. . . . Nobody quite feels like going up on the poop to carry on the argument with him. But although we are cowed our discontent is undiminished. There is good reason for our complaint. The dish objected to actually is a mixture of the morning's left-over porridge, the rice that remained from lunch, a few tasteless potatoes and carrots, and several enigmas. The taste is standardized by the addition of three times too much sugar. The Scandinavians have a sweet tooth, but none of the men on our ship, rough as they are, disguise their hostility to the infamous dish of blah.

It is no idle talk that the food is bad. Apart from the bread, margarine, and coffee, there is nothing that really justifies ordinary wear and tear on our jaws. London *[Jack London, a nickname for a crew member; not the famous author]* and I have threatened the steward until he allows us to go to the *kabyss [galley]* and toast our bread on the hot oven face. Apart from the scattered nibblings, I am holding body and soul together solely on toast and coffee—four thick slices of burnt bread each meal. The meat I simply cannot eat. Acute hunger has forced me to try, but it has only resulted in those painful, horrible little salt-meat boils. The fish is tasteless and safe, but stinks so strongly of ammonia that it gives me no appetite whatever. Sometimes we have pancakes which are tasty but not very sustaining. At lunch one day I fortify myself a little with two potatoes mashed with my margarine. But this is a strain on the margarine. The steward still refuses to give us more than the allotted weekly rations of margarine and sugar. With sugar for the pancakes, and toast every meal, it takes as much as I can do to carry on. Useless to plead hunger to the steward. "I ain't got it" is his only reply. I long for a plain stew and jam. We never get stew, and have had jam twice—a spoonful for each man to go with his Easter pancakes away back in the Roaring Forties. Although only in his early twenties, this fat Finnish steward is a big fellow with a pig of a temper. He sees the point of an argument only when it is demonstrated with the aid of a capstan-bar or a rope with a heavy wood block tied to the end of it. . . .

In these doldrums we are finding more than ever the extreme boredom of our long isolation. After all, we are no more than high-spirited youngsters, and it is becoming increasingly difficult for us to grin and bear it. We are already the most unreasoning, unreasonable, childish, selfish, ill-tempered, cantankerous, dirty, slovenly, greedy body of fellows anybody could wish to see assembled at once. Most of our resilience was washed away or frozen stiff away down south, and what little remains is steadily melting in the tropics. More than ever the slightest incident assumes grave importance in our eyes. We see offense in everything, and many of us are on snarling terms.

The Frog accused Jack London of taking as long as he could to cut himself a slice of bread, thereby impeding the progress of the Frog's meal. They fought bitterly about it, until London made the Frog's nose bleed and half-stunned him with a thwack on the ear.

Yervy accused somebody of hiding a tin of condensed milk in his chest with intent to defraud the others. The accusation led to a brawl with knives until the others separated the duellists.

"The boys won't stand a thief," Bertil told me when we were discussing it over coffee." Once, when I was in another ship, one of the boys stole another's money from his chest. The crew found him out and went to the Old Man and asked to be allowed to deal with him as they thought fit. The Old Man said they could, and so the boys tied him to a rope and threw him overboard and kept him there for half an hour. The water was pretty cold, and the thief was half-dead before they hauled him inside again.

"Bawstead don't no steal more," suggested Gosta, with his mouth full of stolen officers' biscuits.

The Last Leg

12

[Ships scantily provisioned and long delayed in the doldrums could be very short of food, such as it was, as they entered the North Atlantic, the last quarter of their voyages. The crews and officers often fished when weather permitted, usually for bonito, if there were any about, but fish are naturally scarce in the infertile waters of the doldrums. A vessel moving at any speed, also, was unlikely to catch fish. And in the heat of those latitudes any fish caught could not be preserved as a reserve for lean times. Alan Villiers experienced hunger in 1929 on the tedious voyage of the Grace Harwar.*]*

We were now becalmed. We were still two thousand miles from Falmouth; the few items of food we still had—a few potatoes, some beans, and one or two other small things—were insufficient for another week. We had prospects of being another month at sea. The outlook was not bright, though we still carried on with our daily tasks and got the ship ready to come into port. There was more trouble with the second mate who broke down again. We were pretty despondent about it all. And there was always the leak.

The steamers became thicker. We saw their lights on the horizon at night. We tried to Morse some of them, but we had so weak a light that they could not read what we said. It is doubtful if some of them were aware, even, of the fact we were attempting to signal. One was a big passenger steamer, French, by the look of her. It was in the evening, hazy. She quite likely did not see us. She was long way off; her smoke betrayed her to us, but our sails would blend with the haze and make us most difficult to pick out. The twilight was the worst light, both for lookouts and signallers.

We were 123 days out before we had assistance. On the night of that day—Sunday, August 18, 1929—we picked up the lights of a steamer coming from ahead. We signalled her with the Morse as soon as she was near enough. She saw! She answered! She changed her course and came nearer.

It was all hands on deck immediately. We backed the mainyard, swung out the port life boat, hastily manned, and with the Captain himself at the tiller, set off for the strange steamer which had come to a stop about a mile off, waiting for us. It was pitch dark. There was a moon, but it was obscured by heavy clouds. It was a curious sensation, being out on the North Atlantic in a life boat at night. There was a fair swell, and a little rain began to drop. There was not much wind just then. The ship, a curious and romantic shape looming out of the night with her towers of sails black against the sky and the white half-round of her poop gleaming wet in the rain, slipped back into the blackness which closed around her. The steamer flashed a searchlight on the sea, now and again, both to search for us and to guide us. We pulled steadily, not noticing the distance. We came closer, and saw the huge bulk of the steamer, strangely silent with her engines stopped, dipping and falling in the swell above us. They had a line down, right round their ship, to make our coming alongside easy. We came to the foot of the rope ladder and grabbed the line. The steamer's people lined her decks. It was so dark that we could not see her name.

They had everything ready for us. They lowered food into the boat, and threw us tobacco and newspapers. They gave us a case of milk, two cases of preserved meat, a sack of sugar, several sacks of vegetables, and half the carcass of a cow. They threw us down all the spare tobacco they had, and in the intervals shouted down to us something of themselves, while we shouted in reply something about us. They were the Scottish steamer *Orangeleaf,* they said, Invergordon to Trinidad, to load bitumen for British roads. Our Captain clambered aboard up the rope ladder; no one else went. A fireman came down and gave us a huge cake which the cook had baked for the stokehold gang that day, being Sunday. We accepted it gratefully, aware that cakes probably did not often come those firemen's way. We each ate a small piece of it; the rest we kept for shipmates still aboard. We asked the steamer's people if they knew anything of the other sailing ships in the wheat race from Australia. They didn't know much. They told us that the *Herzogin Cecilie* had been over a hundred days but had beaten the *Beatrice* again. They didn't seem to know any of the other ships.

We were not alongside long. The Captain came down the ladder again, and the food was all stowed into the boat in a few moments. We prepared to cast off and pull back to the *Grace Harwar* again, now a mile and a half or more. It had breezed up a little and was raining more heavily. The boat was well loaded; it was a long pull.

A sonorous voice called down from the steamer's bridge to hang on to the line and swing out from the ship's side a bit; they would tow us back. That was grand. We swung out, riding the swells abreast of the steamer, while her engines began to turn and we set slowly off together for our old full-rigged ship. Was there ever such a tow at sea? A four-thousand ton steamer, upon her voyage of prosaic trade, going out of her way to tow the tiny life boat of a full-rigged ship across a mile and a half or so of North Atlantic ocean in the middle of a rainy night back from a borrowing excursion! It was a fine thought of the steamship's captain; they towed us right to the counter of our old full-rigger, leaving us under her very stern, as neatly as if they had been a motor boat and not a big steamer, unused to such manoeuvres. They flashed their searchlight on the side of the ship to show us the way; a moment or two they stayed there, within a biscuit's throw of the sailing ship, while we slipped around her counter and came to the boat falls hanging over the side. Then with cheers and encouraging blasts on their siren, they were off once more upon their voyage. Twenty minutes later there was nothing of the steamer to be seen.

"Pleasant voyage!" the sonorous voice had called from the bridge as the *Orangeleaf* slowly swung under our stern, getting under way again.

We shouted back something in return, and though it was almost midnight when we were back aboard our own ship, the cook got a fire going straight away and we fell to on that beef and made some coffee with sugar and milk in it—luxury of luxuries!

I had the midnight wheel, when the cooking was done. I took a handful of the beef and a mug of coffee to the wheel with me. It was fine to have something to eat again, and the name of the *Orangeleaf* was blessed among us.

— · — · —

[After passing through the doldrums, the fine sailing weather of the north-east trade winds could restore the spirits of the crew and gave life back to the ship and a promise of a rapid arrival in port. Even our chronic grumbler, Ken Attiwill, became inured, with time and experience, to the realities of life on the Archibald Russell *and perhaps in the trade winds began to enjoy himself, if only a little.]*

Steering seems greater fun now, and I am growing to like the job. There is a thrill in holding the ship straight with a fair sea running and the yards close-hauled, steering without the compass and with only a faint tremor in the upper windward corners of the sails to act as a guide to the course. If you go too close to the wind it may blow back into the sails and stop the ship or turn her about, and if you don't go close enough to the wind, you are liable to lose valuable speed. It is an acquired trick—difficult to seize when the skipper stands beside you doing nothing beyond asking you, in the name of the deity, if you can't keep her full; plead with you, for the sake of the deity, to leave out some of the curves; threaten you, before the sight of the deity, with strangulation if you don't bloodywell ease her over; and leave you, to the mercy of the deity, unhappy in the knowledge that a poor bloody worm would wriggle to death trying to follow you.

But it is something different to the other work of the ship. That requires only brawn, but steering requires a mixture of brawn and brain. It is, to my mind, the only real remaining shred of romance about the old romantic windjammer. . . .

Time passes quickly . . . the endeavour to keep the ship straight, the alluring sight of the bounding waves outside, and the occasional glimpses of the hopeful northern horizon as the ship plunges forward and the sails rise and belly before the strong breeze. Romance is coming to the ship as the end approaches. There is a steady list of some fifteen degrees to port and the northeast trade grows in strength. We are logging two hundred miles a day or more. Waves are encroaching on the decks again, and we are putting on more clothes and adding our half-forgotten oilskins and laughing at the waves.

Northward through the north Atlantic, spreading the sea into white foam by day and showering phosphorescence by night as our blunt bows cut steadily through. Freshness in the air, the sun on high—fragrance of England in blossom time. Northward to Europe! Homeward bound! . . .

—·—·—

[Even the most efficient of mates, driving the crew under the pressure of time to complete the refurbishment of the ship, could be frustrated by the capriciousness of fate, as W. H. S. Jones observed.]

By the time we were across the Equator the furbishing of the ship was almost finished. The masts, yards, deck-houses and boats had been painted, the rigging blacked down, the teakwood rails and other brightwork varnished, and the decks holystoned as white as snow. All that remained to be done was to paint the bulwarks. This task now occupied the watch on deck, after we had passed through the pully-hauly of the Doldrums and picked up the N.E. trades.

Only one of our pigs, taken on at Tacoma, remained alive. The others had met their fate in succession at intervals, with the usual piercing screams emitted by hogs when they perceive the butcher's intention to convert them into pork. The ship's cook, known in sailing-ship parlance as the "Doctor", had the task of despatching the hogs to their doom, an operation performed by him with a long knife, while two seamen assisted to hold the victim, with his trotters tied.

The sole survivor was a large but active hog, which roamed the decks at will, and was something of a pet to the men forward, as he promenaded, released from his sty for exercise, and poked his snout with little grunts into all the nooks and corners, for ever hopeful of finding something more than his rations to eat.

Only the Doctor disliked Porky the Pig, who was constantly grunting over the door-sill of the galley, looking for scraps in the most likely place to find some. To get rid of him the Doctor had a playful habit of dropping a few spots of hot water on his back.

One afternoon, in the Mate's watch, the men were at work, spread out at intervals along the snow-white deck, painting the bulwarks. It was a sultry tropical day. Each man had his pot of paint standing on a square of canvas on the deck near where he was painting. The Doctor was sitting on the water-barrel, inside the galley door, reading a Charles Garvice. Porky the Pig as usual was roaming around on deck. He poked his head into the galley door and grunted, just as the Doctor had reached a thrilling incident in the romance.

Annoyed at being disturbed, the Doctor reached for a dipper, and dropped a splash of boiling water on the pig's back.

With a squeal of rage and pain, Porky took off at full gallop along the deck on the starboard side. In his wild career, before the sailors had time to think, he overturned five pots of paint, rolling them on their sides, to spill the paint far and wide over the white holystoned planks.

"Catch him! Head him off! Grab him!" yelled the sailors, too late, as the infuriated swine continued his career around the after-hatch and along the deck on the port side, dripping paint and leaving his hoof-prints in paint there also.

Hearing the commotion, I put my head outside the cabin door just as the Mate clumped down the poop-ladder and saw the full extent of the damage. For a moment, but only a moment, he was speechless. Then he spat to leeward over the rail, raised his hands, with clenched fists above his head, and gave expression to one of the choicest specimens of nautical invective it has been my privilege to hear.

"God almighty!" he said, piously. "Just look at the havoc done by that bloated carcass of mobile ham, at the instigation of an imbecile spud-barber!"

The Old Man came out on deck, and, instantly sizing up the situation and its further possibilities, bawled out: "Catch the damn pig! Grab him by the hind legs! Hitch a rope round his neck!"

Easier said than done, as catching a pig is not part of a sailor's routine. From all directions the seamen converged on Porky, who had his brief moments of triumph, as he dodged between their legs and wriggled out of their grasp, squealing as their yells and dives at him increased his fright. At last he was secured and trussed up. His flanks and legs were still dripping paint.

As no one could think of any effective way of cleaning the paint off him, he breathed his last that evening.

Next day, over a dinner of roast pork, the Mate admitted that he was not a bad animal after all. The men who had to get down on their hunkers to holystone the decks, until all the paint-patches were cleaned up, could also derive whatever satisfaction was possible from the last issue of fresh pork on that voyage.

—·—·—

[After a vessel bound for Europe passed through the northeast trade winds, she came to the westerlies of the northern hemisphere. Frederick William Wallace sailed across the North Atlantic as a passenger in 1920 on the Rus-

sian ship Grand Duchess Maria Nikolaevna. *The* Grand Duchess *originally had been the British* Hesperus, *a vessel much more like the·smart clippers of the 1860s than the utilitarian vessels built at the end of that century. Jack Spurling, the marine artist, incidentally, had been a sailor on the* Hesperus *after his near-fatal fall from aloft. Frederick Wallace was an experienced mariner and had skippered fast and graceful fishing schooners of Atlantic Canada. He described how the* Duchess, *then nearly fifty years old, could still sail when she had a breeze. All vessels returning to Europe got a good push from the westerlies in the final days of their voyages.]*

After drifting all day in the rain, the wind came piping out of the west-sou'west at seven in the evening. With the yards squared, the old clipper began to snore before it and was soon footing out at 8 knots. Is this our real westerly at last?

When the moon came up, I went forward on to the fo'c'slehead to view the ship in the light of it.

It was a night for the gods! Out on the bowsprit one views the old clipper in all her charms in the light of the moon. Rushing along over the heave and dip of the big Atlantic swell, she is rolling her scuppers under while her masts swing across the stars in a 40 degree arc. Below my perch, the sharp bows go roaring into the black water, turning up a furrow of foam which gleams and sparkles like snow in the moonlight.

The great foresail bellies over my head in a mighty arch of ivory, rigid and motionless. Tier upon tier, the other parallelograms of canvas rear aloft, full rounded, and as immobile as though carved in marble. There is no sound from these towers of yard and sail—nought but the creaking of a parrel, a bird-like cheeping of leather against iron. Halliards, sheets and braces stretch like bars of steel as they hold yards and canvas to the wind.

Aloft, there is the rushing sound of the wind pouring under the foot of the sail; under the bows and around the hull are the thunder and growl of the parted waters which increase in volume as she plunges into the great black swells heaving across her path.

Under the arch of the foresail, one can see the whole length of her

as far aft as the man at the wheel. The decks are a patchwork of shadows which shift and play as she swings in the seas.

———·—·——

*[The sight of fishing vessels working the shoal waters of the continental shelf
was often the first confirmation seamen had that their ship was approaching
landfall, for their officers rarely told them the ship's position. With luck, a
fisherman might supply the ship with a very welcome abundance of fresh
fish—in exchange for tobacco or even salt meat (!), if the ship had any left.
P. A. Eaddy recorded the excitement of the event.]*

One of the boys from the other watch rushed into the fo'c'sle one
day to call us at one bell, a quarter to twelve, and he could hardly talk
for excitement.

"Come along, hurry out and see all the trawlers; they are all around
us!" he cried, and sure enough, when we got on deck there were fully
half a dozen large trawlers all fairly close to us.

The Old Man beckoned to the man at the wheel to put his helm up
a bit, and run down to the nearest one.

On getting within hailing distance, the Old Man got his megaphone and called out, "What is my position from Fastnet Light?"

We all waited on the tip-toe of excitement for the answer. Back it
came across the intervening stretch of water in real good "Old Country" English.

"Seventy-five miles nor'west, Captain."

"Thank you," responded the Old Man.

"Have you got any hard tobacco and a bottle or two of 'Old Scotch,'
Captain?" next called the trawler skipper. "If you can let me have some,
I'll fill your boat with fresh fish when you send her over."

"Right you are," our skipper shouted.

He turned inboards, yelling to the Mate. "Back the main yards, Mr.
Craddock, and put a boat over the side."

Willingly we ran to the main braces and backed the yards, and then as the ship lost her way, we lowered one of the boats off the for'ard house over the side.

The steward came along with a small bag of tobacco, whiskey, and some salt junk.

"Over the side, four or five of you," said the Mate, naming several of us as boat's crew, and over we climbed into the boat, the Mate quickly following, and soon we were pulling across the long heaving rollers towards the nearest trawler.

On reaching the decks, the trawler's cook came along to us as our Mate was talking to the skipper, and calling us to follow him, he took us to the galley, and said, "I'm sure you fellows could go a bit of fresh tucker—there you are, help yourselves."

Well, if ever a meal was enjoyed by anyone, that one was by us. We had fresh roast beef, fresh potatoes, and above all things, cabbage, and then a great big plateful of rice pudding with eggs in it.

I've enjoyed many a good meal since that, but none have ever quite come up to the dinner aboard that trawler, after one hundred and fifty-three days of deep-water fare.

The trawler's crew gathered round us as we ate, and gave us the latest happenings ashore. We were keen for any news, as from the second of January to the beginning of June is a long spell to be cut off from the world. . . .

We drank it all in like veritable Rip Van Winkles.

"Come on, boys, lay along here, and give a hand to get the trawl aboard," called our Mate, and what we lacked in skill in handling trawls, we made up for by hard pulling as the fish came up alongside.

Once on deck, there seemed to be tons of fish, and as the skipper had promised, they nearly filled our boat with them.

"Drop aft with your boat, mister, and we'll give you a tow over to your ship," said the trawler skipper, and hanging on astern of the trawler with a long line, we were soon alongside our old ship once more.

Somehow, viewing her from the boat, she looked altogether different, and not at all like the familiar old floating home we had been living aboard all this time as seen by us every day from her decks.

In spite of our cleaning and painting she looked battered and weather-worn, especially for'ard, where the [ice] damage had been done, and every time she rolled great patches of sea-growth were exposed on her boot-topping below the waterline.

Hooking on to the davit falls, we were soon on deck giving a hand to the rest of the crowd in hoisting the boat in.

What a meal of fish all hands had for tea that good night! Our Irish cook was nearly distracted by the constant raids made on his galley for more fried fish.

"May the devil fly away wid yer," he called to some of the boys whose demands were incessant. "Sure, and its a foine thing that we're nearly home, or you'd go hungry for fat to fry all your fish in, me lads, me jewels."

—·—·—·—

[The few ships returning to Europe in the 1930s followed converging courses as they approached Queenstown, Ireland, or Falmouth, England, where they received orders to their discharge ports. Several ships might thus come together in the last few days of the long voyages. Ken Attiwill's Archibald Russell *came upon two,* Penang *and the four-masted barkentine* Mozart, *as she completed her journey in 1929 from Australia.]*

The *Penang* . . . lay across the path of the setting sun, and seemed strangely, piteously symbolic of her race. Vanishing, on the horizon—the horizon of the setting sun. An inspiring picture on the horizon, sails agleam and almost golden in that bright patch of sunlight, masts bending under the weight of wind-filled canvas. A curse forever, but still a thing of beauty! If the vanishing race of square-riggers could but pause there like that for all to see her distant beauty—always on the path of the setting sun—people like Jack London and me would never have to look back on them bitterly, with the bitterness of disappointment and disillusionment. They have done much for us, the ships. . . . It is a great pity to remember them as Jack London and I shall remember them.

A score of years ago the Seven Seas abounded with barques and barquentines, clippers and schooners. Today most of them that are left sail the Baltic, and that only in the summer months. Their trade routes can be counted without exhausting the fingers of one hand. Their usefulness other than for training purposes is gone, their glory is a coffined thing, and slowly but surely the waves are claiming them.

The great Australian Grain Race—that grand, fearless struggle to be the first to Europe with the season's grain—is but a dejected shadow of what it was twenty, fifteen years ago. In another five—possibly ten—years there will be no high sails to span the horizon—nothing but their ghosts to bend before the whining Westerlies, to race madly through the roaring forties—nothing but the ghosts of dead ships to fling themselves recklessly into the waves and along those familiar, trackless courses.

— · — · — · —

[The English Channel in the summer could be a very difficult place for sailing ships. Calm and fog and a lot of ship traffic made the shipmaster's life one of anxiety at the end of an anxious voyage. Rex Clements's Arethusa *had a trying time making her way toward port.]*

By the 2nd of the month we estimated our position to be, by dead reckoning, a few hundred miles from the mouth of the Channel. We began to keep a sharp lookout for passing vessels and the first sight of land. The breeze died down in the course of the day and a film of mist spread over sea and sky. It gradually grew thicker, till we were feeling our way across a grey sea between eddying walls of fog, by the help of wandering airs that only just sufficed to give us steerage way. The foghorn was sent for'ard and its mournful blasts quailed on the air every minute.

The air grew chilly and the damp, drifting mist that covered every-thing was most depressing. Our progress, moreover, was slow; we could hear nothing and see nothing, and how long these conditions were going to last there was no means of knowing.

Fog is common enough in the Channel and neighbouring regions in the summer months and adds another hazard to the navigation of those traffic-laden waters. Far more dangerous to the mariner than gales is fog. It is the most bewildering of the many difficulties with which he has to contend . . . the "Arethusa" . . . just escaped being sent to the bottom by a blundering German liner.

We were creeping blindly along, feeling our way down vistas of eddying fog-smoke, when we heard a pulsing throb and the low swish of water. We looked round and the little fog-horn on the foks'le head coughed violently in response to Neilsen's hurried manipulating. Sud-denly a giant shape loomed up out of the mist, standing directly down on top of us. Neilsen worked his wheezy toy of a fog-horn frantically and we jumped unbidden to the braces. There was no time to do any-thing, the steamer was almost into us and old Jamieson and the mate were heaving hard at the helm.

It was touch and go; only a few yards separated the two vessels, when there was a clatter of bells aboard the steamer and she swerved sharply to port. She missed our stern by only a few feet, travelling at near twenty knots. We read her name on the bows as she tore past—the "Deutschland"—at that time the crack vessel of the Norddeutscher Lloyd. For a moment she towered above us like a colossal wraith of the sea, then melted rapidly into the mist. . . .

This unlucky fog disgusted everybody. To be so near home and yet compelled to creep along at a snail's pace, unwitting where we were, was most tantalizing. Every watch we hoped to sight land and watch after watch drew to an end and left us still disappointed. To add to our discomforts the cumbersome deep-sea had to be hove every hour.

A slow, but very safe, method of navigation is this. The three L's—

log, lead, and latitude—are the three points of the mariner's creed, and there's a cast-iron conviction among underwriters that with a proper use of the lead no vessel would ever be lost through stranding *[going aground]*.

We used it ad nauseum; went through the performance every hour until we were sick of the sight of the long blue sinker and wet coils of line.

The mainyard would first be backed, stopping the way of the ship....

As soon as the cast was taken the mainyard was squared again and the ship stood on her way. It was a wet, monotonous job and had to be carried out with wearisome regularity every time the bells marked the passage of the hours.

The results of the lead were very unsatisfactory; we couldn't by their aid ascertain our position with any certainty; some of the men said we were heading for the Channel, others not. The skipper directed our course towards where he conceived the Scillies *[the westernmost English islands]* ought to be and we crept along at the rate of a few knots. We were on soundings, as the hundred fathom line that fringes the British Isles and North West Europe is called, and that is all we knew. The skipper, no doubt, could have given a shrewd guess at our position, but everybody for'ard was quite in the dark and opinions varied from the neighbourhood of Ushant to St. George's Channel.

The appearance of the sea gave no indication. It might be thought that the shoaling of the water, from the great depths of mid-ocean to a score or two of fathoms, would have been visible in its altered colour and appearance, but it is not so. The clammy fog made extended observation impossible and, as far as the surface was concerned, "soundings" or "mid-sea" looks much the same....

All through the 4th and 5th of May the numbing fog held. Under shortened sail, with a constant use of the lead, we drifted on, with eyes and ears alert, but still with no signs of land. We were almost beginning to think that the British Isles had sunk at their moorings and that nothing but water stretched endlessly in every direction. On the after-noon of the latter day the little breeze freshened and by imperceptible degrees the fog began to melt away. Slowly the air grew clearer and clearer, bringing with it an ever-widening horizon. The sails now were kept steadily filled and the pleasant babble of water arose overside.

It was in the second dog-watch and just about dusk, as Burton and I were sitting in the half deck smoking our "barrel blend," that we heard a shout from for'ard and a stir among the men on deck. We made for the door and ran full tilt into Gilroy. His face was alight and his arm outstretched—"There she is," he said excitedly, "England!"

We rushed out. There was still a pale clear light lingering over the sea's face to the ring of the horizon and as we ran to the rail to look ahead there winked, far away, a pin-point of light. Bright, lonely and unmistakable, it flashed for a moment and was gone. But it was enough. Yonder over the darkening sky-line was England and that light was the double flash of the Bishop, the farthest-flung outpost of her shores and the beacon-light of home!

My heart leapt within me to see this outermost Atlantic sentinel of my native land. All the weariness of the last few days was forgotten and we gathered in little groups and fell a-talking of when we should reach Falmouth, where we should go to discharge and what we should do when we got home. The recurrent flash grew ever brighter and more distinct, full sail was piled on the old barque and course was altered to bring the Scillies abeam.

All that night we stood to the north east, dipping along at not more than five knots, which was all the speed our weed-covered hull would let us attain to. Next morning we were abreast of the toe of England, with a number of fishing vessels in sight. . . .

All that night under easy sail we cruised off and on. With the first streaks of dawn in the sky and the outline of the coast growing clearer to the nor'ard, we bore up and shaped a course for Falmouth. We picked up our pilot—a stalwart West country-man—with round Saxon speech on his tongue—as we closed the land, feeling, as he clambered over the rail, that here at last was a tangible link with home and that our voyage was just about over and done with.

A fair and pleasant county is Cornwall, and justly beloved of sailors. The grand cliffs of the Lizard and Kynance, with the chequerboard of green fields about them, are most often the first speck of English land the returning wanderer sees....

Past the Manacles we went ... to the little white town of Falmouth lying snuggly on the slopes of its beautiful bay.

Fair and green it looked on that bright spring morning. The harbour was full of shipping, both outward and homeward bound. A big Yankee barquentine was lifting her anchor as we came in, her white cotton canvas gleaming in the sun and the tinkle of the windlass pawls sounding musically in the air.

As soon as our anchor was down the captain went ashore and we were quickly boarded by a host of bumboatmen with all sorts of things to sell. Good it was to taste tobacco again, and we sat around and smoked pipe after pipe of strong black Irish roll in silent contentment.

— · — · —

[Ray Wilmore, by his own account, had had a wonderful experience on the beautiful John Ena. *The captain offered him a job as able seaman (after only one voyage!) on her next voyage. Wilmore did not take it, but he found it hard to leave the ship when the time came.]*

It was a morning I shall never forget. If you have never been entirely away from civilization, out of sight of land, out of touch with family and friends, business and the world at large, cooped up on a small ship with a handful of fellow seamen for three and one half months—if you haven't been through these things, it will be difficult for you to imagine the thrill of coming back into a world of people, activities, business and pleasures. And yet, there is much about this beautiful Queen of the Seas—the thrill as she answered to the touch of my hand on her helm; the sheer joy of sailing before a stiff breeze; the majesty of the balmy tropic nights; the excitement of the battles against the elements; the risks and dangers and hardships; all this mixture of emotions and conditions, intermingled and following upon each other in unexpected and surprising succession—yes, there is much about it all that I shall miss, and I think I can understand now why men of the sea love it and their ships; also why they hate it and curse it and everything connected with it; why they leave it but keep coming back to it, loving it for and in spite of all its vagaries . . . why those who do leave the sea after short, unsuccessful ventures again go down to it and why those who stay ashore die of sheer loneliness or broken hearts, having given up their first love.

—————

[Sir James Bisset, at age five in 1888, was taken to see the great steam-powered wonder ship Great Eastern *in Liverpool at the time sailing vessels still dominated the ocean commerce of the world and some of the old clippers still sailed the seas. He went to sea in 1898, intending to make a career in sail, but after four years, at the end of his "time" as an apprentice, he realized that the end of sail was in sight. He switched to steam and lived to command the greatest ships of our age, the* Queen Mary *and* Queen Elizabeth. *Thus he saw the apogee and the extinction of sail. He commented on the end of sail, and what might have been.]*

Though voyages such as this were described, in the shipping columns of newspapers, as "uneventful" unless deaths or serious damage occurred, they were eventful enough for the men before and abaft the mast, who had to work the ships from port to port, encountering ever-changing circumstances, afloat and ashore.

In this narrative I have told of the daily events in a seafarer's life under sail, as accurately as I can recall them after more than fifty years; but I am reminded that such great changes have occurred, at sea and on land, in that period, that the way of life here described may seem to modern readers to have been crude and callous.

It was not considered so at the time, but was perfectly normal. Perhaps, in the year 2,000 A.D., the customs of the mid-twentieth century may seem crude to the people of that time, because everything that is "modern" must eventually become out of date.

Sailing-ship days and ways were "on the way out" in 1904, and this fact was being borne in upon my comprehension in this, my first and last voyage as an officer in sail.

I had made up my mind to go into steam, if possible, for I could forsee that the glorious days of sail were drawing rapidly to a close, and that the mentality of the sailing-ship men was adversely affected by the depressing thought that all their skill and science, so laboriously acquired, was of little avail against the competition of mechanical power.

Inventive mechanical skill was never applied to the handling of sail, but only to abolishing sail as a means of propulsion. The power of the winds would no longer be captured and tamed for men's ocean transits. It would be disregarded; yet possibly a time may again come when wind-driven craft of handy size may be seen on ocean routes, with mechanical devices for handling sail (such as motor winches for all hauling), auxiliary screws to work through the doldrums and into and out of ports, a higher freeboard to avoid flooded decks, water ballast that can be mechanically pumped in and out, electric lights and refrigeration, and possibly nylon sails and cordage, aluminum or other light metal yards, "push-button" control, and radio and radar, and many other devices which would enable the power of the winds to be harnessed with the aid of machinery and the labor of only a few men in the crews.

If such a time should come, the lore of the old sailing ships, which were worked entirely by manual labor, will have been worth preserving. The introduction of steam propulsion made manually-handled sailing ships obsolete, after it was found initially that crude combinations of steam and sail, such as those in the *Great Eastern,* presented some practical difficulties; yet it should not be forgotten that the world's first mammoth ship used her engines as an auxiliary to her sails, or vice versa. If engineers and inventors had studied the actual problems of handling sail, they could possibly have devised some method of continuing to use the power of the winds; but it was not to be, and sail went into discard.

Men who obstinately clung to a way of life that was rapidly becoming obsolete were creatures of habit—either in the fo'c'sle or under the poop. Conditions of employment for the fo'c'sle hands were such that only "drifters," who could find nothing better to do, were available to be picked up as required, in ports far and wide. Many of them were signed on drunk; yet, when they found themselves at sea, they turned to manfully and cheerfully, in the great traditions of their calling.

The masters and officers of sailing vessels sensed, even more than the men before the mast, that their profession now offered little or no scope for advancement. The Captain and Mate in the *County of Cardigan* were morose from the continual worries and frustrations imposed upon them by the nature of their occupation. The Captain's pay was twelve pounds a month, and the Mate's seven pounds a month: no great reward, this, for the responsibilities put upon them and the ordeals and worries they endured. Their surly behaviour was no inspiration to me as an example to be emulated. If, by remaining in sail, I could look forward only to becoming as soured as they, the prospects were not enticing.

It was for reasons such as these that, as I studied for my First Mate's examination while the *County of Cardigan* plowed eastward across the Pacific Ocean, I decided that this would be my last voyage in sail, and that, on returning home, I would look for a billet in a steamer.

— · — · —

[Holger Thesleff is our only witness to the voyages of the Pamir *and* Passat *in 1949, the last commercial voyages under sail around Cape Horn. What, now, he asked, was the future for the officers who had grown up in sailing*

ships, and understood them, and knew how to take them to the farthest, stormiest reaches of the sea and to bring them home again from around the world?]

One November evening I ran into the *Passat*'s first mate in Helsinki. He was one of the last to be paid off and was then passing through on his way to Mariehamn and home. We sat in a little restaurant down by the harbour and sipped our beer while a radio-gramophone played a tango and the tables round filled with sailors from a steamer in the dock. We had to speak loudly merely to make ourselves heard.

"What was that you said, three years it is since you were last home?" I asked, merely to have something to say.

"I saw the old woman and the kids a year ago in Antwerp. They went there. . . ."

"What are you going to do now?"

"It'll be good for me just to see them."

"But are you going to try and sign on in some steamer or other?"

The mate did not answer. He sat silent for a long time while the tango turned into a polka and the uproar around us grew. Then he looked up from his glass.

"Yes, what do you think one should do? I'm not the only one; there are many there at home who have been to sea since they were quite small and have it in their blood. We know a lot about sailing ships, but steamers. . . ." The mate made as though to spit, then restrained himself, and went on: "Even if there is a chance of finding a suitable steamer, it may easily take years to do so. One doesn't just go anywhere or to any sort of job naturally. I've worked and slaved ever since I was small, but I haven't yet got enough put aside to be able to buy a small vessel. And anyway that doesn't pay so well as it used to. And fishing doesn't pay."

"Become a boat-builder. You can make things with your hands, use them to build new boats!"

"Everybody can't begin building. No, one must get to sea if there's to be any meaning in the whole damned thing at all."

A professional, a specialist trained for the life, was out of work. Our talk turned to other matters that did not touch us closely, then suddenly the mate stood up and said:

"No, now I'll go and buy my ticket."

I went part of the way with him. We sauntered along the pavement with neon lights mirroring themselves in the wet surface of the asphalt. We stopped to look at the new model of some make of car, considered the dresses in a shop window; clumsy we were, bumping into the harassed people in our way, and many were the apologies I had to mutter during the short walk.

The rain streamed off the mate's slouch hat and from the skirts of his overcoat as he walked along with bowed head, seeming to be listening to distant sounds. As we parted, he mumbled:

"I just *can't* forget those ships."

APPENDIX A: The Ships in Which the Authors Voyaged

(Dimensions in gross tons and feet and inches)

A. J. Fuller, wood full-rig ship. Built 1881, Bath, Maine. 1,849 tons. 229.3 x 41.5 x 26. Three skysails. Sunk in 1918 by a steamship while at anchor in fog in Seattle harbor.

Arapahoe, ex *Steinbeck*, ex *Durbridge*, steel full-rig ship. Built 1892, Glasgow, Scotland. 2,201 tons. 276.8 x 42 x 24.2. Wrecked off Akun Head, Alaska, May 22, 1928.

Archibald Russell, steel 4m bark. Built 1905, Greenock, Scotland. 2,354 tons. 291.3 x 42.9 x 24. Broken up, 1948.

Arethusa, steel 3m bark. Built Greenock, Scotland.

Bengairn, ex *Pass of Brandar*, steel 4m bark. Built 1890, Glasgow, Scotland. 2,127 tons. 280.5 x 42.1 x 24.4. Destroyed in First World War.

British Isles, steel full-rig ship. Built 1884, Glasgow, Scotland. 2,394 tons. 308.9 x 43.9 x 24.8. Disintegrated in South America in the 1930s.

County of Cardigan, steel full-rig ship. Built 1887, Liverpool, England. 1,323 tons. 229 x 37 x 22−27.

County of Pembroke, steel 3m bark. Built 1881, Sunderland, England. 1,098 tons. 221 x 35 x 20−29.

Denbigh Castle, 3m bark. Built in Wales.

Elginshire, steel 4m bark. Built 1889, Dumbarton, Scotland. 2,160 tons. 285 x 40.5 x 24.7. Single t'gans'ls. Broken up, 1922.

Grace Harwar, steel full-rig ship. Built 1889, Port Glasgow, Scotland. 1,816 tons. 266.7 x 39.1 x 23.5. Broken up, 1935.

Grand Duchess Maria Nikolaevna, ex *Hesperus*, iron full-rig ship. Built 1873, Greenock, Scotland. 1,777 tons. 262.2 x 39.7 x 23.5. Broken up, 1923.

Herzogin Cecilie, steel 4m bark. Built 1902, Bremerhaven, Germany. 3,111 tons. 314.8 x 46.3 x 24.2. Wrecked, Devon, England, 1936.

John Ena, steel 4m bark. Built 1892, Glasgow, Scotland. 2,842 tons. 312.9 x 48.1 x 25. Broken up at Los Angeles, 1934.

Lawhill, steel 4m bark. Built 1892, Dundee, Scotland. 2,816 tons. 317.4 x 45.0 x 25.1. No royals. Disintegrated and finally broken up at Laurenco Marques, 1957.

L'Avenir, steel 4m bark. Built 1908, Bremerhaven, Germany. 2,754 tons. 278.2 x 44.8 x 26.5. Disappeared at sea in 1938 as *Admiral Karpfanger*.

Mandalore, iron full-rig ship. 265 x 39 x 23. Rigged with skysails.

Moshulu, ex *Kurt,* steel 4m bark. Built 1904, Port Glasgow, Scotland. 3,120 tons. 335.3 x 46.9 x 26.6. Preserved at Philadelphia.

Olivebank, steel 4m bark. Built 1892, Glasgow, Scotland. 2,795 tons. 326.0 x 43.1 x 24.5. Sunk by a mine in the North Sea, 1939.

Pamir, steel 4m bark. Built 1905, Hamburg, Germany. 2,798 tons. 316.0 x 46.0 x 26.2. Lost at sea, 1957.

Parma, ex *Arrow,* steel 4m bark. Built 1902, Port Glasgow, Scotland. 3,091 tons. 327.7 x 46.5 x 28.0. Broken up, 1936.

Passat, steel 4m bark. Built 1911, Hamburg, Germany. 3,130 tons. 322.0 x 47.2 x 26.5. Preserved at Travemunde, Germany.

Penang, steel 3m bark. Built 1905, Bremerhaven, Germany. 2,019 tons. 265.7 x 40.2 x 24.3. Torpedoed off the Irish coast, December 8, 1940.

Penrhyn Castle, steel 3m bark. Built 1882, Bristol, England. 1,367 tons. 238 x 36 x 21. Went missing May or June, 1915, between Cape of Good Hope and Australia.

Pommern, ex *Mneme,* steel 4m bark. Built 1903, Glasgow, Scotland. 2,376 tons. 294.8 x 43.4 x 24.5. No royals. Preserved at Mariehamn, Åland Islands, Finland.

Ross-shire, steel 4m bark. Built 1891, Greenock, Scotland. 2,257 tons. 289.1 x 41.2 x 24.4. Burned Christmas Eve, Pisagua, Chile, 1900.

Tusitala, ex *Inveruglas* ex *Sierra Lucena* ex *Sophie,* iron full-rig ship. Built 1883, Liverpool, England. 1,684 tons. 260.4 x 39 x 23.5. Broken up, 1938.

Viking, steel 4m bark. Built 1907, Copenhagen, Denmark. 2,670 tons. 293.8 x 42.5 x 23.2. Preserved at Gothenburg, Sweden.

Winterhude, ex *Mabel Rickmers,* steel 3m bark. Built 1898, Bremerhaven, Germany. 1,972 tons. 267.2 x 40.5 x 24.1. No royals. Broken up, 1949.

APPENDIX B: The Twist of the Sails

[The Pamir *and* Passat *were sold to shipbreakers in 1951. A German shipowner then bought them with the intent of using them as cargo-carrying training ships. He installed engines in both and in 1952 sent them off with cement to Brazil, to return to Germany with iron ore. The propellors of both dropped off early in their voyages, much to the satisfaction of the sail-favoring crews if not to the owner.*

Hilary Tunstall-Behrens had served in Royal Navy minesweepers during the war. He had been in the first Outward Bound training course in 1941, and in exchange for setting up a similar program in Germany in 1951, he was allowed to sail on the Pamir. *He described the characteristic "corkscrew" of sails that is evident, and perhaps puzzling, in almost all pictures of square-riggers.]*

In a windjammer the royal yards are trimmed further aft than the t'gallants and the t'gallants further aft than the tops'ls, so that looking up the mast the sails skew round like a corkscrew. The amount varied according to the ideas of individual masters, but it was generally recognized that the performance was improved by it. Why it should be more efficient is still a matter for conjecture and argument among seamen.

A possible explanation is that the *apparent* wind changes direction between sea-level and the top of the mast. The higher you go the further aft it draws. The friction on the sea slows up the wind to a small extent, and in theory at least the wind has a greater velocity at the top of the mast than on the deck....
As the *true* wind increased in strength, the *apparent* wind changed direction towards the *true* wind, it drew aft. The royals then should be trimmed further aft than the courses if they are to have a similar slant to the *apparent* wind.

A more convincing argument is as follows. A royal yard is only about half as long as a lower yard. All the sails naturally have a curve which deviates from the straight line of the yard at the head increasingly towards the foot. The royals, t'gallant sails and tops'ls have a yard below them to which they are sheeted home. This helps to keep the sails flat; nevertheless the curve from the leading edge of the sail is undeniable and the longer the yards the greater is the angle formed between the line of bellying canvas and the straight line of the yards. This is even more pronounced on the courses where there is no yard to which the tack and sheet are bowsed home. The aim when trimming the sails according to this theory, is to line up the leading edges or rather planes. To do this correctly the lower sails, being the bigger, will be braced up more than the upper, which are smaller and have not such a pronounced curve.

When the wind was abaft the beam, sailing masters often exaggerated the twist or set of the sails. In this case it was said to let the wind screw up the mast and get clear for the wind behind it to have its maximum effect and pass on. The problem of getting rid of bags of wind caused some masters to cut holes in their sails even. It was reckoned that they increased efficiency. In those days proof of such an experiment was bound to remain one of opinion; like many other experiments it was never taken up universally, though a turn of speed could win a great deal of money for a captain and better his position.

———·—·—·—

[Holger Thesleff offered this comment on the corkscrew set of sails, as practiced on the Passat.*]*

Four-masted barques are bad sailors on the wind. Without bracing very hard up they will scarcely go closer than five and a half points, that is to say, about sixty degrees; and, as they make a lot of leeway, up to ten degrees, they are obviously not suitable for beating. For that reason when we sailed on the wind in the north-east trades we kept a good deal of twist on the sails and to that certain extent lessened her angle towards the wind. The sails should always, especially when speed is required, be braced with a twist, which means that the lower yards are braced closer than the upper, so that seen from below the rigging reminds you of a spiral stairway. The theory behind this is the same as that for setting the screw of a propeller aslant. This twist also serves to balance the ship on the helm by keeping the mizzen sails more closely braced than the others. This lessens the tendency to luff, but also the angle to the wind.

Attiwill, Ken. *Windjammer*. New York: Doubleday, Doran & Co., 1931. Copyright © 1931 by Ken Attiwill. Reprinted by permission of Doubleday, a division of Random House, Inc.

Barker, Roland. *Tusitala*. New York: W. W. Norton & Co., 1959. Copyright © 1959 by Roland Barker. Reprinted by permission of W. W. Norton & Company, Inc.

Campbell, Neil. *Shadow and Sun*. London: George Allen & Unwin Ltd., 1947. Copyright © 1947. Reprinted by permission of HarperCollins Publishers Ltd.

Greenhill, Basil, and John Hackman. *The Herzogin Cecilie: The Life and Times of a Four-masted Barque*. London: Conway Maritime Press, 1991. Reprinted by permission of B. T. Batsford Ltd.

Hurst, Alex A. *Ghosts on the Sea Line*. London: Cassell & Co. Ltd., 1957. Copyright © 1957 by A. A. Hurst. Reprinted by permission of Ros Hurst, heir of A. A. Hurst.

Hurst, Alex A. *The Call of High Canvas*. London: Cassell & Co. Ltd., 1958. Copyright © 1958 by A. A. Hurst. Reprinted by permission of Ros Hurst, heir of A. A. Hurst.

Karlsson, Elis. *Mother Sea*. London: Oxford University Press, 1964. Copyright © 1964 by Oxford University Press. Reprinted by permission of Oxford University Press.

Karlsson, Elis. *Pully-Haul*. London: Oxford University Press, 1966. Copyright © 1966 by Oxford University Press. Reprinted by permission of Oxford University Press.

Lubbock, Basil. *Round the Horn Before the Mast*. London: John Murray, 1902. Reprinted by permission of John Murray (Publishers) Ltd.

Thesleff, Holger. *Farewell Windjammer*. London: Thames and Hudson, 1951. All rights reserved. Reprinted by permission of Thames and Hudson.

Villiers, Alan J. *By Way of Cape Horn*. New York: Henry Holt & Co., 1930. Copyright © 1930 by A. J. Villiers. Reprinted by permission of Laurence Pollinger Limited and the Estate of Alan Villiers.

Villiers, Alan J. *The War with Cape Horn*. New York: Charles Scribner's Sons,

1971. Copyright © 1971 by Alan Villiers. Reprinted by permission of Laurence Pollinger Limited and the Estate of Alan Villiers.

Wallace, Frederick William. *Under Sail in the Last of the Clippers.* Boston: Charles E. Lauriat Co., 1936. Reprinted by permission of Brown, Son & Ferguson, Ltd.

Wilmore, C. Ray. *Square Rigger Round the Horn.* Camden, Maine: International Marine Publishing Co., 1972. Copyright © 1972 by International Marine Publishing Co. Reprinted by permission of Mrs. H. W. Timmerman, heir of C. R. Wilmore.

Woollard, Claude L. A. *The Last of the Cape Horners.* Ilfracomb, U.K.: A. H. Stockwell, Ltd., 1967. Reprinted by permission of E. H. Woollard, heir of C. L. A. Woollard.

The editor attempted by various means to contact authors or publishers of all sources. Those efforts were not successful for a number of sources.

Aback. The condition of a square-rigged vessel when the wind is on the front, or wrong side, of its sails.

Abaft the Beam. Any direction from a ship that is more than 90 degrees from the bow but not directly behind or astern of the ship.

Aft, or *Abaft.* Toward the stern.

Aneroid. A barometer that responds to air pressure acting on a metallic box containing a partial vacuum, rather than on a column of mercury.

Arm the Lead, To. To fill a depression in the bottom of a sounding lead with tallow for the purpose of obtaining a sample of the ocean bottom.

Athwart. Across a ship.

Backstay. In a square-rigged ship, a wire leading from the top of a mast to a point on the side or rail behind the mast and supporting the mast against forward tension.

Ballast. Heavy, cheap material used to weight down a ship so as to provide stability to it.

Ballast, In. The condition of a vessel without cargo but partially loaded for stability with ballast in the form of rocks, sand, or perhaps water in special ballast tanks.

Barque, or *Bark.* A three-masted vessel square-rigged on the first two masts and fore-and-aft rigged on the third.

Barquentine, or *Barkentine.* A vessel of three or more masts, of which the foremast is square-rigged and the others are fore-and-aft rigged.

Baulks. Heavy wooden or metal beams.

Beat to Windward. To sail into the wind by tacking back and forth.

Belay, To. To tie a rope to a secure point.

Belaying Pin. A hardwood or metal rod to which running rigging is tied or belayed.

Belaying-Pin Rail. A rack along the inside of the bulwarks in which belaying pins are inserted.

Bell, or *Bells.* The system of keeping time on a ship. The ship's bell, near the steering wheel, is rung each half hour with a characteristic number of strokes. Midnight is eight bells, 12:30 is one bell, 1:00 is two bells and so on until 4 A.M., which is eight bells. Then the sequence starts again for each four-hour period, which always terminates in eight bells.

Bend, To. To fasten a sail to a spar, whether a yard, mast, gaff, or boom, or, in the case of staysails and jibs, to a stay.

Bilge. The lowest part of the interior of a ship's hull.

Binnacle. A structure, usually in front of the steering wheel, that houses the compass, lamps for the compass, and small iron bars that correct the compass for magnetic deviation.

Block. A pulley with up to five sheaves, the grooved wheels within the pulley on which the rope or cable turns.

Bobstay. A heavy wire or chain that runs down from the end of the bowsprit and is shackled to the bow near the waterline.

Boom. The spar on the lower edge of a fore-and-aft sail.

Bosun, or Bo'sun. A junior officer responsible for maintenance on deck and in the rigging. A corruption of boatswain, that is, boat lover.

Bow. The forward end of a ship.

Bower. An anchor, sometimes a spare, carried at the bow.

Bowsprit. The spar projecting forward from the bow of a ship from which sails are set.

Braces. Running rigging used to swing the yards in the horizontal plane.

Brace, To. To swing the yards horizontally to set them at the proper angle to the wind.

Bracewinch. A mechanical device to which lower-yard braces were attached and that would simultaneously wind in and wind out the braces on each end of yards.

Brig. A two-masted vessel square-rigged on both masts.

Bright Work. The varnished and polished woodwork about the decks of a ship; the steering wheels, cabin trim, the binnacle, ladder railings, bucket racks, skylights, and so on.

Bristol Fashion. Very well cared for.

Broach-To, To. The act of a ship swinging out of control in heavy weather such that it turns across the wind and sea. Waves then approach from the side rather than the stern or bow. A broaching or broached ship is very vulnerable to seas breaking on board and smashing her hatches, often a fatal situation.

Bulwark. The side of a ship above the main deck.

Bumboatman. One who went off to newly arrived ships in a harbor, or even offshore, in a small boat that carried a variety of goods and foods for sale to sailors often lacking basic necessities, or anxious for small luxuries or fresh food after months at sea. Tobacco was always in demand. The ship's captain often agreed to pay the bill, to be reimbursed out of the wages owed to the sailors.

Bunt. The center part of a square sail.

Bunt Line. A line attached to the foot of a square sail and running up the fore side of the sail to the yard and then to the deck. The line assists in gathering the sail to the yard before furling.

By-the-Wind. The manner, when handling sails, of securing lines to belaying pins such that the lines may be released and handled quickly. Also, the situation of a ship when it is sailing as close into the wind as possible.

Cable. A nautical unit of measure: 720 feet in the United States; 608 feet in England.

Caps. Metal rings or bands around the masts to which are secured the lower topsail and lower topgallant yards. The caps also secure upper masts to lower masts.

Capstan. A cylinder that revolves on its vertical axis and that is set at various points about the deck. It is geared to provide mechanical advantage when seamen push against bars, also called longbars, inserted in its head. Chains, wires, or ropes are wound about it and, under strain, are pulled when the capstan is turned. The capstan is used for heavy jobs such as weighing anchor, hoisting yards, or tightening the sheets of the largest sails.

Cathead. A structure on each side of the bow for the purpose of lifting anchors on board.

Catspaw. The ripple of the slightest breeze on an otherwise flat-calm sea.

Chanty, or *Shanty.* A traditional sailors' song, of various kinds for particular jobs, usually sung to make work easier.

Clew. A lower corner of a square sail.

Clew Garnet. A tackle attached to a lower corner of the lowest square sails, for hauling up the clew of the sail to its yard.

Clew Line. A tackle attached to a lower corner of an upper square sail, for hauling the clew of a sail up to its yard.

Clew-Up, To. The act of hauling the lower corners of a square sail up to its yard by means of clew lines or clew garnets.

Clewed-Up. The condition of a square sail when its lower corners are hauled up by clew lines or clew garnets to its yard.

Close-Hauled. The situation of a ship when it is sailing as close into, or as near to, the wind as possible—when its sails are hauled as close in as possible.

Course. A foresail, mainsail, or crossjack of a square-rigged ship—the largest and lowest sails.

Crossjack, or *Cro'jak,* or *Cro'jik.* The largest and lowest sail on the mizzen mast of a square-rigged ship.

Crosstrees. Metal or wood structures attached to the upper end of lower masts or topmasts and set at right angles to the length of a vessel to support the tops.

Davits. Curved wood or metal structures projecting from a ship's side from which small boats are suspended, or are lowered to or raised from the water.

Dead Eye. A round device of hardwood pierced with holes and spliced into the ends of shrouds and backstays. A twin would be attached to the ship's rail. Lanyards are rove through the pair and when hove taut, would exert the proper tension on the stays and shrouds.

Dog-Watch. Either one of two two-hour watches between 4 P.M. and 8 P.M.

Doldrums. Ocean regions near the equator characterized by calms or intermittent light and variable winds, with occasional heavy rains and brief squalls.

Donkey Engine. A small steam engine and boiler on the deck of some ships, used for getting cargo in or out, or for other jobs, such as raising an anchor, when extra power is needed.

Donkey's Breakfast. A cheap mattress of typically poor cloth and stuffed with straw, characteristically found in sailing ships.

Earing. A metal ring at each top corner of a square sail for hauling taut and securing the sail to the end of its yard. Also, the lashing for that purpose.

Falls. The tackles consisting of lines and blocks (or pulleys) that suspend and raise or lower small boats from davits or anchors from hawse pipes to the deck.

Fathom. Six feet.

Fid. A bar of metal or wood that fits into the lower end of a topmast or topgallant mast and carries the weight of the mast when it rests on the trestletrees. Also, a pointed tool used for separating the strands of wire or rope.

Fid, To Ship the. To place a fid in its proper position to support an upper mast.

Fife Rail. A rail, usually of hardwood, around three sides of the foot of a mast, and fitted with holes for belaying pins to which running rigging is secured.

Fish, To. To bring an anchor to the rail and secure it. Also, to temporarily mend a broken spar with lashings.

Flare. The curvature of a ship's side that spreads upward and outward from the waterline to the gunwale. A ship with flare is wider at the maindeck than at the waterline.

Flinders Bars. Iron bars used to correct compasses for errors caused by the iron in ships.

Flukes. The flat parts of an anchor that dig into and grip the sea bottom.

Foot Rope. A wire suspended horizontally below a yard on which seamen stand while furling sail or working on a yard.

Fore-and-Aft Rig. A vessel with sails usually rigged parallel with the length of the hull. Such a vessel could also carry a square sail.

Forecastle, or *Fo'c'sle.* The crew's quarters, in Cape Horners usually a deck house behind the foremast.

Forecastle Head. A short deck in the bow of a vessel raised above the main deck. From here the jibs and anchors are handled.

Forepeak. A small compartment furthest forward under the forecastle head.

Fore-Rigging. All the running and standing rigging associated with the foremast.

Fore-Sheet. Tackle at a lower corner of the foresail. Used to keep the sail full of wind and pulling.

Foreward, or *Fore.* Toward the bow.

Freeboard. The height of a ship's rail at its lowest point above the water.

Full-and-By. The condition of a ship when it is sailing as close to the wind as possible ("by the wind") with its sails full and drawing.

Futtock Shrouds. Metal rods secured at their lower ends to a band on a mast and running outward and upward to the edges of a "top," and fitted with crossbars or ratlines as footrests for climbing over the top.

Gantline, or *Girt Line.* A line running through a single block at the top of a mast to hoist up sails or other gear.

Gasket. A line used to secure a furled sail to its yard.

Gig. A small boat carried by a ship and used in port by the captain when going ashore.

Gig-Tag. Swedish for clew garnet.

Gipsy-Wheel. An auxiliary drum fitted outside the main frame of a winch or windlass and used for handling chain when anchoring.

Going-About. The process of tacking.

Gooseneck. A device that secures a spar to its mast and permits the spar to swing.

Greybeards. Huge breaking waves prevalent off Cape Horn.

Gudgeon. A fitting that supports and secures the rudder to the hull and permits it to turn.

Gunwale. The top edge of the bulwark of a vessel.

Halfdeck. The accommodations for apprentices.

Halyard, or *Halliard* (Haul yard). The tackle by which yards, or sails, are hoisted or lowered.

Handy-Billy. A light, portable form of tackle.

Hawse-Pipe. An opening at the bow through which an anchor chain passes.

Hawser. A towing rope.

Heave, To. To throw, or to pull.

Heave-To, To. To stop a ship's forward motion by turning into the wind, usually by putting the sails aback on one or more masts.

Holystone. A block of soft stone used for scouring the deck.

Holystone, To. The act of scouring decks with holystones.

Hove: Thrown, or pulled in.

Hove-Short. Pulled up tight.

Hove-To. The situation of a ship when it is motionless in the water by the manipulation of the sails, but not at anchor.

Jackstay. A metal rod along the length of the top of a yard. The square sail and other gear are secured to the jackstay, and it provides a handhold for seamen on the yard.

Jib. A triangular sail set in front of the foremast.

Jibboom. In some vessels, a spar that projects beyond the bowsprit to which jibs are set.

Jigger. The fourth mast, as on a four-masted bark.

Kedge. A relatively light anchor, often used to move a vessel in the absence of other power.

Keelson. A longitudinal strengthening structure running from the bow to the stern on the inside and at the bottom of a ship.

Knot. One nautical mile per hour. A nautical mile is 6,080 feet.

Lay, To. To go.

Lazarette. Storage space between decks near the after end of a ship.

Leach, or *Leech.* The after edge of a fore-and-aft sail, or the vertical edge on either side of a square sail.

Leach Line. A tackle for hauling the leach of a sail up to a yard or in to a mast.

Lead. A lead weight, generally of 7, 14, or 21 pounds, for determining the depth of the ocean bottom under a ship.

Lead Line. A strong, light line to which the lead is attached, and which is marked at standard intervals for depth measurements.

Lee, or *Leeward.* The side of a ship away from the wind, or the direction from the ship toward which the wind is blowing.

Lie-To, To. See heave-to.

Lighthouse. A structure, usually located near the after edge of the forecastle head, that shelters and displays the port or starboard navigational lights, the only navigational lights normally displayed by a sailing vessel.

Limbers. Holes through the frames of a vessel to allow bilge water to drain to the intakes of pumps.

Liverpool House (or *Section*). The midships deck, extending the full width of the vessel, in a vessel with raised forecastle, poop, and midships decks.

Log. A device for measuring a ship's speed. Also, an official record of a vessel's voyage.

Log Line. A light line on a reel and attached to a wooden triangle that, from time to time, is dragged astern of a ship. The line is marked at specific intervals by knots, and the rate at which the knots are unreeled indicates the vessel's speed.

Marks, Plimsoll. Legally required indicators often welded on the outside of the hull to indicate the proper waterline when a ship is fully loaded.

Marline. Tarred light line used for many purposes in the rigging.

Marline Spike. A wooden or metal pointed hand tool used for separating the strands of wire or rope when splicing.

Mastheaded. The situation of a sail or gear when it is hoisted as high as possible.

Mizzen. The third mast.

Mudhook. An anchor.

Norddeutscher Lloyd. The preeminent German shipping company early in the twentieth century.

Number, To Make a. Every large merchant vessel in the world is assigned a four-letter identification code called a "number." Signal flags can represent that code. When encountering another vessel at sea, a ship would hoist the flags for its code, thus "making its number" and identifying itself to the other vessel. This was an important routine before the days of radio. When making port, a vessel could thereby report that it had met another ship at such-and-such a position, thus relieving anxiety about ships on long, extended passages.

Oakum. Tarred hemp or jute fiber used for caulking seams in wooden ships.

Orlop. A partial lower deck, not the full length of a ship.

Parcel, To. To wrap tarred canvas strips around previously wormed wire. Part of the process used to protect wire from chafe.

Parrel. A device that attaches a yard to its mast and allows vertical and horizontal movement of the yard.

Pawls. Heavy metal fixtures on a capstan that prevent it from turning in the wrong direction.

Pinrail. A wide rail or narrow platform inside the bulwarks with holes to receive belaying pins to which running rigging is attached.

Pintles. Heavy metal pins attached to the forward edge of a rudder and inserted into gudgeons. The rudder turns upon its pintles, supported by the gudgeons.

Police. A sailor on watch and standing by to do errands for the officer of the watch.

Poop. Aftermost deck, raised above the main deck.

Poop, To, or *Pooping.* The act of a following wave breaking over the stern of a vessel and washing forward over the poop deck.

Port. When facing forward, the left-hand side of a ship.

Port Tack. The condition of a sailing vessel when the wind is coming from the port side. It is then on the port tack.

Pully-Hauly. The frequent and tiring turning of sails to meet the ever-changing shifts of wind in the doldrums.

Quarter. That part of a ship at which the rail curves toward the stern, or a direction from the ship about 45 degrees from the stern.

Rail. The top edge of bulwarks.

Ratlines. A series of lines or metal rods secured horizontally on the shrouds that serve as foot rests for seamen ascending or descending the rigging.

Rigging, Running. All the moveable wires, rope cordage, chains, and blocks (or pulleys) by which the sails are set and controlled.

Rigging, Standing. All the (generally) fixed wires and chains by which the masts are secured and braced.

Roach. The concave lower edge of a square sail.

Roaring Forties. That zone of the southern hemisphere between 40 and 50 degrees latitude and characterized by strong west winds and high seas. Also, the winds themselves.

Robands. Lines used to secure sails to jackstays.

Rose Box. A device with screens at the intakes of pumps.

Rove, To. To lead or thread a line through fittings of various kinds.

Rovings. Light lines used to tie together various kinds of fittings, for example, jibs to hoops on stays.

Royal. Masts, sails, and rigging next above the topgallant masts and rigging.

Scuppers. Shallow, gutter-like depression around the edge of the ship's deck. Also, holes through the bulwarks to drain water from the decks.

Scuttle. A small opening, or its cover, in a deck or bulkhead to provide access to storage space.

Sennit. Braided line in various forms, as flat, square, or crown sennits, used for rope or bag handles, or decoration.

Serve. To wrap tarred line tightly around wire, previously wormed and parcelled, for protection against weather and chafe. "Worm and parcel with the lay; turn and serve the other way."

Serving Mallet. A tool with a spool of tarred line at one end and a groove to fit on rope or wire at the other, and rotated around wire as the wire is served, or wrapped, with the tarred line.

Sheerlegs. A triangular weight-handling structure consisting of two spars or girders fastened together at the top and with their lower ends spread out to form a base. The spars are steadied by guys, and the hoisting tackle is suspended from the apex.

Sheet. A line or tackle secured to the lower corners of a square sail, or the lower corner of a jib or staysail, or the boom of a spanker, and used to control the proper angle and "fullness" of the sail to the wind.

Ship. In the strict sense, a vessel that is square-rigged on each of three (or even four or five) masts. In the general sense, any ocean-going vessel.

Shrouds. Part of the standing rigging, shrouds are heavy wires secured to the hull near the bulwarks and to mast tops to provide lateral support to the masts.

Skot. Swedish for sheet.

Skysail. A square sail set above a royal. Common in clippers but very rare in the last square-riggers.

Soundings, To Take. To measure the depth of water under a ship.

Sound the Well, To. Every sailing ship had a pipe (the "well") running from the main deck to the lowest part of the hull through which the ship's carpenter could drop a metal rod and from it determine the amount of water in the hull.

Spanker. The lowest fore-and-aft sail on the after mast of two-, three-, or four-masted square-riggers.

Square-Rig. Vessels with sails mostly set from yards and at right angles to the length of the hull.

Stanchion. In steel ships, a vertical structure, often a heavy pipe, to reinforce frames, decks, or bulwarks.

Starboard. When facing forward, the right-hand side of a ship.

Starboard Tack. The condition of a sailing ship when the wind is coming from the starboard side. She is then on the starboard tack.

Stay. Parts of the standing rigging, stays are wire supports running from the top of a mast forward and down to a forward mast, to the deck, or to the bowsprit or jibboom. They provide fore-and-aft support for masts.

Staysail. A triangular fore-and-aft sail set on a stay.

Stern. The after end of a ship.

Stirrups. Wires attached at intervals along a jackstay by which a foot rope is suspended on which sailors stand when working at the yards.

Strap, or *Strop.* A wire or rope loop usually used for securing a block or other gear to another part of the rigging.

Sweeps. Extra-long oars.

Tack. A tackle leading forward from the lower forward corner of a course. Used to keep the forward edge of the sail taut when beating into the wind. Also, on a fore-and-aft sail, the lower corner close to the mast or stay.

Tack, To. To change the direction of a sailing vessel by swinging the bow into and through the wind.

Tackle. A combination of blocks (pulleys) and line (either rope or wire) used for creating extra power when hauling on sails or yards or lifting boats or anchors. When used for boats or anchors, the tackles are called "falls."

Taffrail. The rail at the stern of a ship.

Top. A small working platform usually at the juncture of a lower mast and a topmast.

Topgallant, or *T'gallant,* or *T'gans'l.* Mast, yards, sails, and rigging next above the topmast and topsails in a square-rigged ship.

Topmast. Masts in large ships were very rarely (if ever) of one piece. Each mast consisted of two or three sections fastened together, topmasts above lower masts and topgallant masts above topmasts. The points of conjunction, where two sections overlapped, were called doublings. Earlier ships usually had three sections. The last windjammers with strong steel spars usually had two, with the lower and topmasts of one piece and a topgallant mast above them.

Trade Winds, or *Trades.* The zones of very constant northeast or southeast winds and fair weather found north and south of the doldrums in all oceans. Also, the winds themselves.

Trestletrees. Longitudinal supports bolted to the upper part of lower masts and topmasts. They support tops, topmasts, crosstrees, and topgallant masts.

Truck. A round block of wood at the highest point of a mast.

Tumblehome. In a cross section of the hull of a vessel, tumblehome is that curvature above the waterline that slopes upward and inward toward the centerline of the vessel. A ship with tumblehome is narrower at the main deck amidships than at the waterline.

'Tween Deck. The deck between the main deck exposed to the weather and the cargo holds. Often the 'tween deck was only partially planked over.

Waist. The low, midsection of the main deck.

Watch. Ships' crews are divided into teams called "watches." On sailing ships there were two watches, the port watch under the first mate and the starboard watch under the second mate. Also, a watch is a period of time for work on deck, usually four hours, but only two hours—"dog watches"—from 4 P.M. to 8 P.M.

Wear, To. To change the direction of a sailing vessel by turning the bow away from the wind and the stern into the wind until the vessel presents its opposite side to the wind.

Weather. The side of a ship, the windward side, upon which the wind is blowing, or the direction from which the wind is blowing.

Westerlies. The zones of usually west winds. Also, the west winds themselves.

Winch-Brake. A brake on a bracewinch or anchor windlass.

Windlass. A form of winch adapted for hauling in an anchor cable.

Windward. The side of a ship toward which the wind is blowing, or the direction from the ship from which the wind is blowing. The opposite of leeward. ("I see a wreck to windward, and a lofty ship to lee"—old ballad.)

Worming. To lay light tarred line along the grooves between strands of wire to fill in the hollows before parcelling and serving the wire.

Yard. A horizontal spar of wood or metal that supports a sail on a square-rigged ship.

Yardarm. The end of a yard.

BIBLIOGRAPHY

Sources of Narratives

Attiwill, Ken. *Windjammer.* New York: Doubleday, Doran & Co., 1931.

Baines, Frank. *In Deep.* London: Eyre & Spottiswoode Ltd., 1959.

Barker, Roland. *Tusitala.* New York: W. W. Norton & Co., 1959.

Bestic, Albert A. *Kicking Canvas.* London: Evans Brothers Ltd., 1957.

Bisset, James. *Sail Ho.* New York: Criterion Books, 1958.

Brown, Dewar. *Alow and Aloft.* New York: Putnam, 1954.

Butlin, C. M. *White Sails Crowding.* London: Jonathan Cape, 1935.

Campbell, Neil. *Shadow and Sun.* London: George Allen & Unwin Ltd., 1947.

Clements, Rex. *A Gypsy of the Horn.* London: Heath Cranton Ltd., 1924.

Eaddy, P. A. *Hull Down.* London: Andrew Melrose, 1933.

Hurst, A. A. *Ghosts on the Sea Line.* London: Cassell & Co. Ltd., 1957.

Hurst, A. A. *The Call of High Canvas.* London: Cassell & Co. Ltd., 1958.

Hutton, W. M. *Cape Horn Passage.* London: Blackie & Son Ltd., 1934.

Jacobsen, Betty. *A Girl Before the Mast.* New York: Charles Scribner's Sons, 1934.

Jones, William H. S. *The Cape Horn Breed.* New York: Criterion Books, 1956.

Karlsson, Elis. *Mother Sea.* London: Oxford University Press, 1964. (Voyages of the *Herzogin Cecilie* and *Penang.*)

Karlsson, Elis. *Pully-Haul.* London: Oxford University Press, 1966. (The 1926 voyage of the *Herzogin Cecilie.*)

Learmont, James S. *Master in Sail.* London: Percival Marshall, 1954.

Lubbock, A. Basil. *Round the Horn Before the Mast.* London: John Murray, 1902.

Muncaster, Claude. *Rolling Round the Horn.* Boston: Charles E. Lauriat Co., 1933.

Newby, Eric. *The Last Grain Race.* Boston: Houghton Mifflin Co., 1956.

Riesenberg, Felix. *Under Sail.* New York: The MacMillan Co., 1919.

Schmitt, Lou A. *All Hands Aloft.* Berkeley, Calif.: Howell-North Books, 1965.

Sheridan, Richard Brinsley. *Heavenly Hell.* London: Putnam, 1935.

Stevenson, Paul Eve. *A Deep Water Voyage.* Philadelphia: J. B. Lippincott Co., 1897.

Stevenson, Paul Eve. *By Way of Cape Horn.* Philadelphia: J. B. Lippincott Co., 1899.

Thesleff, Holger. *Farewell Windjammer.* London: Thames and Hudson, 1951.

Tunstall-Behrens, Hilary. *Pamir, a Voyage to Rio in a Four-masted Barque.* London: Routledge and Kegan Paul, 1957.

Villiers, Alan J. *Falmouth for Orders.* New York: Henry Holt and Company, Inc., 1929. (A voyage of the *Herzogin Cecilie.*)

Villiers, Alan J. *By Way of Cape Horn.* New York: Henry Holt and Company, Inc., 1930. (A voyage of the *Grace Harwar.*)

Villiers, Alan J. *Grain Race.* New York: Charles Scribner's Sons, 1933. (A voyage of the *Parma.*)

Wallace, Frederick William. *Under Sail in the Last of the Clippers.* Boston: Charles E. Lauriat Co., 1936.

Wilmore, C. Ray. *Square Rigger Round the Horn.* Camden, Maine: International Marine Publishing Co., 1972.

Woollard, Claude L. A. *The Last of the Cape Horners.* Ilfracomb, U.K.: A. H. Stockwell, Ltd., 1967.

Further Reading
A. Other Personal Narratives of Twentieth-Century Windjammers

Barker, James P. *The Log of a Limejuicer.* New York: The MacMillan Co., 1936.

Bednall, Warren. *Strange Sea Road: The Story of a Sea Venture.* London: Jonathan Cape, 1936.

Bourne, Pamela. *Out of the World.* London: Geoffrey Bles, 1935.

Course, A. G. *The Wheel's Kick and the Wind's Song.* London: Percival Marshall, 1950.

De Mierre, H. C. *The Long Voyage.* New York: Walker and Company, 1963.

Desmond, Shaw. *Windjammer: a Book of the Horn.* London: Hutchinson, 1932.

Eriksson, Pamela. *The Life and Death of the Duchess.* Boston: Houghton Mifflin Company, 1959.

Hauser, Heinrich. *Fair Winds and Foul.* New York: Liveright Inc. Publishers, 1932.

Holmes, James William. *Voyaging: Fifty Years on the Seven Seas in Sail.* Lymington, Hampshire, U.K: Nautical Publishing Co., 1970.

Johnson, Irving. *The Peking Battles Cape Horn.* New York: Sea History Press, National Maritime Historical Society, 1977.

Lindsay, J. Murray. *By the Wind.* London: Angus and Robertson Ltd., 1963.

McCulloch, John Herries. *A Million Miles in Sail.* New York: Dodd, Mead and Co., 1933.

Newby, Eric. *Grain Race: Pictures of Life before the Mast in a Windjammer.* London: George Allen and Unwin, Ltd., 1968. (Mostly photographs.)

Newby, Eric. *Learning the Ropes.* London: John Murray Publishers Ltd., 1999.

Seligman, Adrian. *The Slope of the Wind.* London: Seafarer Books, 1994.

Spiers, George. *The Wavertree: An Ocean Wanderer.* New York: South Street Seaport, 1969.

Stenhouse, J. R. *Cracker Hash: The Story of an Apprentice in Sail.* London: Percival Marshall & Co., Ltd., 1955.

Villiers, Alan J. *The Sea in Ships.* New York: William Morrow and Co., 1933. (111 photographs.)

Villiers, Alan J. *Last of the Windships.* New York: William Morrow and Co., 1934. (208 photographs.)

Villiers, Alan J. *The Set of the Sails.* New York: Charles Scribner's Sons, 1949.

B. Historical Background and Technical Reading for the Cape Horners

Churchouse, Jack. *The Pamir under the New Zealand Ensign.* Wellington, New Zealand: Millwood Press, 1978.

Colton, J. Ferrell. *Windjammers Significant.* Flagstaff, Ariz.: J. F. Colton & Co., 1954.

Course, A. G. *Windjammers of the Horn.* London: Adlard Coles Ltd., 1969.

Derby, W. L. A. *The Tall Ships Pass.* New York: Charles Scribner's Sons, 1937; London: Jonathan Cape, 1937.

Edwards, Kenneth, Roderick Anderson, and Richard Cookson. *The Four-Masted Barque Lawhill.* London: Conway Maritime Press, 1996.

Greenhill, Basil, and John Hackman. *The Grain Races: The Baltic Background.* London: Conway Maritime Press, 1986.

Greenhill, Basil, and John Hackman. *The Herzogin Cecilie: The Life and Times of a Four-masted Barque.* London: Conway Maritime Press, 1991.

Hurst, Alex. A. *Square-Riggers: The Final Epoch, 1921-1958.* Brighton, Sussex, U.K.: Teredo Books, 1972.

Kahre, Georg. *The Last Tall Ships.* New York: Mayflower Books, Inc., 1978.

Lille, Sten, and Lars Gronstad. *The Finnish Deep-water Sailers.* Pasi, Finland: Etela-Suomen Kustannus Oy, 1980.

Lubbock, A. Basil. *The Last of the Windjammers,* 2 Vols. Glasgow, Scotland: Brown, Son & Ferguson, 1927, 1929.

Lubbock, A. Basil. *The Nitrate Clippers.* Glasgow, Scotland: Brown, Son & Ferguson, 1932, 1966.

MacGregor, David R. *Square Rigged Sailing Ships.* Watford, Herts., U.K.: Argus Books, 1977.

Pearse, Ronald. *The Last of a Glorious Era.* London: Syren and Shipping, Ltd., 1969.

Schulz, G.T. *Sailing Round Cape Horn.* New York: Dodd, Mead and Co., 1954. (No narrative; 224 drawings of a Laeisz ship, including detailed drawings of rigging.)

Underhill, Harold A. *Deep-water Sail.* Glasgow, Scotland: Brown, Son & Ferguson, Ltd., 1952.

Villiers, Alan J. *The Way of a Ship.* New York: Charles Scribner's Sons, 1953.

Villiers, Alan J. *The War with Cape Horn.* New York: Charles Scribner's Sons, 1971.

Waters, Sidney D. *Pamir, the Story of a Sailing Ship.* Wellington, N.Z.: A. H. and A. W. Reed, 1949.

Spencer Apollonio is a marine biologist with an indelible early memory of a four-masted cargo schooner under full sail on a beautiful day on the coast of Maine. He studied the biology of the waters of the Canadian Arctic and the Gulf of Maine for forty years, and for more than twenty years he has sailed whenever possible an ancient, wooden, gaff-rigged sloop along the coast of Maine. He has *always* been interested in old sailing vessels. His two sons, Tom and Taylor, are licensed merchant marine officers.

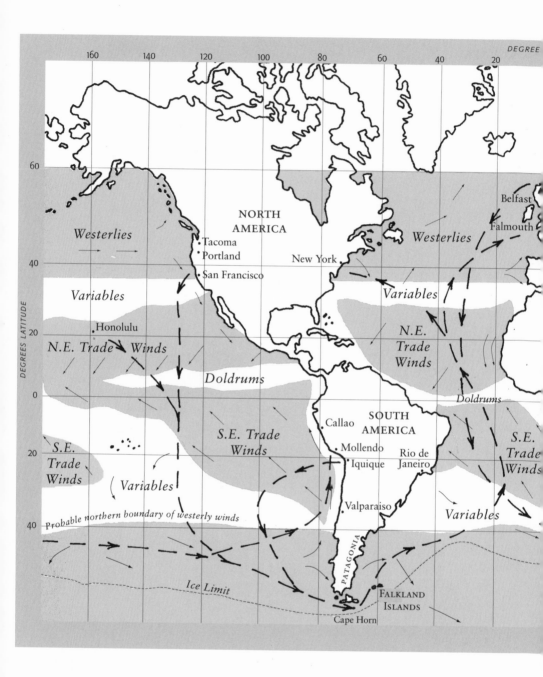

Chart of the World's Wind Patterns and Sailing Ship Passages